THE NELSON PROFICIENCY COURSE

Revised Edition

Susan Morris, Alan Stanton

Nelson

Nelson English Language Teaching
100 Avenue Road
London NW3 3HF

An International Thomson Publishing Company

London • Bonn • Boston • Madrid • Melbourne •
Mexico City • New York • Paris • Singapore • Tokyo

First published by Nelson ELT 1990

This edition published 1993

ISBN 0-17-556683-6
NPN 9 8 7 6 5 4 3

Printed in Hong Kong

Contents

To the Student

The Nelson Proficiency Course is a complete preparation for the Cambridge Certificate of Proficiency in English. It is designed for students who have reached at least the level of Cambridge First Certificate. The course places particular emphasis on developing your vocabulary and improving your ability to understand authentic English, through the use of substantial reading passages and listening material.

The course consists of a Students' Book, two cassettes, and a Teacher's Book (containing notes for teachers, answers and tapescripts). There is also an optional Workbook of additional grammar and vocabulary exercises.

The Students' Book has twelve units, each based on a particular theme. The themes of Units 7–12 are related to the themes of Units 1–6. For example, *Unit 8: Survival and Endurance* is thematically related to *Unit 2: Danger and Risk*. In this way, you have the opportunity to consolidate what you have learned in the earlier units.

The units are similar but not identical in pattern, but each unit contains the following sections:

Lead-in This introduces the unit topic and stimulates thought and discussion. Vocabulary building exercises prepare you for the vocabulary that you will encounter in the rest of the unit, and that you will need in order to talk and write about the theme.

Theme one This is the first of three 'theme sections' which explore different aspects of the unit topic. Typically, it is based on a substantial reading text, with varied types of comprehension questions, and authentic listening material. Practice in writing summaries based on a text is provided in one of the theme sections in each unit.

Language awareness This section focuses on particular aspects of the English Language, such as puns and clichés.

Theme two A second theme section, again using authentic reading texts and listening material, but providing a different perspective on the unit topic.

Grammar This section deepens and extends your knowledge of English grammar, using a deductive approach which encourages you to think about and discuss the language in focus.

Theme three A final theme section, providing a fresh approach to the unit topic while continuing the development of reading and listening skills.

Talking points Opportunities for discussion, using the vocabulary and ideas encountered in the unit.

Writing Throughout the course there is a variety of realistic writing tasks, including letters and narrative, descriptive and discursive compositions. These are accompanied by helpful hints on content, organisation, style and exam technique.

Literary approaches Each unit has a poem or piece of prose by a well-known writer (such as Yeats, Defoe or Sylvia Plath) giving you a taste of the richness and variety of English literature.

Follow-up This section, at the end of each unit, consists of exercises providing practice in the format of Papers 1 and 3 of the Cambridge Proficiency examination, while testing what you have learned in the unit.

Unit one

The Way We Live Now

Lead-in

A Look at the following statements drawn from statistics about Britain at the end of the twentieth century.

Are you surprised by any of the statements?

How does the situation in Britain compare with that in your own country?

1 The population of Britain is expected to rise to 60 million in 2005 from just under 57 million in 1987.

2 Life expectancy at birth is now 72 for men and 78 for women.

3 Britain has more people aged over 60 than any other EEC nation.

4 63% of homes are owner-occupied and the number of people owning their own homes has almost doubled since 1961, but 12,000 families were homeless in 1986 and 10% of the population live alone.

5 Most people work 35– 40 hours in a five-day week, with over 10% of the workforce being self-employed.

6 Women comprise 43% of the workforce and the percentage of women working outside the home is more than 50%.

7 In the 4 years to 1987, 946,000 people left Britain and 1.1 million came to stay.

8 The non-white population is 2.4 million.

9 Children start school at the age of 5 and must stay at school until the age of 16.

10 Weekly attendance at Church of England services is 1.1 million and there are 1.5 million Muslims in the UK.

11 Cars, motorcycles and taxis account for 83% of all journeys. Buses and coaches take less than 10% of all passengers, and trains only 7%.

12 The major killer diseases in Britain are heart disease and cancer.

Britain Today

B What do people in your country do when they are not working?

Do you think the British spend their time differently?

Listen to the tape and make notes about the things mentioned in the list below. Make use of any statistical information given to you.

1 Eating
2 Drinking
3 TV watching
4 TV ownership
5 Video
6 Telephones
7 Central heating
8 Washing machines
9 Cars
10 Cinema
11 Books
12 Newspapers:
national
regional

C Complete each sentence with one of the words or phrases given.

shanty towns	commute	debt	violence
battering	booming	tough	recession
racial tension	hostel	image	racist
high-flyers	status	slum	suburbs
rural depopulation	ghetto	subsistence	squats

1 In Britain today many young graduates want to get a job with high ....

2 The .... of high earners is enhanced by the purchase of a luxury car such as a Porsche.

3 The financial centre of London, the City, is full of highly-motivated young .... who are eager to make a lot of money as quickly as they can.

4 All successful business people know how .... life at the top is.

5 When the economy is ...., everyone seems to benefit.

6 In times of ...., it's the poorest that seem to suffer most.

7 The ease with which British citizens can get credit has led to increasing .... within society at large.

8 For those living at .... level, even buying essentials is a struggle.

9 Mary lives in a(n) .... with sixty other students.

10 Penniless students in large cities try to save money by living in ...., that is, houses which they find to be empty.

11 Financial problems can lead to stress within the family and .... between family members.

12 Wife-............................ is a particularly unpleasant form of violence.

13 In certain inner-city areas .... sometimes occurs between different ethnic groups.

14 Members of ethnic minorities trying to find jobs often complain about .... attitudes on the part of employers.

15 A poor, densely populated area of a town or city lived in mainly by one racial group is called a(n) ....

16 In Third World countries .... have grown up on the outskirts of major cities to house poor workers who have migrated from the countryside.

17 In the developed world run-down and derelict housing in the inner city where people still live is called a(n) ....

18 Throughout the second half of the twentieth century there has been a steady move to the cities. In many areas this has led to ....

19 People working in large cities often like to live away from the centre in pleasant ....

20 People who work in the city centre but live outside have to .... to work everyday.

D Complete the text using the words and phrases given.

emulate	allure	doorstep	metropolis
accommodation	veneer	social life	self-image
stuck	provinces	made the break	rush hour
metropolis	pace	landmarks	keep your wits

A View of the City
If you grow up in the .... *(1)* then capital cities have a very special .... *(2)*. They represent sophistication, choice and freedom. When you've settled in the city, you can think of the people back home as 'country cousins' who 'live in the sticks'. They haven't experienced life as it should be, in the city.

And what have you gained by moving to the .... *(3)*? First, a major change in .... *(4)*. You're one of the special ones, you've .... *(5)*. All those famous places that were previously just names read in the paper or seen on TV become familiar personal .... *(6)* glimpsed as you go to work or explore the capital developing your .... *(7)*. You're never .... *(8)* for something to do – everything's there, on your new .... *(9)*: discos, night-clubs, pubs. If you're culturally minded, there are museums, cinemas, theatres, concerts. And then the people! You never know who you will meet and where. Their status and lifestyle are something you want to .... *(10)*.

Of course, there are shocks. The cost, for one thing, of things like .... *(11)*, transport and entertainment. The crowds, especially during the .... *(12)*. The fast .... *(13)* at which everyone lives. But you soon learn to .... *(14)* about you and develop the special .... *(15)* that city living requires.

Theme one: *Family Life*

Jean's Day

A Listen to Jean describing her day and look at the pictures (**a–f**). Which pictures are correct in every detail?

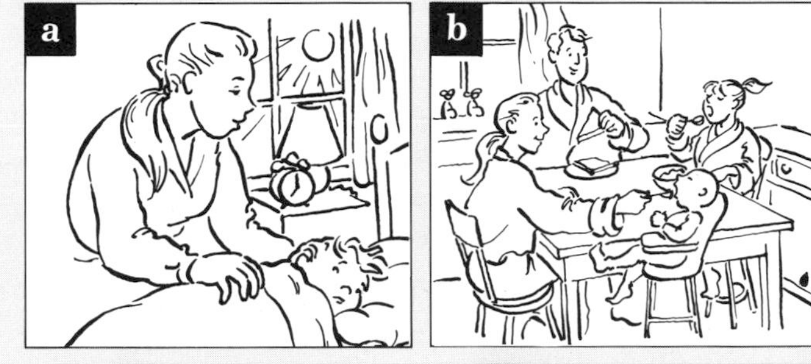

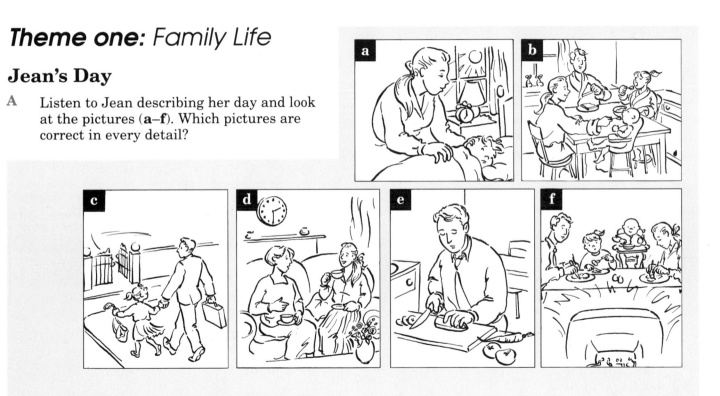

B Discuss with a partner:

What constitutes a successful life?

In the lives of successful people, what is the relationship between work and family life?

Now read the text quickly to find out how far the life of the couple described matches your ideas.

The Odd Couple

The story of Charlotte and John Fedders rocked Washington. It had all the ingredients: success, money, ambition, image-obsession and violence. It has become a modern fable, a cautionary tale that flashes a warning beacon throughout a whole upper echelon of tough young men pushing their way to the top, at the expense of their families.

Charlotte and John were the archetypal successful Washington couple. He was a young lawyer zooming up the status ladder in the fast lane. They were a crisp, clean-living Catholic couple with five young sons, living in a gleaming colonial-style mansion. From the outside they seemed to have it all: the best country clubs, the best Catholic private schools for their children, the best privately catered parties. He was selected for a top job which brought him into the public eye.

Then John Fedders' life fell apart. Or, at least, his image of it, which for him was the same thing. His private life had always been a catastrophe but one well hidden. The last straw for his wife came the day he started to turn his violent rage against his eldest son.

Charlotte Fedders filed for divorce. She hoped for a quiet divorce without dispute. But her husband wanted to battle it out. Perhaps he thought no one would notice an obscure hearing in a small courtroom in Maryland. But the *Wall Street Journal* sent a reporter to write the story, and what a story it was. Fedders had beaten his wife often and savagely. He thumped her repeatedly when she was pregnant. He ran the household with a set of iron rules: no one was permitted to enter the house in shoes; his sons had to do thirty press-ups whenever they came into the room. He was obsessively mean about money. Charlotte got virtually none for herself and the children. And yet she worried frantically about their rising debts. They lived way beyond their means.

The day after the *Wall Street Journal* ran the story, John Fedders was forced to resign. The story ran extensively on nationwide television. It rang new alarm bells. It showed that battered wives were not necessarily poor or confined to ghettos. Charlotte learned for the first time the FBI statistics: four women are beaten to death every day in America by husbands or lovers.

Charlotte got her divorce. John Fedders took a lower paid job and paid $12,000 a year to Charlotte and the children. The older children all worked and contributed their money to the household. Charlotte earned a little in a flower shop, but they were hard pressed. Then a publisher asked her to write the awful story of her life. But just before the book was to appear John Fedders took her back to the divorce court to try to get his puny payments to the family reduced. On top of that, he wanted 25% of the proceeds of the book on the grounds that he was the star of it. Everyone expected him to be laughed out of court. Imagine the shock when the court accepted his plea and did award that 25%.

Charlotte Fedders now seems like a self-confident and articulate woman. She makes speeches on battered wives up and down the country. Her book is a fascinating but dispiriting read. She was a poor, clinging pathetic creature who invested everything in her husband and her children. She thought as a young nurse that she would never find a husband with the sort of earning power that her family expected. When tall, handsome, athletic, clever Fedders looked on her with favour she thought she didn't deserve to land such a big fish. But he spied in her what he wanted: obedience, adoration, inferiority yet a sufficiently cultivated veneer for social acceptability. No danger of equality here.

It is a terrible pattern: this story has caused such a stir in America as it forces attention on the family life of the high achievers. When gilded young husbands work all the hours under the sun, who takes the strain? Who bears the brunt of all that bottled frenetic activity? What do wives and children have to tolerate in order to keep a man on the upward path?

(Polly Toynbee, *The Guardian*)

C Discuss with a partner how the writer of the article views the role of a wife in the families of high-flyers.

D Find a word or phrase in the text which, in context, is similar in meaning to:

Paragraph 1
1 shocked
2 moral story
3 serving as a warning
4 level
5 to the detriment of

Paragraph 2
6 perfect example
7 racing
8 spotlessly clean/shining
9 large expensive house

Paragraph 3
10 the final blow

Paragraph 4
11 hit
12 practically
13 much more expensively than could be afforded

Paragraph 6
14 under pressure
15 insignificant
16 for the reason

Paragraph 7
17 depressing
18 perceived
19 surface

Paragraph 8
20 takes the strain

E Now read the text again and answer the following questions.

1 What reaction did the story of the Fedders cause in Washington?
2 Why?
3 Briefly outline John Fedders' career.
4 Describe the impression that his lifestyle with his family would have made on outsiders.
5 What made his wife divorce him?
6 What fact caused the divorce to receive publicity?
7 What was John Fedders' relationship with his sons like?
8 Explain why the divorce aroused such widespread interest.
9 Give two reasons why John Fedders went back to the divorce court.
10 What was the judgement of the court on the final issue?
11 What picture of Charlotte Fedders emerges before and during her marriage?
12 And after her marriage?

Civil Cases

F Read the following text, but do not attempt to fill the gaps until you have listened to this judge talking about his experiences in matrimonial cases. Then complete the text with a suitable word or phrase according to the information on the tape.

The type of civil cases the judge enjoyed most were those concerned with .... *(1)* where he could make his own decision. The most depressing were the .... *(2)* cases. He often had to deal with applications for .... *(3)* to stop a man .... *(4)* his wife. He also had to act in cases of the .... *(5)* of relationships where children were involved and to decide what were the best .... *(6)* for them. He sometimes had to make the difficult decision to .... *(7)* men to visit their children if the wife was given custody, and he, as the judge, felt that visits might be harmful.

Language awareness: *homophones*

English, like other languages, has a number of words which have the same pronunciation, but a different spelling and a different meaning. Look at the following examples:

My ***son*** *is now seventeen years old.*
The ***sun*** *was shining brightly.*

A ***male*** *deer is called a stag.*
The ***mail*** *usually arrives at about nine o'clock.*

In these examples, the words *son / sun* and *male / mail* have the same pronunciation. The meaning and spelling are clearly different. Native speakers of a language rarely confuse which word is being used, even though the sound is the same, because they use the context to help them predict the word they are about to hear. The existence of homophones can give rise to plays on words or puns. You can learn more about these in later units.

What homophones can you think of in your language?

A Look at the following list of words, and see if you can think of a homophone for each word given. When you can, make a meaningful sentence using the homophone.

1	sail	*5*	mist	*9*	boy	*13*	hole
2	grown	*6*	side	*10*	no	*14*	cue
3	fought	*7*	made	*11*	night		
4	war	*8*	court	*12*	soared		

B The homophones in Exercise **A** have only one syllable, but the following words also have homophones. Can you identify them?

1	ceiling	*3*	whether	*5*	hire
2	morning	*4*	principle		

C The following words have more than one homophone. Can you find at least two for each word?

1	praise	*3*	wear	*5*	sent
2	right	*4*	pair		

D In the following sentences, there is a deliberate mistake. One of the words has been written instead of a homophone which would be correct. With a partner, see if you can correct the sentences.

1 Everyone working on the building sight has to wear a hard hat.

2 Waist not, want not.

3 Robert saw his former girlfriend in the street and walked passed her without acknowledging her.

4 The water comes from a sauce high up in the mountains.

5 The ship tied up at the key and the crew began unloading.

6 I always enjoyed cornflakes for breakfast, but muesli is my favourite serial now.

7 In England, you cease to be a miner at the age of 18.

8 Tom rode across the lake, a distance of six miles. He just wasn't used to it, so the next day his back was aching.

9 The top button has come off my shirt. I'll have to sow on another before we go out.

10 There was a whale of pain from the patient as the doctor attempted to put his dislocated shoulder back into place.

Theme two: A Place to Live and Work

Living in Oxford

A Listen to Helen talking about living in Oxford, now and as a student.
Make notes to complete the table, giving an indication of the good and bad points.

a **b**

NOW		AS A STUDENT	
Good Points	**Bad Points**	**Good Points**	**Bad Points**

B Before reading the text, discuss with other students:
Are there many immigrants in your country?

Do many people emigrate from your country?

What factors cause people to go and live in another country?

What do they expect to find?

What attitudes do they encounter and what treatment do they receive?

How do they view their homeland?

Now read the following text in four minutes and pick out four significant facts about the life of Irish immigrants in London.

Little Has Changed on the Streets of London

The number of people emigrating from Ireland is currently estimated at 30,000 annually. There is no doubt that the bulk of young Irish emigrants end up in London. And while some of their problems are unique to this generation, many of them work in the same jobs and live in the same conditions as endless previous generations of emigrants to Britain.

While some Irish take their degrees to London and use them to get jobs in the burgeoning service industry, for many others who left school in their teens and experienced months, if not years, of unemployment their second act on reaching London is to sign on for social welfare. Their first, and most difficult, is finding somewhere to live.

Social welfare benefits, when they include a rent allowance, are better in England. For a young unemployed man or woman, living at home with little or no unemployment assistance in Ireland, this can seem an attractive proposition, offering independence, a subsistence income and at least the hope of a job in a city where unemployment, while real, is a lot lower than in Ireland. Many young Irish emigrants go straight on the dole when they arrive in England. Some find jobs fairly quickly, others remain on the dole for months.

Andrew Fox is living on the dole, and is also in receipt of housing benefit. And he is living in relative comfort, as he's staying in Conway House, the hostel for young Irish men run by the Catholic Church in Kilburn. This costs £50 a week for bed and breakfast, and all the young men there spoke glowingly of the facilities it offers and the welcome they receive from staff. There was a 300 per cent increase in demand for places in this hostel in the first six months of last year.

But those who get into Conway House are the lucky ones and there is a six month time limit on residence there. It has a capacity for just 300, a drop in the ocean, and thousands of young Irish emigrants live in squats across north London. The squats are empty houses, many of them owned by the local council. They may be being prepared for sale into the private sector. Sometimes the council boards up the windows or removes the stairs, and the electricity is usually cut off. The conditions vary widely in the squats, from those in houses which are in good condition and where the illegal tenants are painters and decorators and do the place up, to those in bad repair where the squatters live on mattresses on the floors – in rooms lit only by candles. If they reconnect the electricity they face arrest and charges for stealing it.

Jobs are easier to come by than homes. But many of the jobs involve hard work, long hours and no security or protection. This is particularly true in the building trade. London is experiencing a building boom and many of the subcontractors are Irish. Like in the 1950's, there are queues of young men outside the Irish pubs and cafes in Kilburn, Camden and Cricklewood at 5.30 on Monday mornings, waiting to be driven to a site maybe miles away. Often there are hundreds of young Irish men and even if they do get work they rarely get back before 7 p.m. Wages are paid cash in hand. The men are not taxed and while they don't tell the contractor they are signing on, he doesn't ask either. And if they are injured, they are not insured.

Sister Joan Kane of the Haringey Irish Community Centre deals with the homeless many of them single men who have worked on the buildings all their lives. 'Some of the men in their forties coming in here worked very, very hard on the casual labouring scene. Then they got injured one day doing very heavy work. Now they're on the rootless scene. The casual scene is still going strong. The thing is, it's Irish employers exploiting Irish people. It's very degrading too, if you're passed over.'

Loneliness as well as the need for practical help ensures that many Irish people stick together. One of the subjects discussed at a seminar on emigration in Kilburn was the trauma experienced by Irish emigrants, revealed in statistics which showed a dispropor-tionately high number of Irish admissions to mental hospitals. One of the reasons for the sense of alienation was the sense of being foreigners in England and the hostility they experienced from many sections of the media and the police. Those who leave the country voluntarily are more likely to adapt well than those, in the majority, forced to do so out of economic necessity. Most of those who attended the seminar in Kilburn were in no doubt about the category they belonged to. 'I love Ireland', says Andrew Fox. 'I wouldn't have left it, only there was no work there.'

(The Irish Times)

C Read carefully through the text again and explain the meaning of the following phrasal verbs:

1 end up *(line 5)*

2 sign on *(line 19)*

3 cut off *(line 69)*

4 do up *(line 73)*

5 come by *(line 80)*

6 passed over *(line 116)*

In paragraphs 7 and 8, what words can you find that deal with negative experiences and feelings?

D Now read the text again and choose the best answer to the following questions.

1 The majority of emigrants from Ireland to London

A have useful qualifications
B encounter problems typical of the late twentieth century.
C get jobs in service industries.
D are in the same position as their predecessors.

2 What young Irish people want when they emigrate to London is to

A have a better chance of finding work.
B get somewhere to live.
C enjoy life in an international city.
D live on the social security system.

3 The problem with Conway House is that

A you cannot have lunch and dinner there.
B only Irish people stay there.
C it is not possible to stay more than six months.
D it is too expensive.

4 The building trade is a popular source of work because

A the wages are good.
B no questions are asked.
C the rate of tax is very low.
D the employers are Irish.

5 The trauma experienced by Irish emigrants is demonstrated in the fact that

A the Irish in London tend to stick together.
B many Irish people are arrested by the police.
C the media is biased against the Irish.
D mental illness among Irish immigrants is higher than average.

Grammar: the word

A Look at the verbs and their subjects in the following sentences and divide them into three groups on the basis of the characteristics they have in common. When you have sorted them into groups, say what these characteristics are.

1 No news is good news.

2 People in the town were delighted at the school's success in the radio quiz.

3 Tuberculosis is a disease that killed many people before a suitable cure was found.

4 The Government have decided to reduce social security payments drastically.

5 What is the fastest means of transport in a city?

6 Cattle were grazing in the field and birds singing in the hedgerows: it was an idyllic scene.

7 Physics is to become a compulsory subject in school under new legislation just approved.

8 The local Planning Authority have decided to turn down May and Tim's application for an extension to their house.,

9 The team were most put out with the result of the match, which they lost by ten goals.

10 The police are investigating the sudden disappearance of a schoolgirl.

B Now look at the following newspaper headlines, and complete the sentence under each to explain what the headline means. Take care to use a suitable form of the verb.

1 CABINET DIVIDED ON ARMS SPENDING
The cabinet ....
....

2 RABIES CONCERN WITH THE OPENING OF THE CHANNEL TUNNEL
Rabies ....
....

3 THREAT TO BRITISH ATHLETICS FROM SOUTH AFRICAN RUNNER
British athletics ....
....

4 AIDS DANGER TO BABIES
Aids ....
....

5 FAMILY KILLED IN MOTORWAY PILE-UP
A family of six ....
....

6 BOMB ATTACK ON ARMY BARRACKS IN NORTHERN IRELAND
The barracks ....
....

7 HEALTH COMMITTEE TO INVESTIGATE SWIMMING POOL RISK
Gloucestershire Regional Health Committee ....
....

8 US INTERVENTION IN HIJACK
The United States ....
....

9 MEASLES A KILLER IN THE THIRD WORLD
Measles ....
....

10 GYMNASTICS TO RECEIVE CASH BOOST
Gymnastics ....
....

11 COLLEGE LECTURERS OUTRAGED BY CUTS
Staff ....
....

12 WRONG DIAGNOSIS LEADS TO DEATH OF AUTHOR
The diagnosis ....
....

Non-count nouns

C No doubt you are aware of expressions like the following:

a piece of { paper / chalk / bacon / advice / cake

Using the word *piece* is quite acceptable here, but sometimes we want to use a more precise word. The words given below in the list on the left are more precise than *piece*. Match each one with a word from the list on the right.

slice	paper
rasher	chalk
sheet	bacon
stick	advice
word	cake

D Now complete the following sentences avoiding the words *piece*, *bit* or *item*.

1 This soup would taste better if you added a .... of salt.

2 A .... of butter added to the soup before serving adds to the flavour.

3 There wasn't an .... of truth in the accusation made against the employee.

4 Lady Winters enjoys a .... of sugar in her tea.

5 Getting out of the bath, Henry slipped on a .... of soap and hurt his head badly.

6 Husbands and wives often have different ideas about how to treat a .... of toothpaste, some squeezing methodically from the bottom and others starting at the top.

7 John borrowed a large .... of money from the bank to finance his share dealings.

8 Joan is so houseproud. You never see a .... of dust when you visit her house.

9 We've bought a .... of land on the south coast and plan to build a house there for our retirement.

10 What I really fancy eating now is a .... of chocolate.

11 The enthusiastic audience gave the speaker a .... of applause.

12 It's always unpleasant to hear people using .... of abuse.

13 .... of laughter could be heard from the girls' dormitory.

14 We watched the bank manager's face for the slightest .... of interest in the project for which we needed finance.

15 As a .... of our respect, please accept this gold watch on your retirement.

E Certain words, often thought of as uncountable, such as *coffee* and *cheese* may be found with the article or in the plural form. In the following sentences, choose the appropriate form.

1 If you want to lose weight, you must not eat any of the following *food / foods*.

2 The new delicatessen sells a wide range of *cheese / cheeses*.

3 We're a bit short of *tea / teas*. Could you get some when you're shopping?

4 You'll find the cooked *meat / meats* over there on the counter, next to the olives.

5 Two *vodka / vodkas* please.

6 There is a great diversity of ethnic origin in the *people / peoples* of the former Soviet Union.

7 If I drink *coffee / a coffee* I get a headache.

8 This is *wine / a wine* that has quite a reputation in Australia.

Theme three: *Work and Study*

Schools

A Listen to these four young people talking about the schools they go to and complete the table by putting a tick if the information is correct.

	1 Claire	2 Stephen	3 Terry	4 Robbie
1 Who obviously enjoys school?				
2 Who is taking exams soon?				
3 Who walks to school?				
4 Who mentions sport or physical activity?				
5 Who lives at school?				
6 Who does project work?				
7 Who is critical of their school?				
8 Who goes to school on Saturday?				

B The text which follows has been 'jumbled' so that it is not in the correct order. Read through the text and decide which paragraph goes with the times given.

1 6.15 a.m.
2 7.45 a.m.
3 8.45 a.m.
4 10.45 a.m.
5 12.30 p.m.
6 2.35 p.m.
7 6.00 p.m.

Just Another Day At The Office

Paragraph a
Time to inspect your platoon not so much for bull but well-being. You make eye-contact with each man. A look can often tell you something you should follow up later. You tell one of your Corporals to take them off on anti-tank weapon training leaving you to discuss the day's programme with your senior NCO. He's a Sergeant six years older than you whose knowledge and experience you have learned to respect greatly.

Paragraph b
Your bed has been made and your room cleaned but your dirty clothes are a matter for you and the regimental washing machine. Exhausted but with a quiet mind you sit down to write a report on a Corporal who's asked permission to apply for a commission. His career could depend on what you write. You're thinking deeply, pen poised, when there's a knock on the door. 'You haven't forgotten we're playing squash before supper?' The Corporal's application will get better attention in the quietness of the evening. Meanwhile there is someone who deserves a good thrashing on court.

Paragraph c
However often you walk into the dining room you always feel the tradition. Sitting at the table are many of the colleagues who will become lifelong friends. Afterwards there's just time to flick through a newspaper in an armchair built uncompromisingly for masculine comfort.

Paragraph d
Your alarm buzzes for the second time. A freezing mist lies heavily over the camp. Your radiator is barely warm. From the room next door a worn-out tape of Dire Straits shakes another young officer awake. On your left you can just hear Mozart's Flute and Harp decorating the morning. With close friends like this, who needs a radio? You wash, shave, pull on a track suit and jog over to your platoon's block. Outside, twenty-two bleary-eyed soldiers await your arrival. What are you going to torture them with today? They'd know if they'd bothered to look on the notice board: an eight-mile run.

Paragraph e
During the coffee break you bump into an Army Air Corps Officer who's just flown in by helicopter. He's hacked off that a unit he was due to do abseiling exercises with next week has suddenly been redeployed. Your mind races. 'Hang on.' You'll need an instructor and permission from your Commanding Officer but your men will get a day's abseiling ninety feet down from a hovering helicopter. They're really knocked out when you tell them after a radio codes lecture just before lunch.

Paragraph f
Armed with a stop watch, map, compass and notepad you drive in your third-hand Alfa Sud to some woods in the next county. As you run through the empty landscape, it starts to rain. But in two hours you're back in the car. You've planned another day's training.

Paragraph g
A quick shower and you change into uniform. You walk past portraits of distinguished generals to breakfast in the mess.

(Advertisement for Army Officers)

C Now answer the following questions.

1 What is the effect of the title in relation to the rest of the advertisement?

2 Comment on the use of the word *torture* in *Paragraph d*.

3 Why did the officer need a shower at 7.45 a.m.?

4 What effect is created by the portraits of the generals in the mess?

5 Why did the officer inspect his men at 8.45 a.m.?

6 What is the relationship between the officer and his senior NCO?

7 What does *Paragraph e* tell you about the way you can organise things as an army officer?

8 How do the soldiers react to the news about the abseiling?

9 How does the officer spend the afternoon?

10 What does the officer do before dinner?

11 And after dinner?

12 In a brief paragraph, outline the major features of the life of an army officer as illustrated by this advertisement.

Talking points

A Look at these houses and compare them. What are their key features?

What do you think the interior of each house would be like?

What do you think is the lifestyle of the occupants of each house and what is your opinion of each house?

B When a sample of house-buyers were questioned about what they wanted from a house, these were the things they valued: space for entertaining; being near open countryside; living in an area with a high status; security; the house as a good investment; comfort; privacy; a well-fitted kitchen.

What they didn't want was to be: in the inner city; in an area with a reputation for crime, violence or racial tension; in an area with a few social amenities.

How far do these ideas of a good place to live fit in with yours?

C Describe to the class your ideal house, giving details of the interior and exterior.

D Look at the cartoon. What differences do you see in the way the people pictured in the cartoon live?

(The Guardian)

Writing

Summary

A Using the article 'The Odd Couple' on page 4, describe the Fedders' marriage prior to the divorce, in not more than 100 words.

Hints

In other units of the book you will be asked to write a summary on at least one of the reading texts. As this is the first unit, you will be given instructions on how to write a summary with a working model based on the following instructions. Read through the notes and follow the steps in the model summary.

Summary writing cannot be done without thought and reworking. A successful summary shows a thorough understanding of the piece that is summarised, as well as exhibiting sound language skills such as accuracy and range of vocabulary and grammar. When writing a summary, you should always allow yourself plenty of time for thinking, writing and rewriting. The following steps will help you in writing summaries.

1 Read through the text to be summarised *at least twice*.

2 Isolate the information required for the summary.

3 Write down this information in *note form*.

4 Check that the points you have decided on are the ones required by the question.

5 Put the points in the correct order. (There may be a natural sequence, e.g. in a narrative, or you may have to decide on an order to emphasise the points you consider most important.)

6 Write out the information in the form of a paragraph. This is your *first draft* and must not be regarded as the end of the summary writing activity.

7 Check the number of words.

8 If the text is *too long*, you must shorten it, by removing less important information, by combining sentences to reduce the number of words, or by using one word instead of a lengthy phrase. If the text is *too short*, you must lengthen it, by expanding some of the information already given or adding to it, and by elaborating some of the phrases.

9 Check your amended draft for length, content and grammatical accuracy.

10 Write out the correct and final version.

Model

1 *Making notes:*

John and Charlotte Fedders
rich and successful couple
Catholic
five sons
husband high-flyer – wife at home
private schools
top job
rage against son
wife-beating
iron rules for household
John mean with money
rising debts
Charlotte's character – low self-esteem
John – domineering

2 *Ordering and selection:*

a rich successful Catholic couple with five sons
b husband high-flyer, top job
c wife submissive, no positive self-image
d John Fedders mean with money, violent
e contrast of private life and public image

3 *First draft:*

Charlotte and John Fedders were a rich and successful Catholic couple with five sons. The husband was an ambitious high-flyer, very concerned with his image, who landed a top job. His wife, a housewife, possessed a sophisticated veneer yet was in fact submissive and had a low self-image. John frequently attacked her, even when she was pregnant. Charlotte didn't fight against John's violence, but was content to be silent, at least until her son was attacked. While John was a high-spender and got the family into debt, Charlotte and the children were kept very short of money. The story illustrates the contrast between a couple's private life and public image.

(111 words)

4 *Final draft:*
Charlotte and John Fedders were a rich and successful Catholic couple with five sons. The husband was an ambitious high-flyer, very concerned with his image, who landed a top job. His wife, a housewife, was submissive and had a low self-image in spite of a sophisticated veneer. She didn't fight against John's violence but was content to be silent, at least until her son was attacked. While John was a high-spender and got the family into debt, Charlotte and the children were kept very short of money. The story illustrates the contrast between a couple's private life and public image.

(99 words)

Letter

B You have recently left home to start your studies in a college in a town away from home. It is the first time you have lived away from your family.

Write a letter to a friend who is in the same situation in another town. Your letter should be about 350 words long. Include information on the following topics:

- how you are coping with looking after yourself (e.g. accommodation, meals/cooking, doing your own washing, handling your money);
- what your course is like and how it is going (e.g. talk about course content, lectures/classes, how you handle study skills, etc.);
- how you feel being away from your family, how your social life is going and how your lifestyle has changed.

Hints
Remember the technical aspects of letter writing.

Look at the example to check that you are following the correct layout and that you are familiar with the hints provided in the box:

96 Sebastopol Terrace
Sheffield
SH10 7YD
20 October 19– –

Dear Sally

Organise your letter into paragraphs.

Include an introduction and conclusion.

Indent the paragraphs.

Don't forget the common forms of salutation and ending in letters to friends:

Love . . . is the common form for ending a letter from female to female, female to male or male to female.

Best wishes or Yours is more common for male to male.

Love
Maria

This is a personal letter to a friend, and therefore the style will be informal and colloquial.

Which of these sentences is *not* in the appropriate style for this letter?

1 I am more than satisfied with the accommodation that has been provided for me by the university authorities.

2 I trust that your own accommodation meets with your approval.

3 I do my own cooking in a kitchen which I share with a few other students.

4 There's a coin-operated washing-machine in the basement of the hall of residence.

5 It is with regret that I have to inform you that some of the lectures have fallen below the standard I had been led to expect.

Literary approaches

What picture of immigrant life emerges from this extract?

Sour Sweet by Timothy Mo (b.1950)

The Chens had been living in the UK for four years, which was long enough to have lost their place in the society from which they had emigrated but not long enough to feel comfortable in the new. They were no longer missed; Lily had no living relatives anyway, apart from her sister Mui, and Chen had lost his claim to clan land in his ancestral village. He was remembered there in the shape of the money order he remitted to his father every month, and would truly have been remembered only if that order had failed to arrive.

But in the UK, land of promise, Chen was still an interloper. He regarded himself as such. True, he paid reasonable rent to Brent Council for warm and comfortable accommodation, quarters which were positively palatial compared to those which his wife Lily had known in Hong Kong. That English people had competed for the flat which he now occupied made Chen feel more rather than less of a foreigner; it made him feel like a gatecrasher who had stayed too long and been identified. He had no tangible reason to feel like this. No one had yet assaulted, insulted, so much as looked twice at him. But Chen knew, felt it in his bones, could sense it between his shoulder blades as he walked past emptying public houses on his day off; in the shrinking of his scalp as he heard bottles rolling in the gutter; in a descending silence at a dark bus stop and its subsequent lifting; in an unspoken complicity between himself and others like him, not necessarily of his race. A huge West Indian bus conductor regularly undercharged him on his morning journey to work. He knew because the English one charged him threepence more. Chen was sure the black man's mistake was deliberate. He put the threepences for luck in an outgrown sock of his little son, Man Kee. Chen was not an especially superstitious man but there were times, he felt, when you needed all the luck you could lay your hands on.

Chen's week had a certain stark simplicity about it. He had once worked out the fractions on the back of his order-pad, dividing the hours of the week like a cake. He worked seventy-two hours at his restaurant, slept fifty-six, spent forty hours with his wife and child (more like thirty-two minus travelling-time, and, of course, Man Kee was often asleep when he was awake). This was on a rotation of six days a week at the restaurant with one off (Thursday). That day was spent in recuperation on his back on the sofa, generally with open eyes, for his feet ached after the hours of standing. It was hard and the money came at a cost but he wasn't complaining: the wages were spectacularly good, even forgetting the tips.

Follow-up

A Fill each of the numbered blanks in the following passage with one suitable word.

The Self Centre

Amid the green pastures of Dukes Meadow is the Riverside Sports Club, a sprawling synthetic temple to exercise and affluence, its car park filled with BMWs, Mercedes estate cars and a couple of amusing pastel Deux Chevaux. Here the .... *(1)* of keeping fit is soothed by deodorised, five-star comfort; this is where the beautiful people end .... *(2)* after they have become very rich and not .... *(3)* so beautiful as before.

Riverside is the biggest sports club .... *(4)* the country. Here are tennis courts, swimming pool, jogging track and exercise studio where 2,500 people .... *(5)* up for 'Rise and Sweat', 'Legs', 'Tums and Bums' or the 'Fat Burner' work-out. To get in through the front door today you must pay £1,000 for membership, to get .... *(6)* the gleaming foyer with its walnut desk and plastic plants will cost another £60 a month.

This is phenomenally cheap, ... *(7)* to Andy Holmes, Riverside's young and energetic managing director. At Riverside, your money .... *(8)* buy you constant tennis from 6.30 a.m. when the club opens, to midnight when it closes .... *(9)* of the film producers, stockbrokers, solicitors or merchant bankers who come here .... *(10)* put in these sort of hours. It's .... *(11)* for their wives. 'Some of our female members are here every day,' says Andy, 'and the only time they leave .... *(12)* to go to the hairdresser's.' But he is planning to .... *(13)* off their escape route. A beauty salon is to be built. There will be no .... *(14)* to leave at all.

This is why the Riverside exists. For its members it is their 'Third Place', ... *(15)* to go which is not the home or office. An arrangement imported from the United States and designed to remove the tedious responsibility of .... *(16)* up something to do with your 'leisure time'. But even in America, Andy says, Riverside would be exceptional. 'I would put us in the top ten clubs in the States – probably the top ten in the world. We have a total .... *(17)* to cleanliness. Ten full-time cleaners work .... *(18)* day, ventilation is absolutely crucial.' Indeed the club is remarkable for its .... *(19)* of sweat .... *(20)* from a faint breath of chlorine from the swimming pool there is no taint of pungent feet or damp changing rooms. Here all human effort is antiseptic and odourless.

B Finish each of the following sentences in such a way that it is as similar as possible in meaning to the sentence printed before it.

1 There is a six-month time limit on residence at the hostel.

You cannot ....

....

2 Immediately he returned from his run, he had to re-organise the morning schedule.

No sooner ....

....

3 He seemed to be very wealthy.

He gave ....

....

4 He found the pressures of the job intolerable.

He could ....

....

5 I had better prepare for tomorrow's training session now.

It's time ....

....

6 The workers did not arrive home until midnight.

It was ....

....

C Fill each of the blanks with a suitable word or phrase.

1 How you respond to the letter .... you alone.

2 He admitted his crimes .... getting a light sentence.

3 If you .... the notice-board, you would know about today's programme.

4 The story caused .... that the government had to change the law.

5 Nobody expected his claims .... seriously.

6 Most councillors voted .... of selling the land.

D For each of the sentences below, write a new sentence as similar as possible in meaning to the original sentence, but using the word given. The word must not be altered in any way.

1 The ships in the harbour took the full force of the storm.
brunt
....
....

2 Most of the orders will have been processed by Friday.
bulk
....
....

3 They renovated and redecorated the old house.
did
....
....

4 Not much heat came from the radiators.
barely
....
....

5 In this job you have to work long hours.
involves
....
....

6 He was given permission to apply for a special training course.
application
....
....

E Choose the word or phrase (*A*, *B*, *C* or *D*) which best completes each sentence.

1 The words *fought* and *fort* are ....

A homophones *B* homographs
C synonyms *D* variants

2 All applicants for this job must have a university ....

A certificate *B* course
C career *D* degree

3 Their standard of living is barely above .... level.

A subsistence *B* poverty
C assistance *D* welfare

4 Because she has two children Mrs Jones receives £14.50 a week in the form of child ....

A dole *B* payment
C entitlement *D* benefit

5 The Electricity Board has .... off the supply to that house.

A broken *B* cut
C stopped *D* shut

6 During the building .... of the eighties, many new houses were built in Docklands.

A rise *B* surge
C boom *D* bonanza

7 They had been living beyond their .... for several years.

A means *B* money
C resources *D* status

8 Before he started body-building, Charles was a .... 40 kg weakling.

A small *B* slight
C slim *D* puny

9 Because of his work for handicapped people, Michael received a(n) .... from the Queen.

A award *B* prize
C order *D* reward

10 Motorways generally have three or four ....

A channels *B* tracks
C routes *D* lanes

11 Most of the people on the early morning trains are ....

A passengers *B* travellers
C commuters *D* staff

12 The rocket .... up into the air at tremendous speed.

A leapt *B* rushed
C pushed *D* zoomed

13 Lady Margaret suggested putting on a concert and giving the .... to charity.

A proceeds *B* takings
C tickets *D* surplus

14 Every Friday, Andrew signs .... for unemployment benefit.

A on *B* in
C up *D* below

15 After twenty years' .... army officers can retire with a pension.

A duty *B* service
C loyalty *D* devotion

Unit two

Danger and Risk

Lead-in

A Identify the jobs or activities shown in the photos. Describe the dangers and risks involved.

B Life insurance companies will insure people's lives in return for an annual premium. The amount of the premium will depend on your age, sex and health and also on your job. People doing six of the jobs listed on the right would almost certainly have to pay a higher-than-average premium, if they could get insurance at all. Can you identify those six?

electrician	vet
carpenter	missionary
crop sprayer	steeplejack
licensed victualler	wrestler
fisherman	doctor
farmer	jockey

What rewards and advantages do dangerous and risky occupations have that more ordinary jobs do not have?

C Complete each sentence with one of the words or phrases given.

tossed
callous
daredevil
playing chicken
lucky charm
peril
accept the consequences
exposed
thrill
life and limb
drew straws
claims
challenge
endangered
death toll
freak storm
risk
hazardous
jeopardy
take a chance

1. The priest asked us to pray for those in .... on the sea.
2. 'The weather looks bad, but I think we'll .... and go for the summit,' said Chris.
3. Steeplejacks risk .... every working day.
4. On the day that he crashed, Michael had forgotten to take his .... – a rabbit's foot – with him.
5. The accident on the railway line happened when the children were ...., daring each other to cross in front of the train.
6. The Meteorological Office said that the damage had been caused by a(n) ...., which they could not possibly have forecast.
7. EARTHQUAKE .... SIXTY LIVES.
8. HUNGERFORD MASSACRE: .... 16.
9. Cars can be parked here at the owners' ....
10. Deep-sea fishing is an extremely .... occupation.
11. The survivors .... to decide who should go in search of help.
12. The bull .... the matador into the air before goring him.
13. The journalist accused the organisers of the race of showing a(n) .... indifference to the safety of the riders.
14. The future of the race is in .... if the safety record does not improve.
15. The men who rode the motor bikes on the 'Wall of Death' called themselves the '.............................. Riders'.
16. The negligence of the captain .... the lives of the passengers and crew.
17. Speaking from his hospital bed, Nigel said that those, like himself, who engage in dangerous sports just had to .... when things went wrong.
18. Gerald found the .... of driving at high speed completely irresistible.
19. The expedition will set out tomorrow, to face the .... of climbing the last unconquered peak in the Himalayas.
20. The inhabitants of Flixborough were .... to deadly fumes from the chemical factory explosion.

D Complete the text using the words and phrases given.

warning	heedless	numbed	charmed life
odds	relatively	precautions	peace of mind
chances	foreseen	sheer folly	
run	lulls	mistaken belief	
safety records	bravado	safety-conscious	

Taking Risks

Statistics prove that the .... *(1)* of having a serious accident in your own home or car are .... *(2)* high. However, people's perception of the risks they .... *(3)* while engaged in everyday activities is quite low, and this often leads to inexplicable acts of .... *(4)*. 'Familiarity breeds contempt', as the saying goes. People have been known to search for a gas leak using a candle for illumination, for example, or to hold their babies on their laps in the front seat of cars, instead of securing them safely in the rear seat, in the .... *(5)* that they can protect them in the event of a collision. The familiarity of the surroundings .... *(6)* people into a false sense of security, often to such an extent that they do not allow even obvious danger signals to disturb their .... *(7)*. 'I never thought it would happen to me,' is the refrain of those surprised by dangers that could have been .... *(8)* and avoided. However, when it comes to travel by air or train, people are often extremely anxious about the potential dangers, despite the fact that airlines and railways have excellent .... *(9)*, notwithstanding the occasional spectacular crash. The fixed routines necessary for the safe operation of transport systems carry their own dangers, however. It can happen that drivers and pilots, their brains .... *(10)* by the monotony of repetitive tasks, fail to take notice of .... *(11)* lights and signals.

Occasionally, someone, so .... *(12)* of his own safety, so desperate for thrills, or so convinced that he bears a(n) .... *(13)*, will play such deadly games as Russian Roulette, in which even if the .... *(14)* are six to one, the consequences can be fatal. Such games, whether prompted by .... *(15)* or a sort of death wish, cannot be compared with unavoidably hazardous activities such as mountain-climbing and deep-sea diving where taking .... *(16)*, not risks, is uppermost in the minds of the participants.

The main danger to us all lies in the unexpected accidents of everyday life and it is therefore essential to be alert and .... *(17)* while at home or work.

Theme one: *Driving into Danger*

A Motorcycle races (known as TT – Tourist Trophy – races) are held annually on the ordinary roads of the Isle of Man, an island situated between England and Ireland.

Do you think that there are any sports more dangerous than motor-cycle racing?

Why do young people want to race motor bikes? And why do people want to watch such races?

Now read the text on the next page and answer the questions which follow.

Death Race

In 1977 TT was freaky. No one was killed. The organisers and supporters were jubilant: you see, they said, it's not really dangerous at all, and those who say otherwise are just spoilsports who don't understand the freedom of the individual. In 1978 five were killed, which came close to the record, and last year two more died, which was about average.

Even dedicated participants have their moments of clarity about the statistics. 'Wait a minute,' one remarked last year. 'If we stood on the dockside at Liverpool and drew straws, with the same odds, for which two had to die, we wouldn't do it. We'd be horrified. But it's the same thing.' Another distinguished competitor, Mike Hailwood, was wondering last year, finally, what he was doing there: 'What with this and car racing. I have known, I mean known, not just known of, 55 people who have been killed. I don't think you would actually know that many if there were a war on.'

The Isle of Man TT is as blood-stained as any sporting event this side of the Roman circus. No one, evidently, has bothered to keep an account of the lives claimed by the two annual events held on the course, but it is probably very little short of two hundred. The cases of permanent brain damage, paralysis, and the loss of the use of arms, eyes and legs will amount to several hundred more.

Notwithstanding its self-induced obscurity, the public is aware, by now, that the TT is dangerous and probably that it is more dangerous than most other racing events. What it does not know is that the TT is merely the extreme expression of an approach to safety that at times is little short of anarchic. Already this year, perhaps two dozen people have died in motor-cycle sport around the world. Not because it is inherently dangerous (which certainly it is) but because the participants are exposed to insane levels of unnecessary danger. Furthermore, the rules governing medical provision are astoundingly inadequate.

What has happened in motor-cycle racing, for complex historical and psychological reasons, is that power and responsibility have been almost entirely polarised between riders and organisers. The riders, in spite of repeated and strenuous and indeed rebellious attempts to acquire power, have been firmly repressed and find that if they ride at all, they ride on the organisers' terms.

On the other hand, they are assumed, since they take part of their own free will in a dangerous sport, to bear all the consequences of their actions. It is out of this that the anarchy arises. When men and women die, there is no visible investigation, no recrimination, no attempt to apportion blame, or to effect compensation, even when there has been self-evident neglect on the part of the organisers (except in Italy, where the laws of criminal negligence apply). This is so in spite of the fact that large sums of money are made out of motor-cycle racing, and perhaps, indeed, because of it.

A recent incident illustrates the way this moral side-step works. It concerns a quiet Geordie side-car racer, Mac Hobson, and his young passenger, Kenny Birch. During TT practice week in 1978, the word spread quickly that a bump at the top of Bray Hill was causing a lot of excitement. Solos were shaking as they hit it, but side-cars, which have a natural tendency to turn around their side-car wheels, were going sideways, skating and slithering down the road at maybe 130 m.p.h. Everyone knows what happens when a motor cycle changes direction at the bottom of Bray Hill at 150 m.p.h.; but it was something new to have such antics at the top.

The bump was a new pipeline, complete with manhole cover, which had been laid by the Manx authorities during the previous winter. The inspection committee of the Auto-Cycle Union (the governing body of British motor-cycle sport, as well as the organiser of the TT) had seen the bump and asked for its removal. Come practice week, it was still there; practice began.

The ACU worried about the bump. They drew a yellow circle round the manhole, and a long yellow line back towards the oncoming racing traffic. They issued a circular, drawing attention to the new hazard. Side-cars, by that time, were slowing down for the bump and avoiding the manhole cover. Then came the race.

Hobson and Birch headed for the bump for the first time under racing conditions. Under full acceleration, at a peak of adrenalin, they had probably forgotten all about it. There was no slowing down and no room to avoid it. When their outfit left the ground, it turned in the air, bounced on the road, turned again and smashed into a garden wall. Seconds later, Ernst Trachsel, a Swiss competitor, flew through the wreckage. At the bottom of the hill, he too crashed and died. The race was not stopped, even for the purpose of hosing down the road. The press officer soon arrived to announce that there had been an accident, that the ACU would not issue a statement since they didn't know enough about it, but that it definitely had nothing to do with the bump in the road. Advised to produce a statement forthwith, he came back with the ACU's comment that they were sorry about Mac Hobson, Kenny Birch, and Ernst Trachsel, but that what happened was 'part and parcel of a speed sport'. Not even the supporters of the event had expected such callousness. Someone had built a bump into the most critical point on the TT course and a disgusting fatal accident had ensued. But there was no blame, no recrimination, certainly no compensation. The responsibility was assumed to be entirely Hobson's. They have an expression for this: 'The throttle goes both ways,' they say, and: 'Nobody made him race.'

Perhaps the most striking thing about the TT is that we allow it to take place at all. It does not seem entirely compatible with the standards of a civilised community. An Italian journalist recently put it harshly, but fairly, as follows:

'The British are hard to understand. They care about animals and the preservation of endangered species. They hate bullfights because they are uncivilised, but they tolerate the TT. Let me say that it seems to me that the only difference between the TT and a bullfight is that nobody cuts off the ears of fallen riders and presents them to the clerk of the course.'

(Barry Coleman, *The Guardian*)

B Find a word or phrase in the text which, in context, is similar in meaning to:

Paragraph 1
1 strange and unusual
2 overjoyed
3 people who ruin others' enjoyment

Paragraph 2
4 fully-committed
5 eminent

Paragraph 3
6 taken the trouble
7 nearly

Paragraph 4
8 despite
9 only
10 without order
11 astonishingly

Paragraph 5
12 energetic
13 kept down

Paragraph 6
14 mutual accusations

Paragraph 7
15 sliding out of control
16 fun and games

Paragraph 10
17 immediately
18 cruel insensitivity

Paragraph 11
19 remarkable
20 severely

C Now answer the following questions.

1 Why were organisers and supporters of the TT races jubilant in 1977?

2 What is the total number of riders who have been killed in TT races?

3 What, in the writer's view, is the main reason for the high death rate in motor-cycle sport?

4 To what extent are the riders able to influence the organisation of the race?

5 What did the ACU do about the bump at the top of Bray's Hill?

6 Why did Hobson and Birch have an accident?

7 What was the ACU's explanation of the accident?

8 What is meant by '*the throttle goes both ways*'?

9 The TT races are compared, in different parts of the text, to two other forms of sport and entertainment. What are they?

D Summarise in 50 – 100 words the writer's general criticisms of motor-cycle racing.

Accidents

E Listen to Andrew talking about his job, which involves using oxy-acetylene cutting equipment to free people trapped in wreckage. Answer the questions with one word or a short phrase.

1 Where does Andrew carry out most of his work?

2 What type of accident does he mainly deal with?

3 What phrase does Andrew use to describe an accident where a number of vehicles are involved?

4 Does he work alone?

5 What is the worst danger at the scene of an accident?

6 What problem does Andrew often encounter when he is on his way to the scene of an accident?

7 Which emergency service does he express admiration for?

8 Which other emergency service does he refer to?

9 What does he like about his job?

Language awareness: *multiple meanings*

A In the following groups of sentences find the *one* word which fits the gaps in all three sentences. You must use the same word for each sentence without changing it in any way.

EXAMPLE:

a She .... her husband five children.
b That man is such a .... No wonder his wife divorced him.
c This new machine can .... a tunnel at the rate of three metres an hour.

ANSWER: *bore*

1 *a* The .... survivor of the shipwreck managed to stay alive by clinging to a life-raft.
b I enjoy eating fish, and one of my favourites is Dover ...., which I cook in the oven with white wine.
c John's shoes were pretty old and when it started to rain the water began to seep through the left ....

2 *a* Peter's much too .... ever to lend anyone any money.
b What do you .... by implying that I am a liar?
c The .... annual rainfall in Britain is higher than that in Egypt.

3 *a* The .... on page 15 of Dr Mitchell's report shows the figures for perinatal death worldwide.
b Please make ten copies of the proposals that I intend to .... at the meeting.
c With such a large family we had to buy a really big kitchen .... to be able to seat everyone.

4 *a* Make sure you .... well in advance if you want to stay in a hotel on the coast in the summer months.
b This is a .... I have no hesitation in recommending.
c The police have decided to make an all-out effort to .... every motorist who speeds going through the village.

5 *a* The soldier went absent without ....
b I'll make all the arrangements. Just .... it all to me.
c 'Please may I .... the room?'

6 *a* Doesn't it .... you as a brilliant idea to pick out that wonderful green in the carpet in the cushions on the sofa?
b The seamen's .... caused enormous disruption to freight traffic.
c If teachers .... pupils, they must be prepared to suffer the consequences.

7 *a* It's just not .... to give one child all the sweets. Give some to the others too.
b For the children, the most exciting part of the afternoon was the trip to the ...., where they went on rides, bought candyfloss and each won a goldfish.
c Julie has .... hair just like her mother.

8 *a* This meat is deliciously .... It just melts in the mouth.
b The contract was put out to .... and given to the company that produced the most competitive price.
c She bruised her arm quite badly. At first it was too painful to touch, and still felt very .... a week later.

9 *a* The night-watchman decided to .... the alarm when he heard a suspicious noise and suspected there was an intruder on the premises.
b Don't make a .... If you do, I'll hurt you.
c The surveyor was quite sure that the building was ...., so we made an offer for it.

10 *a* The audience was hushed in anticipation as the soprano attempted the top ....
b Please .... that all rooms must be vacated by 11.30 a.m.
c Robert left a .... to say he would be back by ten o'clock.

11 *a* The .... made a mix-up about my standing orders, so my account was overdrawn.
b If you must swim in the river, it'll be safest if you stay near the ....
c You'd be unwise to .... on Frank's doing what he says; he's notoriously unreliable.

12 *a* What sources of money can we .... in order to finance the project?
b We'll have to call in a plumber. That .... just won't stop dripping.
c This porcelain is extremely delicate. The slightest .... and it will break.

13 *a* The man in the .... pleaded not guilty.
b The ship was pulled into the .... by a tug.
c Mary worked for an employer who would .... her wages if Mary broke anything, even if it was quite accidental.

14 *a* The mousse was .... enough to stand on the plate.
b The .... Caroline works for has gone into liquidation, so she's on the job market again.
c The Housing Minister made a .... commitment to the idea that everyone in the country should have a roof over their heads.

15 *a* Looking after the elderly is a .... of love.
b Sally has always believed it was important for organised .... to have the right to join forces to improve conditions.
c You shouldn't expect people to support you just because you're a poet. Don't .... under the delusion that the world owes you a living.

Theme two: All Part of the Job

A What are the risks doctors encounter in carrying out their work?

How can they minimise these risks?

Now read the text and answer the questions which follow.

Hazard at Work

I was nearly killed on Boxing Day. My job nearly got me killed. To start with, it was not a serious incident: one car off the road and two very shocked but not terribly injured passengers. I was giving assistance, that is my job: rural GPs are often called out to traffic accidents because they can sometimes get there first and often help the ambulance crews prepare patients for a long journey to hospital.

The next car down the road changed it all. I saw it coming and had time to think: surely it will stop. I remember the noise as it hit me. No pain at this stage. I was tossed across the road and scrambled up on to the verge. Straightaway I knew that my leg was broken. Well, that's my job too. Still no pain. I didn't want to die, that was my foremost thought. I didn't want to die here on the roadside, so I worried about bleeding to death, about internal injuries or an unsuspected head injury. I waited for the signs of shock and tried not to pass out.

The scene was now full of shouting and crying. No one seemed to notice me. The village bobby arrived on cue. Sure my leg was broken, but I wasn't going to die. Now it hurt.

'Burn out' sums up how anyone in a caring profession can end up responding to chronic job-related stress by loss of concern and complete withdrawal from their work. GPs are not immune. Well, I suffered a 'flash out'. Nothing chronic about this stress. Suddenly, lying there on the roadside with a smashed-up leg, it didn't seem worth it any more.

That was three months ago. I'm still only mobile with crutches. The practice has carried on without me – which is how it should be, for no one is indispensable in a good system. I don't need to be a doctor for a while. My patients kindly showed their concern and wished me well while they took their problems to the locum.

Because I have spent nearly nine years working often in excess of a hundred hours a week, everyone assumes my enforced idleness to be a heavy burden. It isn't. I'm more concerned that I'm not missing my work and that I'm certainly not bored. Does this mean that I don't need to be the doctor permanently?

I know why I like being a GP. I live in a good place and I work for myself. I'm responsible only to my patients, myself and my partner. It is probably useful. It involves practising a set of skills that could never be perfected and so is always a challenge. My staff and local colleagues are good company. It pays well. I get home for lunch every day.

The more nebulous rewards, the sort of things many non-doctors think we do it for – like being in a position to 'help people' – tend to be counter-balanced by the reasons I don't like the job. I get used. I have to try to help with problems that should never have come my way, to which the solutions are invariably political and not medical. I cannot prescribe jobs or better houses or better relationships. I can try to be supportive, but just a few patients can create a mountain of hassles. I'm sometimes over-committed and frequently over-tired. Stress is an everyday problem. My job nearly got me killed.

Three days after I was admitted to hospital my wife went into a different hospital and had our second baby. It is impossible for me to express how unhappy my unforeseen absence made me. I couldn't decide whether to blame the accident (but accidents happen) or my job (but no job is without risk) or just to assume no blame.

Well, the balance remains tipped. Despite the apparent usefulness of being a GP and the satisfaction it gives me, I have discovered that the only certain reason I do it is for my family. Along with paying the mortgage, it allows us to live how and where we like.

Everyone in a caring profession knows that if they do not ration their caring they can end up emotionally and intellectually burnt out. They separate themselves from their families by giving too much. I suppose I'm still bitter because there are few precautions I could take to avoid the way I was almost permanently separated from my family – and at such an important time. My resolve has been questioned. Do I need to be a doctor? The jury is still out.

(Stephen Singleton, *The Guardian*)

B Explain the meaning of these words and phrases from the text.

1 Boxing Day *(line 1)*

2 rural GPs *(line 7)*

3 scrambled up on to the verge *(lines 20)*

4 The village bobby arrived on cue *(lines 33–34*

5 'burn out' *(line 37)*

6 'flash out' *(line 43)*

7 the practice *(line 50)*

8 the locum *(line 57)*

9 the more nebulous rewards *(line 79)*

10 I get used *(line 84)*

11 a mountain of hassles *(line 93)*

12 the balance remains tipped *(lines 108–109)*

13 paying the mortgage *(line 114)*

14 the jury is still out *(line 130)*

C Now read the passage again and choose the best answer to the following questions.

1 Why was the writer at the side of the road?

A His car had been involved in a minor accident.
B He was helping the ambulance crews.
C He could get to the scene before the ambulance.
D He had been summoned to provide medical assistance.

2 The writer suffered

A only a broken leg.
B a broken leg and shock.
C a broken leg, shock and internal injuries.
D a broken, leg, internal injuries and a possible head injury.

3 As he lay injured by the roadside the writer felt that

A there was no point in continuing to be a doctor.
B nobody cared about him.
C he was under too much stress.
D the petrol in the car might catch fire.

4 For the last three months the writer

A has not worked at all.
B has worked but not as a doctor.
C has managed to work on crutches.
D has been able to practise new skills.

5 How many really positive reasons does he find for being a doctor?

A seven
B eight
C ten
D eleven

6 Why do a few patients create so much work for him?

A They take advantage of him.
B Their illnesses cannot be cured.
C He gets overtired.
D He sees them every day.

7 Why did the accident happen?

A There was no particular reason.
B The car was going too fast.
C The doctor was careless because of stress.
D The road was blocked by the first car.

8 The writer believes that doctors and nurses should

A devote themselves completely to their patients.
B accept that they will be separated from their families.
C limit their emotional involvement in their work.
D burn up their energy by working hard.

9 In the future, the writer

A has to go to court to get compensation.
B might decide to give up being a doctor.
C will take precautions against accidents.
D will always feel bitter about what happened.

Fire-fighting

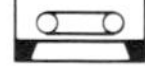

D Listen to Philip talking about being a fireman.

The first time you listen, explain the meaning of the words in the box on the right, which are commonly used by firemen.

1 when the bells go down
2 the appliance
3 multiple calls
4 persons reported
5 hydrant location book

E Now listen again and decide if these statements are *true* or *false*.

1. They are not often called out to big fires.
2. They begin to make plans before they reach the fire.
3. They prefer to be the first firemen to reach a fire.
4. They put on breathing apparatus as soon as they arrive at the fire.
5. They rely on information given to them by the people whose house is on fire.
6. Philip mentions two dangers that firemen face when they enter a burning building.
7. When searching a burning house, firemen always wear a mask, a tank of air and carry a hose with them.
8. Philip searched the house at least three times.
9. If someone has died in the fire, the morale of the firemen becomes very low.
10. The firemen sometimes make jokes when people commit suicide.

Grammar: *present tenses, inversion*

Simple present tense

A Look at these sentences and divide them into seven groups of three.

What are the differences between the seven groups?

1. Water freezes at zero degrees Centigrade.
2. I propose a toast to the bride and bridegroom.
3. Disabled man wins medal for bravery.
4. Walter and Daisy celebrate their 50th wedding anniversary next Saturday.
5. I swear to tell the truth, the whole truth and nothing but the truth.
6. You get on the coach at 10 p.m. and arrive in Madrid at 8 a.m. the next day.
7. He walks in, goes straight up to the barman and says ...
8. Make sure Mr Smith gets these papers before he leaves.
9. He always catches the 7.40 to Victoria.
10. Stay at the hotel until you hear from me.
11. Snow covers South of England.
12. I'll let you know as soon as I have the information.
13. Lofthouse passes to Greaves, who runs for the goal ...
14. She comes back from holiday tomorrow.
15. They live in Barnes.
16. He works out in the gym twice a week.
17. The Earth goes round the Sun.
18. First, I remove the inspection cover. Then I move the red lever and ...
19. Prime Minister flies to New York.
20. Three times three equals nine.
21. I forgive you – this time.

Now write one sentence of your own for each of the seven groups.

Present progressive

B Look at these sentences and divide them into four groups of three.

What are the differences between the four groups?

1. Jack is cleaning the car.
2. The daffodils are coming along nicely.
3. I am going to Poland next month.
4. I'm always forgetting to lock the car.
5. I am making the pastry.
6. We are meeting the solicitors at 10 a.m.
7. He is constantly having bonfires.
8. I am eating out tonight.
9. I am taking the train to the office this week.
10. We are staying in a hotel while the roof of our house is being replaced.
11. I'm forever tidying up after you.
12. The toast is burning.

Now write one sentence of your own for each of the four groups.

Acceptability

C Are any of these sentences unacceptable?

1. Despite John's urgent request, I'm refusing to help him.
2. I'm thinking that you've got the answer.
3. Sally is looking very beautiful.
4. Martina looks great.
5. I'm feeling sick.
6. We are looking forward to seeing you.
7. We look forward to your early reply.
8. We are not knowing all the details.
9. I'm seeing Mr Burgess then.
10. The cost of living rises very fast this year.

Inversion

D Compare these sentences.

We had scarcely recovered from the first attack when the enemy launched a fresh assault.

Scarcely had we recovered from the first attack when the enemy launched a fresh assault.

The effect of inversion is to give more emphasis to the words at the beginning and in this way to give the sentence a more dramatic tone.

Rewrite these sentences without inversion. You will sometimes have to add or change words.

1. Hardly had we stepped off the aircraft when we were surrounded by police.
2. Had I known his true motives, I would never have trusted him.
3. No sooner had we opened the theatre doors than the crowd surged forwards.
4. Were I the owner, I would not give permission.
5. Little did he know that he would never see his own country again.
6. Seldom does this great artist grant us the privilege of an interview.
7. Such was his skill that he could complete a portrait in two days.
8. Never had we seen such an unusual fossil.
9. On no account must you invite him to the house again.
10. Should the photographs be ready, bring them back with you.
11. Only by using a hammer and chisel could we get the box open.
12. Rarely did a day go by without a phone call from mother.

E Now rewrite the following sentences beginning with the word given.

1. He had no idea that armed police were waiting for him.

   Little did he know that armed police were waiting for him

2. If we had counted the money, we would have realised we had been cheated.

   Had we counted the money, we would have realised we had been cheated

3. As soon as they got out of the car the police arrested them.

   No sooner they got out of the car ....

4. We had only just reached the summit when the storm began.

   Hardly ....

5. If this vase were in perfect condition, it would be worth twice as much.

   Were ....

6. He must definitely not be allowed to leave.

   On no account ....

7. It was so cold that we stuffed our boots with dried grass.

   So ....

8. Bears were hardly ever seen during the winter.

   Seldom ....

9. The only way we could cross the river was by floating across on tree trunks.

   Only ....

10. It was the first time the cave had been entered by human beings.

    Never ....

Theme three: *High Risk*

A What forms of gambling are popular in your country?

Are there any restrictions on gambling?

'To be on the wire is life – the rest is waiting'
(Karl Wallenda – high wire artist)

Read the text and discuss in what way the quotation above applies to it.

We all take risks every day of our lives. Driving to work, catching an aeroplane, even crossing the road. These sorts of risk are qualified by actuaries and covered by insurance policies. The insurance company, working on the past record of many hundreds of thousands of instances, calculates the probability of a particular accident befalling the individual seeking cover and sets the premium for the policy accordingly, plus a healthy margin to take care of its operating costs and profits. Exactly as the casinos do. But whereas most prudent people would take out an insurance policy, as a basic part of their game-plan for living, gamblers choose to take a wholly unnecessary and avoidable risk. Seeking risk for its own sake, as a diversion.

Part of the attraction, I feel sure, is the physical sensations offered. Consider simply the case of someone like you or me, planning to spend a night out at the casino. First comes the pleasure of anticipation, thinking through the day about going out to gamble; then perhaps comes the agreeable social pleasure of making arrangements to meet friends, other gamblers; not forgetting the important point of ensuring that you have the money to gamble ... That may well be a nervous-making element, especially if you can't really afford it, or can't afford to lose; then comes the physical sensation, the pitter-patter of excitement as you walk through the doors of the casino, the sight and sound of action in the gambling-rooms ... twitches of nervous tension ... finally the see-saw sensations of each coup, one after the other in rapid succession, as the wheel spins or the dice roll or the cards fall; the exhilaration of winning and the depression of losing.

The same sequence of sensations applies to any other kind of bet, or, for that matter, an investment in the stock market. Currency speculation, which I have tried, is much the best for round-the-clock action: as soon as the market in London closes, the dealing starts up in New York, and then moves to the Far East, and so back to London again. All bets are essentially the same, it is the time scale that's different. However this amalgam of sensations, of anticipation, excitement and resolution, may be described, the impact is in the body, physical.

Such feelings are not limited to gamblers. The same sort of sensations, I suppose, are felt by glider pilots, racing drivers, deep-sea divers, to name but three (operating as it were above, on and below the level of everyday living). The difference is in the pay-off: the thrill of trusting to the wind, speed around the track, piercing the darkness of deep water. When you come to think about it, almost all human activities carry an emotional charge, in varying degrees – the actor going on stage, the politician at a public meeting, the salesman trying to close a deal. In this sense gamblers are not so different. The emotional charge is a common experience, known colloquially as 'getting the adrenalin going'. There is one key difference, though, which distinguishes the activity of gambling from gliding, racing, diving and all the other things that people do when they are enjoying themselves. In all these activities, the pilot, driver, swimmer, or whoever, has trained or practised or worked out the right and the wrong way of doing it, has been taught and tested at some length how to perform and has, in sum, established that he or she is in a position to carry through the action successfully. There may be accidents – freak winds, oil on the track, oxygen failure – but the chances are very strongly in their favour. In gambling it is exactly the opposite! The odds are against the player and everyone knows it. The risk is worse than fifty-fifty. Gamblers who manage to get a fifty-fifty break count themselves lucky!

After all, you cannot win at gambling in the long run, and that is the basic truth and the basic point about it. The very point that makes the motive for gambling such a mystery. Put it this way: suppose you're walking down the street and you meet some fellow who offers to toss a coin with you, heads or tails: the only snag is, when you lose you pay a dollar, when you win, you get paid only 99 cents. You wouldn't do it, would you? You'd be out of your mind to do it. But that is what happens, exactly what happens, when you bet in a casino. I do it, you do it, and everybody does it. That is how the casinos make their huge profits.

So why gamble? The reasons are as many and various as the stars in the sky. I prefer to take the question the other way round. Why do some people not gamble? It's such a widespread trait of human conduct that it might be considered abnormal not to do it. The thought is not new. Gaming in all its forms – casinos, horse-racing, lotteries, card-games – is simply too large an industry to be based on services catering for a deviant sub-group of the population. As the great gambler and early student of probability, Geronimo Cardano (c. 1530) observed, 'Even if gambling were altogether an evil, still on account of the very large number of people who play, it would seem to be a natural evil.'

(*Easy Money* by David Spanier)

B Explain the meaning of these phrases from the text.

1 sets the premium *(line 4)*
2 a healthy margin *(line 5)*
3 game-plan for living *(line 7)*
4 pitter-patter of excitement *(line 15)*
5 twitches of nervous tension *(line 16)*
6 see-saw sensations *(line 16)*

C Find a word or phrase in the text which, in context, is similar in meaning to:

Paragraph 1
1 happening to

Paragraph 2
2 a bet

Paragraph 3
3 24-hour a day activity
4 buying and selling
5 mixture of feelings

Paragraph 4
6 the reward

Paragraph 5
7 the problem
8 mad

Paragraph 6
9 a common characteristic
10 an abnormal minority

D How many different forms of risk-taking activity are mentioned by the writer, and what are they? Do you agree that these activities are comparable to gambling?

E In the introduction to his book the writer says:

'Gambling is a deeply-rooted human instinct, as strong as hunger, thirst or sex. As such, it is my contention that Gambling is Good for you.'

Do you agree with him? Can you think of arguments against his point of view?

Peeping Tom

F Read the following text, but do not attempt to fill the gaps until you have listened to the tape. Then complete the text with a suitable word or phrase according to the information on the tape.

A woman who lived in a .... *(1)* flat was alerted to the presence of a prowler when .... *(2)*. She got up, wearing her .... *(3)*, and saw a man looking through the window. She told him to go away and he replied with some .... *(4)*. The woman started to be .... *(5)* and, terrified, phoned the police. She threatened she would .... *(6)* but the policewoman just .... *(7)*. By the time the police arrived, the man had .... *(8)*, but finally he was found and .... *(9)*.

Talking points

A What are the people in the following four photographs doing?

B Work in pairs.

Student A: dissuade your partner from taking up one of the sports shown, pointing out the dangers.

Student B: play down the dangers and emphasise the pleasure and excitement.

C What are the dangers associated with the following activities and events?
What precautions should you take?
Work in pairs and advise your partner how to carry out these activities safely:

- changing a light bulb
- opening champagne bottles
- letting off fireworks
- using household and garden chemicals
- moving furniture
- deep-fat frying
- mowing the lawn
- using glue
- answering the telephone
- flying on scheduled flights
- travelling on trains
- going to football matches
- breaking down on the motorway.

Writing

Letter

A During a storm, a tree fell on your car and damaged it.

You now have to write to the company that insures your car. Give full details of exactly:

- how and when the accident happened
- what the extent of the damage is
- what action you have taken so far
- what further action will be required.

Establish with the company exactly what the procedure is for the payment of claims.

Your letter should be about 200 words long.

Hints

Look at the two examples of business letter layout given below and notice how they differ from each other and from the layout of a personal letter as seen in Unit 1.

When you write the letter remember:

– this is a formal letter to a company
– you should cover all essential details
–it should be explicit yet concise.

Example a

17 Green Street
Richmond
Yorkshire
YP7 8QT
30 October 19--

Claims Department
Commercial Insurance plc
125 Cornhill
London EC2 8TR

Dear Sirs,

Thankyou
① Say why you are writing
→ indented paragraphs
② Details
③ Conclusion, response required

Yours faithfully

Jane Smith

Jane Smith (Mrs)

Example b

17 Green Street
Richmond
Yorkshire
YP7 8QT
30 October 19--

Mr T Cotton
Claims Manager
Commercial Insurance plc
125 Cornhill
London EC2 8TR

Dear Mr Cotton

Yours sincerely

Jane Smith

Jane Smith (Mrs)

Magazine article

B You have been asked to write an article for a magazine warning holiday-makers about the possible dangers they face on the beach. Using the illustration to help you, write the piece using about 350 words.

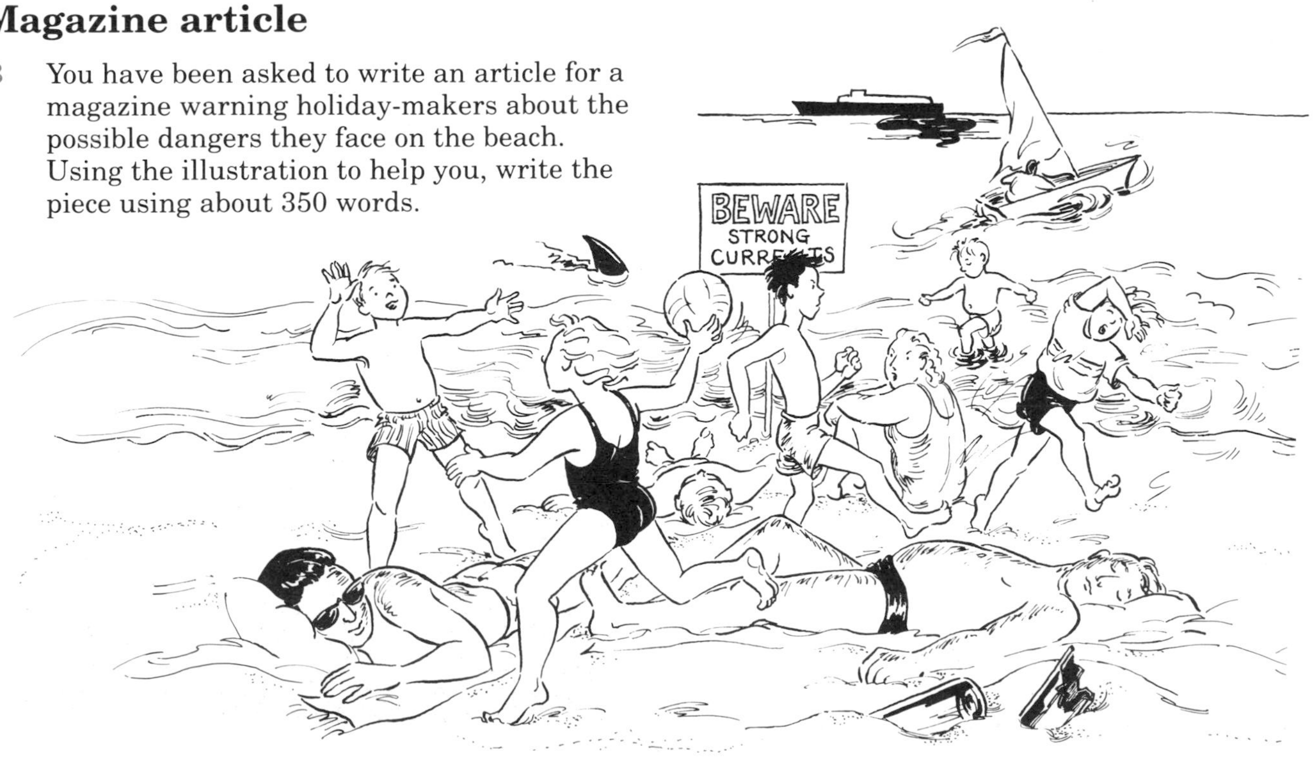

Literary approaches

Who is the speaker in the poem?

What choice has he made and why has he made it?

An Irish Airman Forsees His Death

by W B Yeats (1865 – 1939)

I know that I shall meet my fate
Somewhere among the clouds above;
Those that I fight I do not hate,
Those that I guard I do not love;
My country is Kiltartan Cross,
My countrymen Kiltartan's poor,
No likely end could bring them loss
Or leave them happier than before.
Nor law, nor duty bade me fight,
Nor public men, nor cheering crowds,
A lonely impulse of delight
Drove me to this tumult in the clouds;
I balanced all, brought all to mind,
The years to come seemed waste of breath,
A waste of breath the years behind
In balance with this life, this death.

(from *The Wilds Swans at Coole*, 1919)

Follow-up

A Fill each of the numbered blanks in the following passage with one suitable word.

Gambling
Many people love to gamble, but very few are any good .... *(1)* it. When things go wrong, those ....*(2)* have lost their money blame someone..................*(3)* and shout for help.

For some people the desire to gamble is very strong, ... *(4)* irresistible, in fact. It is possible to become addicted to gambling in the .... *(5)* way that people are addicted to alcohol or drugs. When this happens, as well as losing all their money, gamblers .... *(6)* lose their jobs and suffer many personal difficulties, ...*(7)* as their marriage.................. *(8)* up. They may .... *(9)* to crime to finance their gambling habit.

A very large number of people, perhaps the majority, ... *(10)* bets at .... *(11)* time in their lives. These are usually small .... *(12)* of money which are gambled on the results of football matches, ... *(13)* on horse and dog races. Almost all sports attract some .... *(14)* of betting. In as .... *(15)* as you have to use your knowledge of the sport to decide .... (16) you think the result will be, there is an.................. *(17)* of skill involved. The odds, however, will always be against you and you can only win a fortune by taking a huge .... *(18)*.

The same .... *(19)* for casinos. A gambler may have a .... *(20)* of good luck but the casino always wins in the end – about 20% of the money which is bet stays with the house.

B Finish each of the following sentences in such a way that it is as similar as possible in meaning to the sentence printed before it.

1 Although the car was difficult to steer, Andrew managed to complete the race.

In spite ....
....

2 John finds it difficult to accept that he was responsible for the accident.

What ....
....

3 The number of people killed in motor-cycle accidents during races this year is now twenty-four.

Already this year ....
....

4 This driver failed to win any races last season.

No ....
....

5 He gets his salary plus a company car and free accommodation.

Along with ....
....

6 All members of the team know the risks they face.

Everyone ....
....

C Fill each of the blanks with a suitable word or phrase.

1 Already this year some two dozen motorists .... in accidents on a section of motorway noted for its fog.

2 In any disaster firemen .... their own lives to save those of others.

3 The doctor wouldn't have been injured himself if he .... to the scene of the accident.

4 You could say that anyone taking part in a dangerous sport has to accept the risks, but, ..., it could be argued that the organisers have some responsibility for safety.

5 You shouldn't gamble if you .... to lose.

6 These speakers are not .... with this CD player.

D For each of the sentences below, write a new sentence as similar as possible in meaning to the original sentence, but using the word given. The word must not be altered in any way.

1 The organiser's action almost amounted to negligence.

short

....

....

2 A number of accidents occurred, when the week for practice arrived.

come

....

....

3 The driver had been travelling at over 180 m.p.h.

excess

....

....

4 Up to half a million people may have perished in the earthquake.

claimed

....

....

5 The team is unlikely to reach the summit.

odds

....

....

6 The boxer agreed to take part in the match only on the conditions he himself laid down.

terms

....

....

E Choose the word or phrase (*A*, *B*, *C* or *D*) which best completes each sentence.

1 The manager decided to .... a circular about health and safety matters.

A give *B* issue
C post *D* publicise

2 The gambler is aware of a(n) .... of adrenalin just as the bet is placed.

A acme *B* zenith
C summit *D* peak

3 Fatal accidents are part and .... of a speed sport.

A packet *B* packaging
C parcel *D* package

4 It was the second time in a week that Dr Brown had been called .... to a traffic accident.

A up *B* for *C* round *D* out

5 The survivors of the accident .... a coin to determine who should go and look for help.

A tossed *B* threw
C aimed *D* hurled

6 Nobody had .... such a lack of basic safety precautions.

A guessed *B* expected
C warned *D* previewed

7 The desire to gamble in the hope of winning a lot of money without working for it is a common human ....

A character *B* trait
C need *D* want

8 Before selecting anyone for the mountaineering team consider carefully his or her past .... on mountains.

A qualifications *B* training
C record *D* career

9 Being involved in an accident is just one of the mishaps that can .... an individual.

A happen *B* befall
C hurt *D* upset

10 The lawyer insisted that his clients receive some compensation before blame was ....

A determined *B* decided
C placed *D* apportioned

11 Jack decided to .... £5,000 as compensation for his injuries.

A effect *B* seek
C claim *D* sue

12 The racehorse owner was .... when his horse came in first.

A gleeful *B* jubilant
C stunning *D* boasting

13 Actuaries draw up their statistics on the basis of thousands of different ....

A data *B* information
C moments *D* instances

14 Incompetence was claimed on the .... of the stewards monitoring the competition.

A side *B* behalf
C part *D* half

15 An obstacle had been placed in the middle of the road and the .... accident was blamed on it.

A occurring *B* ensuing
C following *D* resulting

Unit three

Getting and Spending

Lead-in

A Look at the statistics which show the way money is spent according to the income group to which people belong.

What differences emerge from these statistics?

How would you account for these differences?

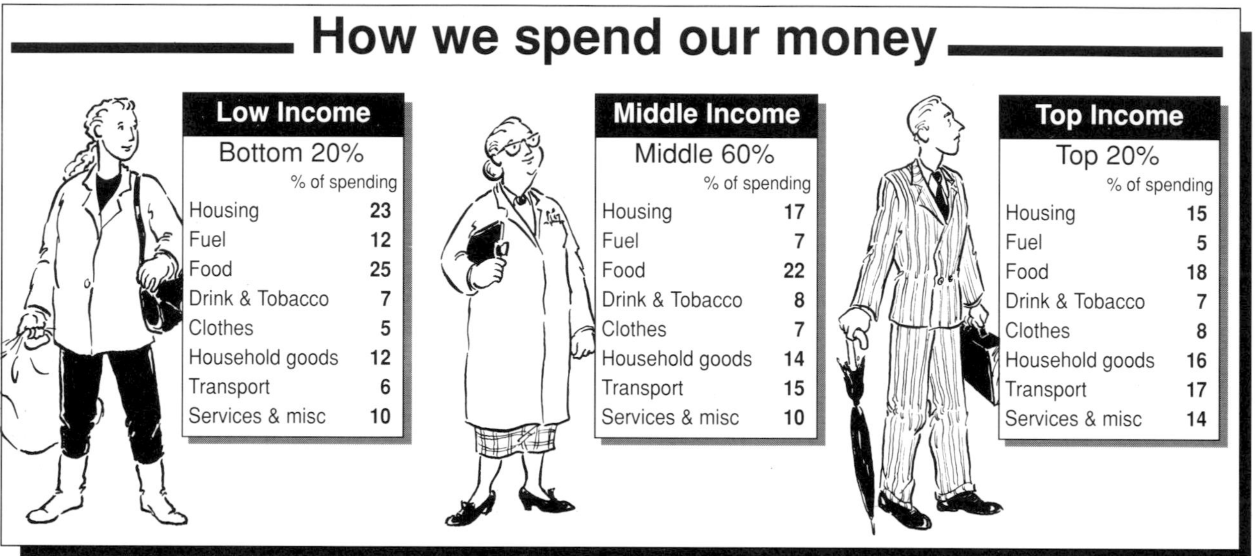

How we spend our money

% of spending	Low Income (Bottom 20%)	Middle Income (Middle 60%)	Top Income (Top 20%)
Housing	23	17	15
Fuel	12	7	5
Food	25	22	18
Drink & Tobacco	7	8	7
Clothes	5	7	8
Household goods	12	14	16
Transport	6	15	17
Services & misc	10	10	14

B Complete each gap in the sentence with one of the words or phrases given.

high earning potential	plough	stockbroker	income tax
wealth	shares	earnings	means
pocket money	cash	in debt	revenue
bonus	commission	poverty	fee
lotteries	credit card	credit	affluent
wages	the pools	budget	
benefit	salary	broke	
loan sharks	liquidation	cheque	

1 In many countries, there is a contrast between the .... of a small number of citizens and the .... of the masses.

2 For people on the breadline, their one chance of becoming rich overnight is to win ....

3 In Australia, basic social services such as hospitals are funded by ...., which provide the government with .... and citizens with the chance of large .... prizes.

4 People in work pay .... on their .... Those who are unemployed receive ....

5 If you are paid by the hour you get .... If you are paid on an annual basis, you get a(n) .... and if you are paid for a particular service you get a(n) ....

6 In department stores, there are three ways of paying for goods: in cash, by .... and by ....

7 Housewives running the family finances have to work within a(n) ....

8 If your expenditure exceeds your income, you will find yourself ....

9 Children frequently receive .... from their parents, and supplement this with part-time jobs such as baby-sitting or paper rounds.

10 Graduates in the 1990's are attracted to jobs with ....

11 One way of investing money is to buy .... in a public company, the prices of which are quoted on the Stock Exchange.

12 A(n) .... can advise you on which shares to buy and sell and carry out these transactions on your behalf.

13 Salesmen get a large part of their income through ...., a percentage based on the volume of sales they achieve. If they achieve sales figures beyond a specified level they may also get a(n) ....

14 People on low incomes sometimes take out loans from .... which they are never able to repay.

15 For some people, living on .... is a normal way of life.

16 Although he earns a lot of money, Tony always seems to be ....

17 Charles's .... lifestyle came to an end when he was made redundant.

18 When the company's major creditor could not pay its bills, it had such high debts that it was forced to go into ....

19 When our company starts making a profit, we shan't take the money for ourselves but will .... it back into the business by buying some up-to-date equipment.

20 People who apply for this grant must undergo a(n) .... test to establish whether they are genuinely in need.

C Complete the text using the words and phrases given.

current account	ready cash	arrears	mortgage
debt	income	rich	pensions
cope	freed	unexpected	
security	overdraft	in reserve	
means	credit cards	potential	

Personal Finances

Many people regard financial .... *(1)* as the most important thing in family finances. This is not the same thing as being .... *(2)*. It means being able to .... *(3)* with the unexpected, being .... *(4)* from the need to think about money, living within your .... *(5)*. For day to day living you need .... *(6)* but you also need a bit .... *(7)* for a rainy day.

The first thing to think about is your .... *(8)* and how much is in it. You don't want to run the risk of having an unauthorised .... *(9)*, it's far too expensive. .... *(10)* can be a helpful way of handling .... *(11)* expenses, but credit is always costly, and of course it's just another form of .... *(12)*. In Britain many people have a very large debt called a(n) .... *(13)*, a sum of money borrowed from a bank or a building society, which many regard as a good way of buying a house.

But if the payments fall into .... *(14)*, your house could be sold to pay off the debt.

Life assurance and .... *(15)* are an important aspect of feeling secure, and if you don't make provision early, retirement can be a financial shock. It's worth foregoing some jam today for a bit more bread tomorrow.

Finally, investments. You need to invest in an area where there is some .... *(16)* for your capital to grow while you still have a(n) .... *(17)*. You could choose shares, unit trusts, or government securities.

If you do all these things, you shouldn't have to worry on a day-to-day level.

Theme one: *Young Consumers*

Pocket Money

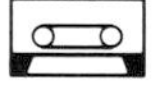

A Listen to these schoolchildren talking about pocket money and how they spend it. Complete the table by making notes on the text. Give precise figures wherever possible and write *'doesn't say'* if the information is not on the tape.

	1 Stephen	2 Claire	3 Robbie	4 Terry
How much do they receive?				
How much do they get from work?				
What kind of work do they do?				
What do they do with their money?				

B Do you think children and teenagers should receive pocket money from their parents?

Should they work or do odd jobs to earn money?

Now read the text and answer the questions which follow.

Paying Your Way

There were red faces at one of Britain's biggest banks recently. They had accepted a telephone order to buy £100,000 worth of shares from a fifteen-year-old schoolboy (they thought he was twenty-one). The shares fell in value and the schoolboy was unable to pay up. The bank lost £20,000 on the deal which it cannot get back because, for one thing, this young speculator does not have the money and for another, being under eighteen, he is not legally liable for his debts. If the shares had risen in value by the same amount that they fell, he would have pocketed £20,000 profit. Not bad for a fifteen-year-old. It certainly beats a paper round. In another recent case, a boy of fourteen found, in the attic of his grandmother's house, a suitcase full of foreign banknotes. The clean, crisp, high-denomination notes looked very convincing but they were not legal tender in their country of origin or anywhere else. This young wheeler-dealer headed straight to the nearest bank with his pockets crammed with notes. The cashiers did not realise that the country in question had devalued its currency by 90%. They exchanged the notes at their face value at the current exchange rate. In three days, before he was rumbled, he took £200,000 from nine different banks. Amazingly, he had already squandered more than half of this on taxi-rides, restaurant meals, concert tickets and presents for his many newly-acquired girlfriends (at least he was generous!) before the police caught up with him. Because he is also under eighteen the banks have kissed goodbye to a lot of money, and several cashiers have had their careers blighted.

Should we admire these youngsters for being enterprising and showing initiative or condemn them for their dishonesty? Maybe they had managed for years with tiny amounts of pocket money wrung from tight-fisted parents. Maybe they had done Saturday jobs for peanuts. It is hardly surprising, given the expensive things that young people want to buy, such as fashionable trainers and computer games, if they sometimes think up more imaginative money-making schemes than delivering newspapers and baby-sitting. These lads saw the chance to make a killing and took it.

Another recent story which should give us food for thought is the case of the man who paid his six-year-old daughter £300 a week pocket money. He then charged her for the food she ate and for her share of the rent and household bills. After these deductions, she was left with a few coins for her piggy bank. 'She will soon learn the value of money,' he said. 'There's no such thing as a free lunch. Everything has to be paid for and the sooner she learns that the better.' At the other extreme there are doting parents who provide free bed and board for their grown-up children. While even the most hard-hearted parents might hesitate to throw their children out on the streets, we all know of people in their late twenties who shamelessly sponge on their parents. Surely there comes a time when everyone has to leave the parental nest, fend for themselves and pay their own way in life? But when is it?

C Find a word or phrase in the text which, in context, is similar in meaning to:

Paragraph 1

1 obliged by law
2 delivering newspapers
3 someone who makes money quickly (but not always honestly)
4 completely full of
5 the value printed on the notes
6 found out
7 wasted
8 damaged

Paragraph 2

9 thinking for yourself and taking action
10 ungenerous
11 for very little money
12 make a lot of money quickly

Paragraph 3

13 something to think about
14 very loving in a foolish way
15 accommodation and food

D

1 Briefly summarise the three stories about children and money which are referred to in the article.

2 Why did the bank lose £20,000 and not £100,000?

3 Is there anything admirable about what the two boys did?

4 What was the father's motive in giving his daughter £300 a week pocket money?

5 In your opinion, what are appropriate amounts of pocket money for children to receive at various ages? When should people cease to be financially dependent on their parents?

Grammar: *simple past tense*

A Divide these sentences into two groups of eight.

What is the difference between the two groups?

1 I'd rather you didn't come tomorrow.

2 I didn't like what I saw.

3 We enjoyed our trip to Norwich.

4 It's time we left.

5 They shot six rabbits and four pigeons.

6 Did you want to see Mrs Jones now, doctor?

7 What did you say your name was?

8 I looked up his number in the directory.

9 You said you knew how to play this game!

10 If I knew the answer I would tell you.

11 Did you phone the estate agent?

12 He took the parcels to the post office.

13 Who did you want to see?

14 I'd very much prefer it if you delivered the sofa-bed next Monday.

15 How much did you pay for the painting?

16 The exchange rate wasn't very good.

Now write three sentences of your own for each of the two groups.

Theme two: *Credit and Debt*

Repayment of a Debt

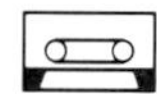

A Read the following text, but do not attempt to fill the gaps until you have listened to the tape. Then complete the text with a suitable word or phrase according to the information on the tape.

The speaker talks about something that happened over .... *(1)* years ago. Her husband's .... *(2)*, whose name was Arthur, ... *(3)* asked her to lend him £ .... (4). He needed the money to repay a .... *(5)* debt. If he didn't pay this he might receive a ....*(6)*. Also, he had decided to leave Britain and join the .... *(7)* but had to sign a form declaring that he didn't owe any money. The speaker .... *(8)* Arthur, ... *(9)* to her husband and decided to lend him the money. She handed it over, in .... *(10)* and in an .... *(11)*, outside a .... *(12)* and felt rather .... *(13)* about this. The debt was not repaid, so the speaker, with the support of her .... *(14)*, sent a letter to Arthur suggesting that he should repay the debt .... *(15)* and that if he did not do so his .... *(16)* would be informed, although they were .... *(17)* to take this step. After .... *(18)* years the debt was repaid in full.

B Look at the following material issued by a bank.

What is attractive about their offer?

Are there any disadvantages that might not be immediately obvious to the public?

BARCLAYS BANK PLC
Customer Services Centre
PO Box 111, Gloucester GL4 7RP

A Sample Esq
1, Any Road
Any Town
Anyshire
XY1 1XY

561 PRIZES MUST BE WON IN OUR £100,000 COMPETITION!

Dear Mr Sample,

I am pleased to confirm that this month's repayment on your Barclayloan will be the last. As you are a valued Barclayloan customer, I am also inviting you personally to enter our big prize Barclayloan competition.

There are literally hundreds of wonderful prizes to be won, so you could stand a good chance of winning. You could be the owner of a luxury villa in the Mediterranean, or visit a Grand Prix venue anywhere in the world.

I appreciate that you may not have wished to commit yourself to a further loan whilst still making repayments. Now that these are completed, however, I hope you will consider using Barclayloan again. Remember, Barclayloans are available for almost anything from garden furniture to flying lessons. And if you are thinking of buying a car - new or secondhand - there is now another excellent reason to choose this fuss-free form of finance:

We'll be giving away 7 nights' free hotel accommodation with every Barclayloan for cars approved between now and 29th July.

C Read the text and discuss whether the use of credit has the same effects in your country as in Britain.

Debt and despair on the dark side of consumer credit

Edward Vulliamy examines how the present boom in borrowing is costing some people their homes and their marriages.

A breed of advice worker braced themselves for a surge in business yesterday after news that the problem they deal with appears to be reaching a point beyond control: figures for June showed consumers owing £3 billion in credit, an increase of more than 10 per cent on the previous month.

Consumer credit – a smart word for debt – has brought the Citizens' Advice Bureaux a massive workload as their clients, unable to cope with repayments and interest on loans and plastic-card shopping, arrive for help.

People have lost their houses, their marriages have broken up, they suffer from stress. It is the new social disease of the spendaholics.

At the Merton Money Advice Service in south London, all social groups come for help, although the unemployed, at 6 per cent in the borough but 38 per cent of the clients, are heavily represented.

Ms Alison Skittrall, an advice worker, says: 'They cannot afford to live off benefits, but they want to try and keep the standards they had before being made redundant.' Nearly a third of all clients had more than 10 creditors, and 18 per cent owed more than £10,000, excluding their mortgages.

Many who come in have 'robbed Peter to pay Paul', trying to cover a multitude of smaller debts by taking out large loans which they cannot afford to repay. Often there is a problem of ignorance. 'People are only looking at the monthly repayment,' Ms Skittrall says, 'never at the interest or at what they will have to pay in total.'

Some of those in difficulties are young – under 24 – and easily tempted into credit by the high street storecard. 'They want to be fashionable, they want a compact disc player, or an auto focus camera. And because the interest is so high on shop cards and on the credit cards, they might take out a larger loan with a bank or a financial company.

'Then it starts to get further down the line, and that is when they come to us. Often too far down the line: they arrive when they are being evicted from their houses, or they have been to court.'

Many run into problems when the fine-tuning of their life 'on tick' is disrupted by quite modest reductions in income. Ms Skittrall had been seeing a woman with eight credit cards, all in debt, plus a bank loan. The woman was 'just able to juggle and keep them going with about £30 a week overtime. Then that went. It was a small but crucial amount, and she fell completely behind on even the minimum payments.'

Mr Chris Bain, of the Birmingham Settlement Money Advice Centre, says: 'I used to be astonished by the problems people came in with and the advertising people are lured with. But I've lost my incredulity now.

'I have a client here with debts of about £13,000, in arrears on all his credit cards, and yet still being offered free gifts by the credit card companies if he felt like putting up his credit limit by another £100.'

Barclays has just started a pilot scheme called Profiles which enables cardholders to acquire points with the money that they spend with their cards. The points accumulate to entitle them to gifts from a catalogue. Barclays is emphatic that the idea shows no signs of exacerbating repayment problems.

However, Mr Bain says the gift system does cause problems with the storecards 'which are shoved down people's throats every time they walk into the big shops in Birmingham.'

Another of his clients had overdrafts with two banks, payments he could not meet on Barclay and Access cards* and a sizeable loan from Barclays Bank, the monthly payment on which alone was four times what was left of his income after essentials. 'Then this man is told that if he was to spend an additional £200 in one of the stores on his storecard, then he'll get a bloody carriage clock. His family is suffering, his marriage has become unstable. Creditors telephone him and visit, so that every time you hear the phone ring, or the door knock, you think it's them. Every time a letter drops on the floor, you think it's them again.

'Of course, there is a degree of self-inflicted harm about it at first, but as it goes on, then so does the advertising, which is an obscenity.'

One of the problems is addiction to optimism, Mr Bain says. 'It just builds up over a period of time. I get people who think they've got this far, so if they're saying "go on holiday on an Access card" then they think why not – I may win the pools tomorrow. Then comes the crunch.'

Advertisements for consolidated loans to swallow up all the little ones – at huge interest levels – nowadays cram the pages of tabloid newspapers.

Mr Bain said: 'I get people who go for what they think is the short-term answer and end up losing their houses. I've had four in the last month who've lost their houses because they got behind, and the building societies wouldn't consolidate the arrears.'

In Liverpool, Mr John Pope dealt with the case of a woman in debt whose monthly repayments had been set, with the finance company's agreement, by the Citizens Advice Bureau for which he worked.

'Then she had a baby, and that required us to have another look at the payments. Instead, the company simply offered her a further loan, the very last thing she needed. We managed to persuade her out of it, but if we hadn't been dealing with it, I don't know what might have happened.'

A spokesman for Barclaycard said yesterday that the company has tightened its vetting procedures, and this June had turned away 38 per cent of applicants for cards, against 24 per cent in June last year.

He added that 43 per cent of cardholders paid their monthly bills without incurring interest. 'We do not want people who cannot afford to use the card, and every credit limit is based on the customer's ability to pay.'

A spokeswoman for Access said that the individual banks offering the facility, rather than the credit card company itself, were responsible for the customers using the card. Any offers or incentives to use the card were not Access's business but that of the subscribing banks.

(Edward Vulliamy, *The Guardian*)

* *Access* and *Barclaycard* are the most widely-used credit cards in Britain.

D Read the text again and find the word or phrase which, in context, is similar in meaning to:

Paragraph 1
1 a period of economic growth
2 causing someone to lose something

Paragraph 2
3 stood firm
4 a forward rush

Paragraph 3
5 fashionable
6 amount of work to be done

Paragraph 4
7 relationships have ended
8 people addicted to spending

Paragraph 5
9 local area

Paragraph 6
10 to be financially dependent on
11 put out of work
12 people to whom money is owed

Paragraph 7
13 mass

Paragraph 9
14 thrown out of
15 been subject to legal action

Paragraph17
16 a positive approach
17 increases
18 the critical moment

Paragraph 22
19 person who speaks on someone else's behalf

Paragraph 23
20 causing to occur

E Now choose the best answer to the following questions.

1 According to the article, *spendaholics* are people who
A suffer from a social disease.
B have spent all their cash.
C have overextended themselves.
D have been conned by credit companies.

2 The unemployed are heavily represented at money advice centres because
A their income is low.
B they try to cling to their former standard of living.
C they have too many creditors.
D their mortgages are too big.

3 Young people find credit tempting for a variety of reasons. Which of the following does not apply?
A It provides easy access to consumer goods.
B It is readily available in the High Street.
C The monthly repayments seem reasonable.
D It is fashionable.

4 People who borrow too much
A have been conned by credit card companies.
B are victims of lack of knowledge.
C are not responsible for their own position.
D need more credit to help them out.

5 The attitude of credit card companies to the increasing problem of debt is
A defensive.
B helpful.
C responsible.
D aggressive.

F In not more than 120 words, outline the factors that lead people to get into debt.

An Account Executive Talks about his Job

G Listen to the first part of the tape and write down your answer to the questions on the next page as a number/numbers (e.g. two) or a number/numbers and one other word (e.g. two weeks).

1. How long can people be in arrears before the accounts representative calls?
2. How long do people take to pay arrears?
3. How many customers does the company have?
4. How many are in arrears?
5. What are the minimum and maximum percentage of people likely to be in arrears?
6. How many reminders are usually sent?
7. How long can customers be in arrears before the company starts legal proceedings?
8. How long do customers have to respond to a letter demanding payment?
9. How long does it take to recover the equipment after the default notice is served?

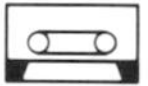

H Now listen to the second part of the tape, which tells the story of one particular customer who got into arrears. Make notes on the following points and re-tell the story in writing or orally.

1. the names used and why they, and the address, were significant.
2. other companies involved.
3. what happened in court: the various charges, the verdict and sentence, mitigating circumstances, the customer's general reputation, the outcome for the company.

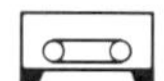

I Listen to the third part of the tape and say whether these statements are true or false.

The company:

1. will only rent TVs to people whose names are on the voters' roll.
2. never installs in certain parts of town.
3. always takes up employers' references.
4. is suspicious of people who want to pay cash.
5. prefers to deliver equipment at a specific time agreed with the customer.
6. prefers customers to have lived at the same address for at least six months.

Language awareness: *loan words*

A English is a language that has always been happy to borrow words from other languages. Many of these 'loan words' have now become an accepted part of the language.

In the following sentences, can you identify the loan words and say what they mean?

1. I've got the afternoon off and I'm going to make use of the fine weather by having a blitz on the garden.
2. Representatives of the leaders of the two opposing armies met at a secret rendezvous to try to negotiate an armistice.
3. The press conference was a fiasco: none of the speakers was adequately briefed to respond to the questions.
4. The military junta was overthrown by guerrilla forces working with help from a foreign power.
5. It's cold outside. Make sure you do up your anorak.
6. The health club provides a gymnasium, a sauna and a crèche.
7. Flower-arranging has always been one of our most popular evening classes but this year it's been rivalled by origami.
8. If you're really hungry I can recommend some excellent restaurants for shish kebab, crêpes, tandoori and dim sum.
9. Mary's become more relaxed since she took up yoga.
10. Christopher won't get on in this company. He's not prepared to kowtow to anyone, even the Managing Director.

B In the following sentences, can you use one of the words given to fill the gaps in the sentences? Use each word only once.

wunderkind	forte	entrepreneurs	raconteur
cuisine	imbroglio	kamikaze	vigilantes
paparazzi	rapport	pariahs	traversing
literati	trekking	genre	patio
bourgeoisie	cache	siesta	résumé
contretemps	crescendo	wanderlust	
née	spiel	macho	

1 The police discovered an arms .... buried beneath the floorboards in the abandoned building.

2 New York subways are patrolled by .... who aim to defend the travelling public against muggers.

3 One of the joys of being retired is being able to have a .... after lunch.

4 If you want to catch a glimpse of London's ...., don't miss the presentation of the Booker prize for the year's best novel.

5 Stephen's a terrific ....: the stories he tells keep his audience spellbound for hours.

6 The new nanny established an immediate .... with the children she was going to look after, so her employers had no qualms about going off on holiday and leaving her in charge.

7 When I told my friends I was going to train as a social worker, they looked at me as if I had said I wanted to be a .... pilot.

8 The Conservative Party has always expected to get the support of young .... who are not unwilling to take risks in order to gain a reward.

9 Before the Second World War in Britain, it was not unusual for divorced women to be treated as ...., not respectable enough to be entertained in polite society.

10 Another girl who left school in 1975, Sarah Taylor, ... Smith, is now living in New York where husband Piers has landed a job with the World Bank.

11 The poor Prince and Princess just couldn't escape from the Press. Even on their honeymoon they were relentlessly pursued by .... eager to photograph them wherever they went.

12 That was one of the most embarrassing evenings I've ever spent. If Michael and his wife have had a .... they might keep it to themselves and not inflict their bad feelings on their guests.

13 Mozart was treated as a .... on his concert tours with his father and sister in his early years.

14 Many couples like to improve their homes by building a .... complete with barbecue for summer entertaining.

15 The new principal's .... style of management caused feelings of resentment and hostility amongst the lecturers.

16 Like many students Angus was grabbed by .... and spent his vacations exploring the Amazon or .... in the Himalayas.

17 The .... is one class in society not conspicuous for its wish to change the status quo.

18 The applause reached a .... then slowly faded away.

19 '*Lean* ....' – our new range of low calorie pop-in-the-oven meals.

20 Aspiring authors are best advised to send a .... of their work and a sample chapter to an agent, rather than approaching a publisher direct.

21 The Junior Minister became involved in a financial .... that eventually led to his resignation.

22 John seems to be a talented pianist when he's playing at home. But the concert in front of parents at the school was not a success. Playing in public is just not his ....

23 I'm afraid that science fiction is not a .... that has ever held any interest for me.

24 It's always fascinating at sales promotions listening to the PR men delivering their ....

25 Students at the Officers' Training School go rock climbing, orienteering and on exercises involving .... difficult country at night.

Theme three: Money Matters

A Before reading the text discuss with other students:

What ways do you know of saving and investing money?

What are the risks and rewards of different types of investment?

What are *shares*?

What do you know about the Stock Market?

An Alternative Way to Save

So you want to be rich, do you? One of the roads to riches can be buying shares quoted on the stock market. Choose well and your investment quickly goes up in value. But pick the wrong one and a chunk of your savings can go down the drain. Many small investors have tried their hands at picking shares then sometimes found they had their fingers burnt and decided to hand their money over to the professionals. But unless you have a five-figure-plus cash sum, it is difficult to find people willing to manage a portfolio of shares for you. A more realistic route is to invest your hard-earned cash in a unit trust. With unit trusts, a saver's money is pooled with other people's cash to buy a range of shares selected and managed by a professional fund manager. You pay an up-front charge, an annual management fee, and every time sales or purchases are made, the dealing costs are deducted from the overall fund value. The attraction is that you hedge your bets – your money goes into a whole basket of different shares, possibly as many as a hundred or more companies. So if one or two companies have a hiccup, your investment can still grow in overall value. If you have investments in a handful of individual shares, you are more likely to suffer if one hits the skids, but if you hit the jackpot there are larger profits to be made.

What type of investor are you?

Your first step is to sort out what kind of investor you are – do you have a lump sum to invest, a few thousand pounds from an inheritance or a redundancy pay-off, or do you want to save money regularly to build up a nest-egg for the future?

Points for lump sum investors to consider:

- The minimum you can invest is typically £1,000 upwards.
- Can you afford to leave the money untouched for several years? A minimum of five years is a good starting point.
- Are you happy to put your money into a 'risk' investment which can go up and down in value?

Points for regular savers to consider:

- The minimum you can save is typically £35 a month upwards.
- Although there are no penalties if you want to cancel, think in terms of saving for a minimum of several years.
- A perk of regular savings is that you get more units for your money when share prices are low. So, provided prices go up again by the time you sell, you gain.

Do you want a regular income?

When returns on building society and bank accounts fall sharply, it's worth looking at the monthly income portfolio based on unit trusts. The advantage is that you are paid a reasonable income return which is likely to increase with a chance of capital growth. In a typical monthly income scheme, a lump sum of £10,000 will yield an income of £40 a month.

Two case histories

1
Three years ago, Jane Weston unexpectedly inherited a few thousand pounds. 'At that time Gemma was just a few months old. I thought it would be ideal to put the money into an investment which would grow in value, rather than just pay me interest,' she says. 'I decided to put the money into a unit trust.' Since she made the investment, it has grown in value by more than 50% and will be used for secondary education in the future.

2
Choosing presents for children is always difficult. So what Jamie Pullen's godmother, Anne Gilbert, decided six years ago was to start a regular savings plan for him. Each year £25 (the minimum is now £40) goes into an account designated for James. Hopefully, by the time he is eighteen, he will have a cash sum built up which should be very useful for him. Jamie's mother says: 'He certainly does not miss one more present – he always seems to get so many and I think he will really benefit from having a cash sum to spend as he starts university, college or working life.'

(Daily Mail)

B Explain the meaning of these words and phrases from the text.

1. go down the drain *(line 8)*
2. tried their hands *(line 9)*
3. had their fingers burnt *(line 11)*
4. a portfolio of shares *(line 17)*
5. hedge your bets *(line 30)*
6. a basket of different shares *(line 31)*
7. hit the jackpot *(line 40)*
8. a lump sum *(line 43)*
9. a nest egg *(line 47)*
10. capital growth *(line 87)*

C Now answer the following questions.

1. What risks are referred to when buying shares on the Stock Market?
2. How does a unit trust work?
3. What are the benefits of a unit trust to the small investor?
4. What two types of investor are described?
5. What two benefits are described for a monthly income portfolio based on unit trusts?
6. How does Jane Weston feel about her investment?
7. What does Jamie's mother think of Anne Gilbert's present?

For Richer, for Poorer

D Listen to this radio broadcast dealing with the subject of differing attitudes to money in couples.

Look at the exercise on the next page and choose the answer which best fits the text.

1 Terry Allison's research revealed that

A money problems caused more problems in marriage than sex.
B women wanted to earn more than men.
C attitudes to money could cause friction between couples.
D couples didn't want to share their possessions.

2 Which word best describes Hannah's feelings about her position?

A overworked
B furious
C exploited
D undecided

3 When Ruth went out with James before they were married she

A enjoyed receiving gifts.
B never offered to pay.
C thought James would always be happy to pay.
D felt overwhelmed by James's generosity.

4 James's attitude to money

A changed radically when he married.
B is that you use it differently at different stages of your life.
C is best described as inconsistent.
D shows that he is basically mean.

5 Anna's upbringing made her

A enjoy spending on luxuries.
B fear not being able to pay the bills.
C careful about money.
D suspicious of big-spenders.

E Now listen to the tape again and find out what words or phrases are used for the following:

1 any subject that polite people do not refer to

2 the major earner in the family

3 the legal document indicating how a person wants things disposed of on death

4 people who are extremely mean with money

5 managed

6 would not even consider

7 a person who is seen merely as a provider of the basic necessities and is not appreciated for it

8 what you earn from work

9 to spend extravagantly

10 to control the money

Talking points

A Two newspaper items about people who won the pools follow. Before you read the articles, discuss with a partner:

What sort of problems do you think they encountered through suddenly becoming very rich?

How do you think you would react in similar circumstances?

Would your attitude to your work or friends change?

What about your lifestyle?

What ways are there in your country for people to get rich?

Is there a moral difference between getting rich through chance, through inheritance or through personal effort?

B Work in pairs. Each of you should read one article, then report the contents to the other and answer any questions from your partner about the text. Then the texts can be discussed with the whole class.

Article a

Win May Have Caused Death

Pools winner Harry Johnson died suddenly yesterday – just seven weeks after scooping a £751,735 jackpot.

He suffered a massive heart attack as he drove to work with his wife Mabel. And last night a leading expert on stress said: 'It is highly likely that the pools win was to blame.' Dr Malcolm Carruthers of the Maudsley Hospital, London, explained: 'It is a recognised syndrome for someone of this age undergoing an abrupt change of fortune to suffer a heart attack.'

Mr Johnson, a 59-year-old woodwork teacher known affectionately to his pupils as 'Bulldog' lived with his school-mistress wife in a small house in Hale, Cheshire. They decided to work until Christmas. Then they planned to buy a new car each, renovate their house and take a holiday. Mr Johnson's friend and deputy head, Ray Drinkwater said: 'Sadly, I don't think Harry got around to doing anything with the money.'

(Daily Star)

Article b

Husband Walks Out On Pools Wife Who Won £368,000

Lovestruck Ian Stenson has walked out on his wife, Janice, who won £368,000 on the pools. He left their luxurious four-bedroom home and moved into a terrace house with his lover. He is supporting himself with the help of a £40-a-week Government grant to run a new business.

Ian, 33, insisted: Our split was nothing to do with the win. I just found someone with whom I had more in common.

It was in October 1984 that secretary Janice became a Vernons winner. The couple moved into a £100,000 home in Birmingham. Ian bought a £25,000 Porsche sports car, and Janice gave up full-time work and did a part-time job instead. Two years later Janice discovered Ian was having an affair. He had kept on his job as a storeman with British Telecom. His new love, 22-year-old Jaquie Burgess, also worked for BT. Now Ian has set up his own company with a friend. The business specialises in fitting telephones and business systems, and has been launched with a Government £40-a-week enterprise grant.

Ian said: 'After the win life should have been a dream, but neither of us had the imagination to get off our behinds and do something. We had a nice house, nice car and everything to look forward to. I felt guilty about leaving, and I wish Janice all the best in future.'

(Daily Express)

C **Role-play**

Work in groups of three.

One of you has just won a considerable amount of money by chance. The news is given to you on the telephone at work. One of you is a colleague who is told the news, and the third person is the boss of the winner.

Act out your reactions to the situation.

Writing

Composition

A Read the following information and then write a composition saying what you did with Aunt Agatha's bequest.

When your aged great-aunt Agatha died, she left you several items as detailed in her will, an extract from which is given below.

When the bequest became known to members of the family, you received a letter from Agatha's brother, your great-uncle Christopher, part of which is given here.

This is the last will and testament of
AGATHA MURIEL JOHNSTON
of Cremorne House The Close Salisbury Wiltshire

1 I revoke all my previous testamentary dispositions.

2 I appoint Arthur Livingstone and Catharine Whiting Solicitors of 10 Lincoln's Inn Fields London WC1 as my executors and trustees.

3 I give all my property whatsoever and wheresoever not otherwise disposed of to my Trustees.

4 To (YOUR NAME) I give the following:

the oil paintings 'House at Sunset' by Teddy Smythe, 'Cornfield' by Roger Carrington and 'Seascape in a Storm' by Beatrice Wentworth;

my diary, kept until my death at Midland Bank, Holborn Circus, London WC 1;

my property of 200 acres at Crewkerne, Northumberland, including the house, Franleigh Lodge, that stands on the site together with all its contents.

As far as the diary is concerned, I think you should be very careful who you show it to. Agatha was a headstrong girl, and discretion was not one of her characteristics when she was living in London in her twenties. She knew a lot of well-known people, knew them rather too well, in fact, and there are many people who could well be embarrassed to learn what she wrote privately. And I mean very well-placed people. Don't on any account let the Press get wind of it. A lot of people might lose their reputations, even if they've now passed on.

The house is another matter. Do with it what you want. If you want to live in an area that the government uses for military exercises, it's up to you. As for the paintings, they are utterly worthless and I would be happy to take them off your hands.

Hints

1 *Organisation:*

title	Make sure you choose one which is appropriate.
paragraph 1	Explain the situation.
paragraph 2	Discuss the most important part of the bequest.
paragraph 3	Discuss the second part of the bequest.
paragraph 4	Discuss the least important part of the bequest.
paragraph 5	Conclusion.

2 *Length:*

This composition should be about 350 words long. If you are not sure what this represents in your handwriting, it will be useful for you to get some idea. You can do this by looking at some old compositions and counting the number of words per page on, say, six pages. Work out, and remember, your average number of words per page. Use this number as your guide. If you become aware of what 200 or 350 words look like in your handwriting, you won't need to count the number of words every time you write a composition within a specified word limit.

3 *Style*

Informal.
No contractions.
Say what you did. Use the past tense.

Letter

B You have received the following letter from your bank. Reply to the bank, explaining how your account came to be overdrawn and indicating what action you have taken or plan to take.

> We wish to inform you that according to our records your current account was overdrawn in the sum of £35.00 as at 10 April.
>
> We regret that we do not feel able to continue payment of cheques drawn on this account until such payment is made to put the account in credit.
>
> We shall be debiting your account with the costs incurred as a result of using an unauthorised overdraft and charging you at the rate of 28p per cheque for every cheque drawn on the account. We shall also be charging you interest on the overdraft.

Literary approaches

Read this extract from a novel and consider these questions.

What role do the coins play in Silas Marner's life?

What attitude does the writer have to Silas?

Silas Marner by George Eliot (1819-80)

Gradually the guineas, the crowns and the half-crowns grew to a heap, and Marner drew less and less for his own wants, trying to solve the problem of keeping himself strong enough to work sixteen hours a day on as small an outlay as possible. Have not men, shut up in solitary imprisonment, found an interest in marking the moments by straight strokes of a certain length on the wall, until the growth of the sum of straight strokes, arranged in triangles, has become a mastering purpose? Do we not wile away moments of inanity or fatigued waiting by repeating some trivial movement or sound, until the repetition has bred a want, which is incipient habit? That will help us to understand how the love of accumulating money grows an absorbing passion in men whose imaginations, even in the very beginning of their hoard, showed them no purpose beyond it. Marner wanted the heaps of ten to grow into a square, and then into a larger square; and every added guinea, while it was itself a satisfaction, bred a new desire. In this strange world, made a hopeless riddle to him, he might, if he had had a less intense nature, have sat weaving, weaving, looking towards the end of his pattern, or towards the end of his web, till he forgot the riddle, and everything else but his immediate sensations; but the money had come to mark off his weaving into periods, and the money not only grew, but it remained with him. He began to think it was conscious of him, as his loom was; and he would on no account have exchanged those coins, which had become his familiars, for other coins with unknown faces. He handled them, he counted them, till their form and colour were like the satisfaction of a thirst to him. But it was only in the night, when his work was done, that he drew them out to enjoy their companionship.

Follow-up

A Fill each of the numbered blanks in the following passage with one suitable word.

The Fast No-fuss Way To Make Your Dreams Come True

You already appreciate the ease and convenience of making everyday purchases using your Trustcard. But now we can also .... *(1)* out with the more costly things too, thanks to the Trustcard Personal Loan Service. For Trustcard holders only, it's the ideal .... *(2)* to borrow up to £7,500 at competitive rates – without fuss, without interview. Quickly and easily, without complicated and time-wasting 'red tape' of .... *(3)* kind.

Just think! With a cheque from Trustcard in your hands, you can enjoy all the freedom and bargaining power of a cash buyer the very next time you make a major .... *(4)*. There'll be no need to pass .... *(5)* real bargains when you see them, and no frustrating wait while you work out where the money will come from. And you're free to spend your Trustcard Personal Loan on almost .... *(6)* you like. On repairs and improvements that add value to your home. On replacing your old car with a new one that costs .... *(7)* to run. On an exotic and refreshing holiday. On attractive additions to the house that .... *(8)* also be worthwhile investments such as antiques and art. Or simply on .... *(9)* with the kind of emergency that, when it occurs can .... *(10)* havoc with even the best-run household budget.

As an existing Trustcard holder we already know that you're more than capable of .... *(11)* your own financial affairs in a sensible way. So we don't require any form of .... *(12)* to set against the amount you borrow, your simple promise to repay your Trustcard Personal Loan is .... *(13)* we need.

Just .... *(14)* your Trustcard itself, our Personal Loan Service represents a more flexible way to borrow and spend. One designed to .... *(15)* your own particular plans. You can choose the amount you require, from £1,000 up to £7,500. And depending .... *(16)* how much you wish to borrow – and what you want to spend it on – you can choose between one and five years to repay.

What's more, a Trustcard Personal Loan makes budgeting easier too. Thanks to the fixed rate of .... *(17)* your modest monthly repayments will never be increased. .... *(18)* you be worried that sickness, accident or unemployment could ever affect your ability to repay, you'll be pleased to know that insurance .... *(19)* to meet these eventualities can be included within your Loan Agreement for only a small .... *(20)* cost.

B Finish each of the following sentences in such a way that it is as similar as possible in meaning to the sentence printed before it.

1 Mrs Brown is not involved in the management of this company.

Mrs Brown has nothing ....

....

2 Although he liked strawberries very much, John couldn't face eating any more that day.

Much ....

....

3 The court made him re-pay the debt week by week.

He was ....

....

4 If she had known the problems money would bring, she would have turned down the prize.

Had ....

....

5 Although some of his shares had gone down in price, he had made an overall profit.

In spite ....

....

6 She was interested in nothing except making money.

Making money ....

....

C Fill each of the blanks with a suitable word or phrase.

1. The situation seems .... crisis point.
2. The stockbrokers to .... she owed money took her to court.
3. The shock of suddenly becoming rich was probably .... his heart attack.
4. He was affectionately .... 'Bulldog' by his pupils.
5. She took it .... that the bank would accept her application for a credit card.
6. Rich ...., he still can't afford to buy an original Van Gogh.

D For each of the sentences below, write a new sentence as similar as possible in meaning to the original sentence, but using the word given. The word must not be altered in any way.

1. Peter's workload is more than he can handle.

   cope

   ....

   ....

2. If you don't pay by the end of the month, interest is charged.

   incur

   ....

   ....

3. The company does not intend to replace this model.

   plans

   ....

   ....

4. There is not much difference between these two vehicles.

   choose

   ....

   ....

5. Margaret is entitled to receive a share of the profits.

   right

   ....

   ....

6. It gave him great pleasure to contemplate the misfortune that had befallen his rival.

   gloated

   ....

   ....

E Choose the word or phrase (*A*, *B*, *C* or *D*) which best completes each sentence.

1 The driver knew his lorry was going to crash and .... himself for the impact.

A held *B* supported
C braced *D* tensed

2 The explorers realised they had reached the .... of no return.

A point *B* place
C edge *D* beginning

3 After his marriage broke .... John lived alone.

A up *B* away *C* apart *D* off

4 Sandra took out a £5,000 .... to buy a new car.

A debt *B* loan
C borrowing *D* credit

5 Martin was .... from the house because he hadn't paid the rent for six months.

A evicted *B* forced
C ejected *D* thrown

6 All applicants will be thoroughly .... for security risks.

A examined *B* vetted
C tested *D* searched

7 The amount you can borrow is .... on your salary.

A based *B* according
C determined *D* depending

8 As a special ...., Tracy was taken to the zoo on her birthday.

A prize *B* reward
C treat *D* gift

9 After her massive pools win, Mrs Jones went on a spending ....

A spree *B* bout
C splash *D* session

10 Peter and his brother don't have much .... common.

A by *B* on *C* together *D* in

11 You must be there at 6 a.m. on the ....

A time *B* dot *C* hour *D* point

12 You need a(n) .... five years' experience before you even think of applying to be manager.

A good *B* excellent
C solid *D* first-rate

13 Eventually, the debts were so bad that the company went ....

A bust *B* crash
C liquid *D* down

14 Unfortunately this model .... to be the most unpopular the company had ever produced.

A developed *B* proved
C turned *D* marketed

15 Sheila paid all the money .... her account.

A to *B* for *C* into *D* by

Unit four

All Creatures Great and Small

Lead-in

A Can you identify and describe these animals? What is their relationship to human beings?

B Do you agree with this statement?

'The time will come when men such as I will look upon the murder of animals as they now look upon the murder of men.' (Leonardo da Vinci, 1452–1519)

C Complete each sentence with one of the words or phrases given.

food chain	balance of nature	predators	vivisection
slaughtered	dwindled	stray	free-range
endangered species	exotic	prey	pests
gruesome details	breeding	pelts	
factory farms	poachers	bait	
species	culled	prevention	

1 Leopards hunt their .... at night.

2 In Britain, monkeys, salamanders and snakes are regarded as .... pets.

3 In most cities, one can see .... dogs, often abandoned by their owners, wandering about the streets.

4 In some African countries, elephants are illegally killed by .... who cut out and sell the tusks.

5 When his animals are fat enough, the farmer sends them to the abattoir to be ....

6 Some philosophers believe that man is intrinsically superior to all animals, whereas others argue that man is simply another .... of animals.

7 On .... animals are usually confined in pens, cages or stalls and not allowed to roam about freely.

8 Mrs Jones always buys .... eggs because she does not like the taste of eggs from hens reared in batteries.

9 He makes his living by .... dogs for show.

10 Some people argue that it is necessary to practise .... on animals in order to develop surgical techniques.

11 The Royal Society for the .... of Cruelty to Animals was established in 1824.

12 Many people do not want to hear the .... of slaughterhouse procedures.

13 In order to attract the tiger, the hunter ties a cow to a tree to serve as ....

14 It takes about sixty-five .... to make one mink coat.

15 The numbers of certain animals, such as tigers and whales, have .... to the point where they are regarded as ....

16 Animals in protected environments, such as National Parks, are often .... to keep their numbers down.

17 Farmers regard rabbits, rats and foxes as ....

18 In the early twentieth century rabbits were introduced to Australia and proliferated because they had no natural ....

19 Intensive hunting of one type of animal can often upset the ....

20 If cattle eat grass growing on polluted land, dangerous chemicals can travel up through the .... until they end up in the bodies of humans.

D Complete the text using the words and phrases given.

fought	well-being	banning	experimental
kept	mistreating	cruelty	entertainment
provides	abuse	resources	interference
right	activists	conservation	
exploited	safeguarded	wild	

Animal Rights

When we think about animals, we usually consider them in relation to human beings, rather than in their own .... *(1)*. For example, people who keep pets are likely to think of themselves as responsible for the .... *(2)* of their animals. If we do not have animals at home, we can still see them in zoos and circuses or on farms, where human beings are very much in control of how they are .... *(3)* and what happens to them. Only animals living in the .... *(4)*, dependent on their own .... *(5)*, and what nature .... *(6)* for their survival, appear to be free from human .... *(7)*.

Do any of these animals have rights? If we look for a moment at today's society, and at the ways in which animals live, it may seem that most people think they do not. There are millions of animals in zoos for us to look at, in laboratories for .... *(8)* use, on farms for us to eat, in circuses for our .... *(9)*, and in the wild for us to hunt. Human beings, it appears, have decided that animals exist simply to be used as they think best.

On the other hand, however, there are many stories in the newspapers and on television about people who have been convicted in the courts for .... *(10)* to animals. There are also reports of zoos being closed down for .... *(11)* their animals, councils .... *(12)* circuses from visiting their areas, demonstrators protesting against hunting, animal .... *(13)* 'liberating' animals from laboratories, and a growing number of wildlife .... *(14)* programmes. So not everyone believes that animals exist just to be .... *(15)*. More and more people are deciding that they do not have the right to use – and often .... *(16)* – animals, but that animals have rights themselves which must be .... *(17)*, and when necessary, ... *(18)* for in the same way that we fight for women's rights, civil rights and all human rights.

Theme one: *Friends or Food?*

Vegetarianism

A Listen to the discussion Tracy has with her parents. Which of the following points do her parents make in order to persuade her not to be a vegetarian?

1 She has always eaten meat before.

2 Her mother is an excellent cook.

3 She needs protein.

4 She should eat solid rather than liquid food.

5 She will lose weight, and already has.

6 She needs a balanced diet.

7 Eating meat has not done Tracy's parents any harm.

8 Most people eat meat.

9 It is expensive to be a vegetarian.

10 Tracy's mother will have to work harder.

B Now listen to the tape again. What points does Tracy make in defence of her decision?

1 She doesn't like chicken.

2 Eating animal flesh is like eating people.

3 Eating meat makes people aggressive.

4 Animals are slaughtered in a very cruel way.

5 It is good to lose weight by eating less animal fat.

6 Proteins are found in other things besides meat.

7 There have always been vegetarians.

8 Vegetarians live a long time.

9 She has perceived something that her parents cannot comprehend.

10 Her mother will not have to prepare special meals for her.

C What was your attitude towards animals when you were a child?

Has it changed over the years?

What influenced you to like some animals rather than others?

Now read the passage and compare your own childhood experience with that described by the author.

Animal Liberation

Our attitudes to animals begin to form when we are very young, and they are dominated by the fact that we begin to eat meat at an early age. Interestingly enough, many children at first refuse to eat animal flesh, and only become accustomed to it after strenuous efforts by their parents, who mistakenly believe that it is necessary for good health. Whatever the child's initial reaction, though, the point to notice is that we eat animal flesh long before we are capable of understanding that what we eat is the dead body of an animal. Thus we never make a conscious, informed decision, free from the bias that accompanies any long-established habit, re-inforced by all the pressures of social conformity, to eat animal flesh. At the same time children have a natural love of animals, and our society encourages them to be affectionate towards pets and cuddly, stuffed toy animals. From these facts stems the most distinctive characteristic of the attitude of children in our society to animals – namely, that there is not one unified attitude to animals, but two conflicting attitudes that coexist in one individual, carefully segregated so that the inherent contradiction between them rarely causes trouble.

Not so long ago children were brought up on fairy tales in which animals, especially wolves, were pictured as cunning enemies of man. A characteristic happy ending would leave the wolf drowning in a pond, weighed down by stones which the ingenious hero had sewn in its belly while it was asleep. And in case children missed the implications of these stories, they could all join hands and sing a nursery rhyme like:

'Three blind mice, see how they run!
They all ran after the farmer's wife
Who cut off their tails with a carving knife.
Did you ever see such a thing in your life
As three blind mice?'

For children brought up on these stories and rhymes there was no inconsistency between what they were taught and what they ate. Today, however, such stories have gone out of fashion, and on the surface all is sweetness and light, so far as children's attitudes to animals are concerned. Thereby a problem has arisen: what about the animals we eat?

One response to this problem is simple evasion. The child's affection for animals is directed towards animals that are not eaten: dogs, cats and other pets. These are the animals that an urban or suburban child is most likely to see. Cuddly, stuffed toy animals are more likely to be bears or lions than pigs or cows. When farm animals are mentioned in picture books and stories, however, evasion may become a deliberate attempt to mislead the child about the nature of modern farms, and so screen him from reality. An example of this is the popular Hallmark book *Farm Animals* which presents the child with pictures of hens, turkeys, cows and pigs, all surrounded by their young, with not a cage, shed or stall in sight. The text tells us that pigs *'enjoy a good meal, then roll in the mud and let out a squeal!'* while *'Cows don't have a thing to do, but switch their tails, eat grass and moo'*. British books, like *The Farm* in the best-selling Ladybird series, convey the same impression of rural simplicity, showing the hen running freely in an orchard with her chicks, and all the other animals living with their offspring in spacious quarters. With this kind of early reading it is not surprising that children grow up believing that even if animals 'must' die to provide human beings with food, they live happily until that time comes.

Recognising the importance of the attitudes we form when young, the Women's Liberation movement has suggested changes in the stories we read to our children. They want brave princesses to rescue helpless princes occasionally. To alter the stories about animals that we read to our children will not be easy, since cruelty is not an ideal subject for children's stories. Yet it should be possible to avoid the more gruesome details, and still give children picture books and stories that encourage respect for animals as independent beings, and not as cute little objects that exist for our amusement and table; and as children grow older, they can be made aware that most animals live under conditions that are not very pleasant. The difficulty will be that non-vegetarian parents are going to be reluctant to let their children learn the full story, for fear that the child's affection for animals may disrupt family meals. Even now, one frequently hears that, on learning that animals are killed to provide meat, a friend's child has refused to eat meat. Unfortunately this instinctive rebellion is likely to meet strong resistance from non-vegetarian parents, and most children are unable to keep up their refusal in the face of opposition from parents who provide their meals and tell them that they will not grow up big and strong without meat. One hopes, as knowledge of nutrition spreads, more parents will realise that on this issue their children may be wiser than they are.

(*Animal Liberation* by Peter Singer)

D Find a word or phrase in the text which, in context, is similar in meaning to:

Paragraph 1

1 have the wrong idea
2 first response
3 carcass
4 prejudice
5 originates
6 opposing
7 separated

Paragraph 2

8 clever (in a bad sense)
9 clever (in a good sense)

Paragraph 3

10 avoidance
11 give wrong information
12 protect

Paragraph 4

13 unpleasant and disgusting
14 unwilling
15 disturb

E Now answer the following questions.

1 What are the four points that the writer makes about children eating meat?

2 What are the two attitudes society expects children to have towards animals and why do they conflict?

3 What attitude towards animals was inculcated by traditional stories and rhymes?

4 In what way are children's picture books misleading?

5 Why is it difficult to change the traditional stories involving animals?

6 Why might some parents not want their children to know how animals are kept on farms?

7 In what sense may children be wiser than their parents?

F In a passage of 50–100 words summarise the problems that parents might face in explaining to their children how animals live.

Language awareness: animal images

A The list on the right contains expressions connected with animals. Match each one with an item from the list on the left, to describe a person who:

1	is more dangerous than he appears	*a*	to smell a rat
2	wears clothes which are too young for her	*b*	to get the lion's share
3	is very clumsy	*c*	as mad as a March hare
4	has a wrong sense of priorities	*d*	to let sleeping dogs lie

5	is in an unfamiliar situation and feels uncomfortable	*e*	mutton dressed as lamb
6	gets two results from one action	*f*	his bark is worse than his bite
7	leaves things as they are and doesn't cause trouble	*g*	to buy a pig in a poke
8	reveals a secret	*h*	to have a bee in his bonnet
9	destroys the source of his wealth	*i*	a wolf in sheep's clothing
10	is a bit obsessed with something	*j*	to kill the goose that lays the golden eggs
11	gets the biggest part	*k*	to kill two birds with one stone
12	is less frightening than he seems	*l*	to let the cat out of the bag
13	buys something without having seen it	*m*	a fish out of water
14	is suspicious about something	*n*	a bull in a china shop
15	is crazy	*o*	to put the cart before the horse

B Match the animal expressions in the list on the left with their definitions in the list on the right.

1	It's a dog's life.	*a*	raise a false alarm
2	This is a fine kettle of fish.	*b*	a poor, wretched existence
3	You're flogging a dead horse.	*c*	an unattractive child that later becomes beautiful
4	These loan repayments are like an albatross round our necks.	*d*	bad words and actions will return to trouble us
5	The chickens will come home to roost.	*e*	a burden we can't get rid of
6	One day you will cry wolf once too often.	*f*	something that cannot be criticised without causing great offence
7	That's one of our sacred cows, I'm afraid.	*g*	what is good enough for one person is good enough for another
8	What is sauce for the goose is sauce for the gander.	*h*	a hopeless pursuit of something that doesn't exist or cannot be caught
9	This test will sort out the sheep from the goats.	*i*	separate the good from the bad
10	This candidate is something of a dark horse.	*j*	a futile activity
11	We used to think she was an ugly duckling.	*k*	a chaotic situation
12	It's a wild-goose chase, I'm afraid.	*l*	someone whose abilities are unknown

C These newspaper headlines all use expressions taken from activities involving animals (e.g. sport, hunting, farming). Can you identify the animal reference and explain the meaning?

1 NEW PRESIDENT TAKES THE REINS.

2 NO LAME DUCKS IN BRITISH INDUSTRY SAYS CHANCELLOR

3 BRITISH GAS PROJECT FALLS AT THE FIRST FENCE

4 NEW MANAGER IN THE SADDLE

5 REBEL MPS RETURN TO THE FOLD

6 EXISTING PRODUCT RANGE A BIT LONG IN THE TOOTH SAYS NEW MANAGER

7 SURREY PUMA A RED HERRING SAY POLICE

8 POLICE BARKING UP THE WRONG TREE

9 MANAGER FEATHERED OWN NEST

10 INFLATION – WE MUST SEIZE THE BULL BY THE HORNS SAYS CHANCELLOR

11 PM SAYS 'I'VE GOT THE BIT BETWEEN MY TEETH

12 LEADER RIDING ROUGHSHOD OVER VIEWS OF PARTY MEMBERS

13 NECK AND NECK FINISH IN LONDON MARATHON

14 TIME TO CHEW THE CUD SAYS DEFEATED CANDIDATE

15 SOLDIERS WERE SITTING DUCKS

Theme two: *The Hunters and the Hunted*

A Which animals are the most dangerous to people?

In what circumstances are people likely to be attacked by animals?

Read the text quickly to find out what has caused the threat to Borivli Park.

Threat to Borivli Park

The killing of a child by a panther on March 13 has once again highlighted the crisis in the ecosystem of the National park at Borivli.

The panther stealthily crept into the tiny 'pada' (hamlet) of Chunabhatti in the wee hours of that Sunday morning and snatched the sleeping girl Rekha Janu Burkhud (aged 4) from where she lay beside her mother, Mainabai.

The family realised that the girl was being spirited away only when she let out a cry, 'Aai mala dhar' ('Mother hold me').

Rekha's father, Janu, and the other villagers then hurled stones at the panther, and chased it for some 150 metres. The animal finally abandoned the child and escaped into the darkness. The girl, however, lost her life.

The park authorities have now set up a crude-looking trap, in the form of a cage with a live dog as bait, but the panther has eluded them. Two forest guards and two villagers stand vigil in the 'pada' every night and the villagers do not stir out after 6 p.m. In fact just two days after killing Rekha the panther, according to the villagers, took away a pet cat from the same 'pada'.

So far, the authorities have doled out Rs 300* to the bereaved family 'out of sympathetic consideration'. A maximum compensation of Rs5000 is allowed under rules, provided the killing has taken place outside the park area. A higher claim for Rekha is being 'reviewed' since the death occurred within the park.

Panthers claimed two victims in 1986 and 1987 and since they struck 'outside' the park, i.e. in Yeoor village, Rs5000 was promptly paid. This time, however, the bureaucrats keep pointing out that the death took place on the wrong side of the boundary.

But the March 13 tragedy is only an early warning signal for the disaster looming ahead. After all, why did the panther attack the four-year-old Rekha?

It is well-established that panthers attack humans only when they are injured, sick or too old to hunt for prey. Their favoured prey are deer and wild boar. Over the years, however, these species have diminished mainly due to poaching.

The hardy panthers have adapted to these developments by preying on dogs, whose number has proliferated following the setting up of stables in Goregaon and elsewhere. In fact, some people claim that the panther mistook the naked Rekha for a dog.

The reaction of the park authorities is predictable. The deputy conservator, Mr S D Sathe, said that the park, which ranges over 103 square kilometres, has too many panthers. Though no study has ever been made, he put the number of panthers at around thirty-five. This figure was based on ocular estimation, he added.

According to Mr Sathe, the park could at best support ten to fifteen panthers. A sum of Rs 1 lakh* had been sanctioned in November 1987 for shifting some of the 'surplus' animals, but this was vociferously opposed by naturalists. In spite of this opposition, two panthers were surreptitiously transported to Melghat in Amravati district.

'If we can't shift the panthers, then let's move out the inhabitants,' the authorities seem to say. Some eleven areas within the park, housing around five hundred persons, have already been declared notified encroachments under the Indian Forest Act. A list of those to be resettled, including people living along the periphery, has been sent to the revenue and forest departments, which are dragging their feet.

But the Adivasis have an organic link with the forest and unlike those on the periphery, are part and parcel of the park. Instead of ejecting these people, most of whom are Warlis and Mahadeo Kolis, the authorities can absorb them in the forest department and settle them in the staff quarters. Those in the periphery can be shifted and resettled in the vicinity so that they are not deprived of their means of livelihood.

While a hue and cry is raised about the so-called notified encroachments, not a word is breathed about the three big temple complexes which have sprung up at Gomukh, near Kanheri caves. These temples have been 'expanding' steadily, and especially on Mahashivratri day there is bedlam in the park.

The right approach towards the problems of the park will have to be holistic, according to Mr Ulhas Rane, honorary wildlife warden for Maharashtra.

The immediate task is to ensure that the park is run in accordance with modern park management techniques, as at the Kanha national park and the Project Tiger reserves, Mr Rane said.

The park at Borivli is under greater threat primarily because it lies in the midst of a bustling metropolis. Government policies have not helped things a bit. Quarrying is conducted on the western boundary of the park, the film city is being developed near the southern end and tourists invade the place from the Borivli side.

The park has a budgetary allocation of only around Rs 70 lakh, with a staff of just 163.

Inadequately financed, poorly equipped and unimaginatively run – that is the state of the park today. When panthers kill four-year-olds, there is talk of shifting out human beings and animals. Different solutions are available and necessary.

(*Times of India*)

* *Rs*: rupees, the currency of India

* one *lakh* = 100,000 rupees

B Choose the best answer to the following questions.

1 On 13 March the villagers of Chunabhatti

A couldn't see the panther in the dark.
B attempted to rescue the girl.
C thought the panther had magic powers.
D expected a panther to attack.

2 Why has Rekha's family not received Rs 5000?

A The park authorities are not very sympathetic.
B They have already accepted Rs 300.
C The amount of compensation depends on where the killing took place.
D The park authorities are still considering a change in the rules.

3 What is the reason for the recent attacks by panthers on humans?

A The panthers in the park are getting too old to hunt their natural prey.
B Poachers have reduced the number of deer and wild boar.
C The number of panthers has increased.
D The villagers are not well protected.

4 Which of the following have the park authorities *not* done?

A They have moved some panthers.
B They have told some people that their presence in the park is illegal.
C They have protested about the three temple complexes.
D They have requested help from the revenue and forest departments.

5 What is the underlying cause of the problems facing Borivli Park?

A Government policies.
B Quarrying.
C Tourism.
D Its proximity to a city.

6 The writer thinks that what the park needs most is

A better management.
B ecological improvements.
C better protection for villagers.
D restrictions on people entering the park.

Hunting rabbits

C Listen to Robert describing what happens when he goes hunting. When you listen for the first time, tick the things that Robert takes with him when he hunts rabbits.

1	ferrets	*7*	a flask of coffee
2	a purse	*8*	a gun
3	nets	*9*	waterproof clothing
4	a spade	*10*	wellington boots
5	an axe	*11*	a dog
6	a knife		

D Now listen to the tape again. Below is a list of the things the hunters do when they hunt rabbits. Can you put them in the right order?

a They have a cup of tea.
b They place nets over the holes in one set.
c They place nets over the holes in another set.
d They kill the rabbits.
e They put the ferrets down.
f They collect up the nets.
g They move on to the second set.
h They hang the rabbits on a tree.

E Now listen a third time and answer these questions.

1 Why is it better to hunt rabbits on a frosty morning?

2 Why must rabbit-hunters be extremely quiet?

3 If the ferret kills a rabbit underground, what do the hunters do?

4 How many rabbits does Robert catch on average?

5 What three things does Robert do with the dead rabbits?

6 Describe what happens in the pub.

Fishing

F Read the text, but do not attempt to fill the gaps until you have listened to the tape. Then complete the text on the next page with a suitable word or phrase according to the information on the tape.

While he is fishing, Joe also enjoys seeing the other wildlife and birds. On one occasion, in order to see a .... *(1)*, he climbed onto an .... *(2)* tree-trunk and looked into the river. In fact, he saw, for the first time .... *(3)*, a beaver, which was unaware of his presence. He realised it was a beaver when he saw its .... *(4)*. He frequently sees .... *(5)* that the beavers have been feeding on. On another occasion an otter looking for .... *(6)* came very close to him. He was particularly impressed when he saw a deer and .... (7) fawns crossing in shallow water. The deer .... *(8)* a king salmon, which became very .... *(9)*, as did the deer. The salmon probably .... *(10)* as much as the mother deer. All these creatures .... *(11)* and there was a cloud of .... *(12)*. This is the most...................................... *(13)* thing Joe has seen while fishing.

Grammar: *passives*

When doing the following exercises, bear in mind these points:

- passive sentences cannot necessarily be turned into active ones, or vice versa.
- passives are quite common, both in speech and writing, and are not necessarily formal.
- some active verbs can express passive meanings.

A The sentences below all have a passive form. Which ones can be changed into the active to produce a sentence which is both acceptable and the same in meaning as the original (without adding additional words or moving too far away from the original sentence)?

1 Shakespeare's plays have been translated into many languages.

2 John Keats was born in 1795 and died in 1821.

3 The gun was dismantled and carried up the mountain by six marines.

4 Two policemen were arrested.

5 The house will be sold by auction.

6 The baseball game was watched by 100,000 spectators.

7 They were married in St Paul's.

8 Hundreds of years ago patients were bled by the application of leeches.

9 You were supposed to have finished by now.

10 A good time was had by all.

11 Illegally-parked vehicles will be wheel-clamped.

12 These seats are meant for elderly or handicapped persons.

B Which of these active sentences can be changed into the passive?

1 The garden measures 10m by 20m.

2 The surveyors measured the field.

3 Twelve million people live in Shanghai.

4 That hat doesn't suit you.

5 The committee are questioning Mr Jones now.

6 The audience laughed at the comedians.

7 This bottle holds 75 cl of water.

8 These jeans wash well.

9 There is all the tidying-up to do.

10 This vehicle costs £15,000.

11 Everyone agreed with the decision.

12 This margarine spreads well.

C Complete these sentences.

1 You are expected to..

2 He is said to have..

3 We were asked to..

4 It is not known how ....

5 It has been reported that ....

6 Robert Browning is considered to be ....

7 It was felt by the committee ....

8 Dr Jones is believed to be ....

9 There are known to be ....

10 He hated being ....

11 The patients waited to be ....

12 He remembered being ....

Theme three: Circus Life

A What do animals do in circuses?

How entertaining would a circus be without animals?

Now read the text quickly and decide what the author's view of the treatment of circus animals is.

Ten Days with the Circus

At Eastbourne the circus was excluded from town sites by the council. At Crowbridge and Tonbridge it was picketed by Animal Rights activists. I read their leaflets and I thought about the issue, and I was free to wander around the entire site for more than a week. I never saw one animal being mistreated, neglected or harshly-trained. Not once.

The five Bengal tigers are the cream of the show. They are moved first, and settled earliest. They are fed with the best of food – if you like oxheads, that is, and they do. They are cleaned, watered, meticulously cared for. And they are trained carefully, gently, repeatedly. Because no one, least of all someone who is locked into a cage with five of them, wants an evil-tempered tiger.

The lions are something else. Martin Lacey and his lions rub heads together in the ring – and outside it, when no one is watching. The lions spend their days in a typical leonine doze awakened only briefly for exercise in the ring, which is more than a typical zoo animal would get. They lead the life of Riley: and they look well on it.

The circus elephant is Rani, and Robert is her trainer. The two are virtually inseparable. If you want to find Robert, you go and stand by his elephant; you don't bother going to his wagon. He'll be with Rani in a few moments.

One cannot criticise the treatment of animals at this circus. The worst thing you could say is that they may, in their private opinions, be discontented. This seems to me a tricky point.

They may indeed be wishing themselves back in the zoos which sold them as surplus to requirements – no, none of them were snatched from the wide open spaces. But we cannot know for certain. One could equally claim that they love the life, or that nothing will satisfy them until they can read Schiller in the original.

Who knows? But while we eat meat, and wear leather and wool, cows, sheep, pigs, hens and dogs are going to work for people. Why not well-treated exotic animals too?

We can never know what an animal is thinking; but if I were one of the ponies, I would know I had it jammy. Compared with the average child's pony, or worse, a busy riding stable hack, these little ones have their hooves up for half the day and work only twice in two ten-minute shows and one training session daily. I have yet to see one of them raise more than a light sweat.

I was half-knackered, though.

For that is it. There is cruelty in the circus. It is extremely hard on people. It is a hard, intermittently dangerous life, with a regular score of little mishaps. While we were visiting, April's luck was out. On the second day she cut her foot while practising in the ring. For the rest of the week she hopped and hobbled, doing as much work as she possibly could on one foot. Stitches out, she was leading the palomino stallion into the stable when he threw his head up and knocked out two of her bottom teeth. She was sobbing on the steps of her wagon during the interval, but in the second half she was in the ring with the juggling act. The only sign she gave was that she kept her bruised lip shut when she smiled. And her eye make-up was a bit smudged from the tears.

(Philippa Gregory, *The Guardian*)

B Are the following statements *true* or *false*?

1 The circus was not allowed to perform in three towns.

2 The circus distributes leaflets about its activities.

3 The tigers are the first animals to arrive on a new site.

4 Mr Lacey rubs the lions' heads together.

5 The lions sleep most of the time.

6 Most of the animals were purchased from zoos.

7 Most of the circus animals, although well-looked after, are discontented.

8 The writer thinks that you can't criticise the use of animals in circuses if you eat meat.

9 The writer thinks that the ponies would have a better life if they belonged to children.

10 During the day the ponies practise standing on their hind legs.

11 April had two accidents in one week.

12 April was not in a lot of pain.

C What do these phrases mean?

1 lions are something else *(line 24)*

2 lead the life of Riley *(lines 32 – 33)*

3 a tricky point *(line 46)*

4 had it jammy *(lines 65 – 66)*

5 have their hooves up *(line 69)*

6 I was half-knackered *(line 75)*

7 a regular score of little mishaps *(lines 79– 80)*

8 April's luck was out *(line 80)*

9 a bit smudged from the tears *(lines 97 – 98)*

Which two of the above phrases would you not use in polite company?

Circus Animals

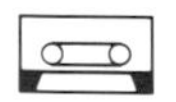

D Listen to Barbara talking about the circus and its animals and choose the best answer to the following questions.

1 What is the main reason the circus prefers to hire rather than own animals?

- *A* They have to change the programme frequently.
- *B* The large animals are expensive to feed out of season.
- *C* It's easy to get the animals from a Safari Park.
- *D* Hired animals come with their own trainer.

2 What happens to the circus animals which are too old to perform?

- *A* They are destroyed when they no longer earn money.
- *B* They are returned to Safari Parks.
- *C* They stay on the circus's farm until they die.
- *D* They are still kept with the circus.

3 Which of the following is not a serious problem when travelling with animals?

- *A* Ensuring that the animals cannot escape if there is an accident.
- *B* Finding suitable food for the animals.
- *C* Ensuring that they do not become hungry and thirsty during a journey.
- *D* Planning which route to take.

4 Recently, problems with anti-circus protesters

- *A* have become worse.
- *B* have become much worse.
- *C* have not been quite as bad as before.
- *D* have been the same as usual.

5 Which of the following do anti-circus protesters not do?

- *A* They demonstrate outside the circus.
- *B* They give out leaflets.
- C They ask circus customers to sign a petition.
- *D* They persuade councils to ban circuses.

6 What does Barbara find particularly annoying about the behaviour of some councils?

- *A* They deprive people of the pleasure of seeing a circus.
- *B* They make it difficult for the circus to make a profit.
- *C* They don't consult the general public.
- *D* They make decisions without consulting the circus.

Talking points

A Compare and contrast the following pairs of pictures.

Home
Sweet
Home

B What attitudes to life are suggested by the following three extracts from animal stories?

Extract a

Once upon a time there were four little Rabbits, and their names were Flopsy, Mopsy, Cotton-tail and Peter. They lived with their mother in a sandbank, underneath the roots of a very big fir-tree.

'Now my dears,' said old Mrs Rabbit one morning, 'you may go into the fields or down the lane, but don't go into Mr McGregor's garden: your father had an accident there; he was put in a pie by Mrs McGregor.'

(*The Tale of Peter Rabbit* by Beatrix Potter)

Extract b

The Mole waggled his toes from sheer happiness, spread his chest with a sigh of full contentment, and leaned back blissfully into the soft cushions. '*What* a day I'm having!' he said. 'Let us start at once!'

'Hold hard a minute, then!' said the Rat. He looped the painter through a ring in his landing stage, climbed up into his hole above, and after a short interval reappeared staggering under a fat wicker luncheon basket.

'Shove that under your feet,' he observed to the Mole, as he passed it down into the boat. Then he untied the painter and took the sculls again.

'What's inside it?' asked the Mole, wriggling with curiosity.

'There's cold chicken inside it,' replied the Rat briefly; 'coldtonguecoldhamcoldbeefpickledgherkinssaladfrenchrollscresssandwidgespottedmeatgingerbeerlemonadesodawater –'

'O stop, stop,' cried the Mole in ecstasies: 'This is too much!'

(*The Wind in the Willows* by Kenneth Graham)

Extract c

'What is the matter?' asked Rikki-tikki.

'We are very miserable,' said Darzee. 'One of our babies fell out of the nest yesterday, and Nag ate him.'

'H'm!' said Rikki-tikki, 'that is very sad – but I am a stranger here. Who is Nag?'

Darzee and his wife only cowered down in the nest without answering, for from the thick grass at the foot of the bush there came a low hiss – a horrid cold sound that made Rikki-tikki jump back two clear feet. Then inch by inch out of the grass rose up the head and spread hood of Nag, the big black cobra, and he was five feet long from tongue to tail. When he had lifted one-third of himself clear of the ground, he stayed balancing to and fro exactly as a dandelion-tuft balances in the wind, and he looked at Rikki-tikki with the wicked snake's eyes that never change their expression, whatever the snake may be thinking of.

'Who is Nag?' said he. 'I am Nag. Look, and be afraid!'

(*The Jungle Book* by Rudyard Kipling)

C *'Stories in which animals speak and behave like humans cause people to develop attitudes which are detrimental to the interests of real animals.'*

With a partner, discuss the arguments for and against this statement.

Writing

Essay

A Write an essay on the following topic:

'Pets: what role do they play in your culture?'

Hints
When you see an essay title like the one above, it's quite common for some people to say they do not know what to say, or even have nothing to say. One way of trying to overcome this problem is to use the idea of a 'buzogram.'

1 In the centre of the page you put your topic, in a box like this:

2 Then you think of any ideas connected with the topic and draw lines radiating from the box with the subject in it. Like this:

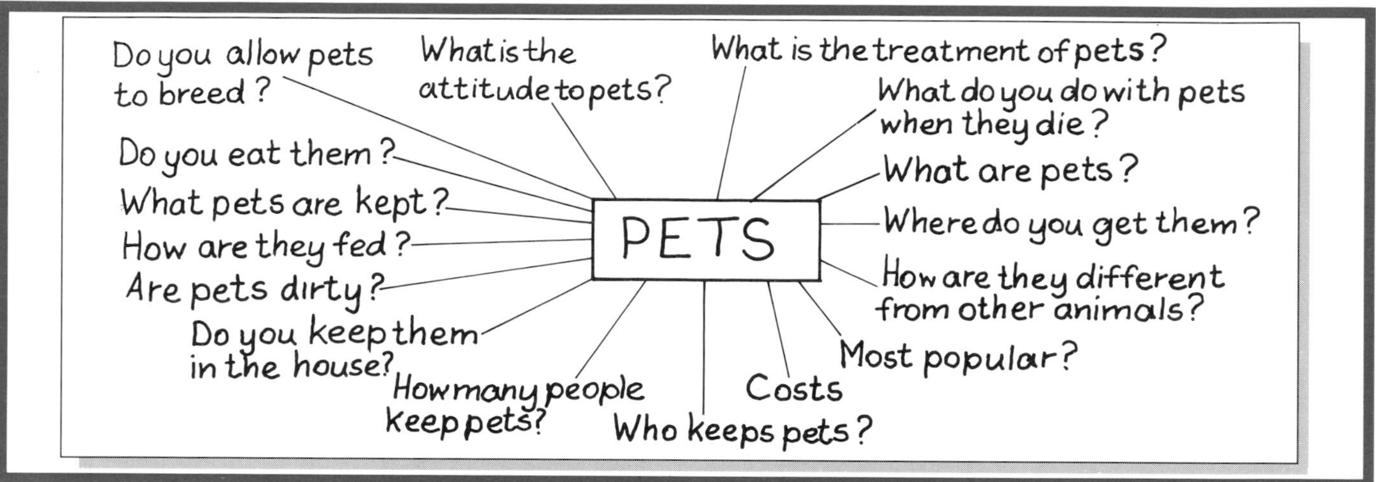

3 Then you can think of sub-sections of your ideas like this:

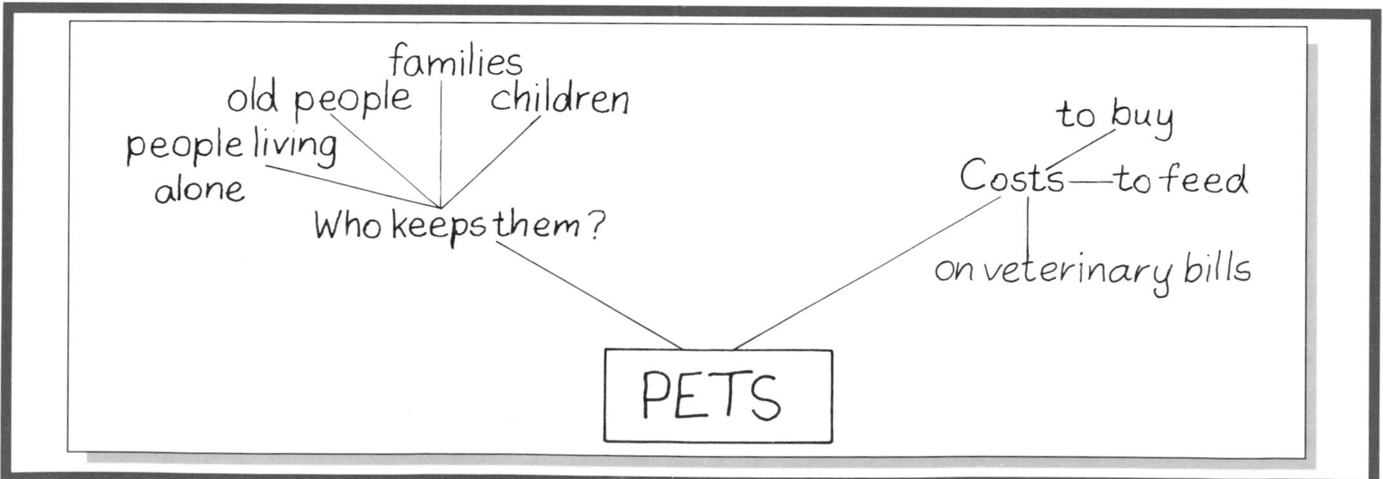

Working in this way, you will probably find you have come up with a lot of ideas.

Now select the ideas you want to discuss.
Group similar ideas.
Put your points in a logical order.
Don't forget the importance of the *introduction* and the *conclusion*.

Letter to a newspaper

B Look at this letter you have read in a newspaper regarding the treatment of animals raised for human consumption. You feel very strongly that the points made are incorrect. Write a letter to a national newspaper protesting against the point of view expressed.

Sir

Before sending a cheque to the Royal Society for the Prevention of Cruelty to Animals in support of their campaign against keeping poultry in battery cages, readers of this newspaper should consider what life is like for chickens which are allowed to wander around freely on farms.

Free-range chickens suffer extremes of temperature and weather which can cause discomfort. In large flocks the pecking order can deprive some of the birds of their food. Hens wander around, free to pick up anything from the ground. Eggs are laid on the ground and it is difficult to keep them clean. Chickens can pick up infections from wild birds and rats and they are vulnerable to attack from predators such as foxes.

All in all, life is surely better for animals kept in cages.

Cyril Roberts
Sale
Cheshire

Hints

1 *Getting ideas:*
Use a buzogram to help you get ideas on what to write and how to organise the information.

2 *Tone:*
formal and very polite, but your indignation must come through.

3 *Facts:*
give facts to contradict those of the article.

4 *Useful phrases:*

I wish to contradict...
I disagree entirely that ...
I wish to protest ...
It is disgraceful that ...
I am appalled to learn that ...
Furthermore, the fact that ...
I was utterly disgusted ...

5 *Layout:*
Follow the layout given for formal letters in Unit 2 (page 35).

Literary approaches

Where is the fox?

What happens at the end of the poem?

The Thought-Fox
by Ted Hughes (b.1930)

I imagine this midnight moment's forest:
Something else is alive
Beside the clock's loneliness
And this blank page where my fingers move.

Through the window I see no star:
Something more near
Though deeper within darkness
Is entering the loneliness:

Cold, delicately as the dark snow,
A fox's nose touches twig, leaf;
Two eyes serve a movement, that now
And again now, and now, and now

Sets neat prints into the snow
Between trees, and warily a lame
Shadow lags by stump and in hollow
Of a body that is bold to come

Across clearings, an eye,
A widening deepening greenness,
Brilliantly, concentratedly,
coming about its own business

Till, with a sudden sharp hot stink of fox
It enters the dark hole of the head.
The window is starless still; the clock ticks,
The page is printed.

Follow-up

A Fill each of the numbered blanks in the following passage with one suitable word.

Owning a Pet

Research findings have now confirmed that owning a cat or dog can drastically reduce the chances of having a heart attack. The theory that pets had a calming effect .... *(1)* their owners had .... *(2)* based on pulse rate readings taken .... *(3)* and after stroking animals. But recent research .... *(4)* out on blood samples taken from 5,700 people .... *(5)* now shown that dog and cat owners have lower levels of cholesterol and free fatty acids (triglycerides) than non-pet owners, as .... *(6)* as lower blood pressure. Vets now suggest that doctors with patients who are at .... *(7)* of heart attacks should .... *(8)* a pet. But it must be a pet the patient can lavish affection on, because the health benefits centre on the amount of love that passes .... *(9)* pet and owner.

Scientists in Australia .... *(10)* risk indicators in people .... *(11)* a clinic offering free coronary risk evaluation. They .... *(12)* asked if they kept a pet. Male pet owners of all ages and women pet owners .... *(13)* 40 to 59 had significantly lower levels of triglycerides. Male pet owners also had significantly lower blood-pressure levels.

.... *(14)* on the research, Dr Bruce Fogle said it appeared that humans .... *(15)* from the unquestioning, 'superabundant' love that animals .... *(16)* their owners. 'I often have mothers who come to my clinic and confide in me that they love their dogs more than their children. It's a different class of love, and human .... *(17)* thrive on it. .... *(18)* to Dr Fogle, the beneficial .... *(19)* of pet ownership dates back to man's primitive past, when in domesticating animals he had to understand .... *(20)* to survive.

B Finish each of the following sentences in such a way that it is as similar as possible in meaning to the sentence printed before it.

1 Children often over-react when they learn that animals are killed to provide meat.

On ....

....

2 It is probable that there will be strong resistance to the ban on shooting.

There is ....

....

3 I didn't see the trainers mistreat the animals.

I didn't see the animals ....

....

4 The panther took the girl thinking she was a dog.

The panther mistook ....

....

5 He estimated that there were thirty panthers in the park.

He put ....

....

6 The tiger was stalking the hunter, who was quite unaware of it.

The hunter didn't realise he ....

....

C Fill each of the blanks with a suitable word or phrase.

1 Many parents believe their children should eat meat .... they won't be healthy.

2 In fairy stories it is quite common for animals such as wolves .... as the enemies of man.

3 The turkeys are allowed to eat .... they find in the forest.

4 Compensation up to £50,000 for loss of life .... under new regulations.

5 Panthers won't attack human beings .... injured, sick or too old to hunt for prey.

6 When the weather is good, ... looking for Claire in the house: she'll be out riding her pony.

D For each of the sentences below, write a new sentence as similar as possible in meaning to the original sentence, but using the word given. The word must not be altered in any way.

1 The young girl died when she was attacked by the panther.

lost

....

....

2 The elephant and its trainer seem to spend all their time together.

inseparable

....

....

3 Toy animals tend to be bears and lions, not cows and pigs.

likely

....

....

4 Don't tell anyone about our plans.

breathe

....

....

5 Any goods in excess of what is necessary can be returned to the manufacturers.

surplus

....

....

6 I know those nursery rhymes because I was taught them as a child.

brought

....

....

E Choose the word or phrase (*A*, *B*, *C* or *D*) which best completes each sentence.

1 My fear of dogs .... from being bitten by a neighbour's alsatian when I was a child.

A bases *B* roots
C stems *D* begins

2 A problem has .... about the best way to treat the virus found in seals.

A roused *B* risen
C arisen *D* aroused

3 Robert has always been very .... towards his pets.

A fond *B* sentimental
C sympathetic *D* affectionate

4 The public feels it has been .... by government statements on the presence of the salmonella virus in chickens.

A misled *B* mistreated
C mishandled *D* misconceived

5 Parents often want to .... their children from the reality of how animals are raised for the table.

A ward *B* hide
C conceal *D* screen

6 A large number of environmental protection groups have drawn attention to the threats to the ecosystem they see .... ahead.

A looking *B* pending
C leering *D* looming

7 .... efforts are being made to save the animals belonging to the bankrupt zoo from being put down.

A stringent *B* strict
C powerful *D* strenuous

8 This report on the beef industry is not free from political ....

A slant *B* bias
C policy *D* angle

9 Children are often given .... toy animals as playthings.

A pet *B* cherished
C familiar *D* cuddly

10 The two pressure groups have .... attitudes on agricultural policy.

A antagonistic *B* conflicting
C competitive *D* clashing

11 When a fire broke out at the stables, all the fire engines in the .... were called in to help.

A whereabouts *B* locale
C environs *D* vicinity

12 The anti-vivisectionists broke into the laboratory and .... made their way to where the animals were kept.

A secretively *B* stealthily
C slyly *D* surreptitiously

13 These animals escaped from a zoo and .... in the wild.

A propagated *B* produced
C proliferated *D* expanded

14 There was a slight .... during the journey when one of the horses broke loose in its box and injured its neck.

A misfortune *B* mishap
C misadventure *D* mischance

15 Because she had been crying, her make-up was ....

A marked *B* wet
C sticky *D* smudged

Unit five

Communicating

Lead-in

Social Settings

a	doctor's surgery	*f*	politics
b	telephone	*g*	law court
c	pub	*h*	church service
d	salesman at work	*i*	weather forecast
e	classroom	*j*	job interview

A Listen to the extracts on the tape and match the social setting where each occurs to those given on the list on the right.

B Examples of four different ways of communicating are illustrated. What are they?

With a partner, think of other ways of communicating and decide in which of the four categories you would put them.

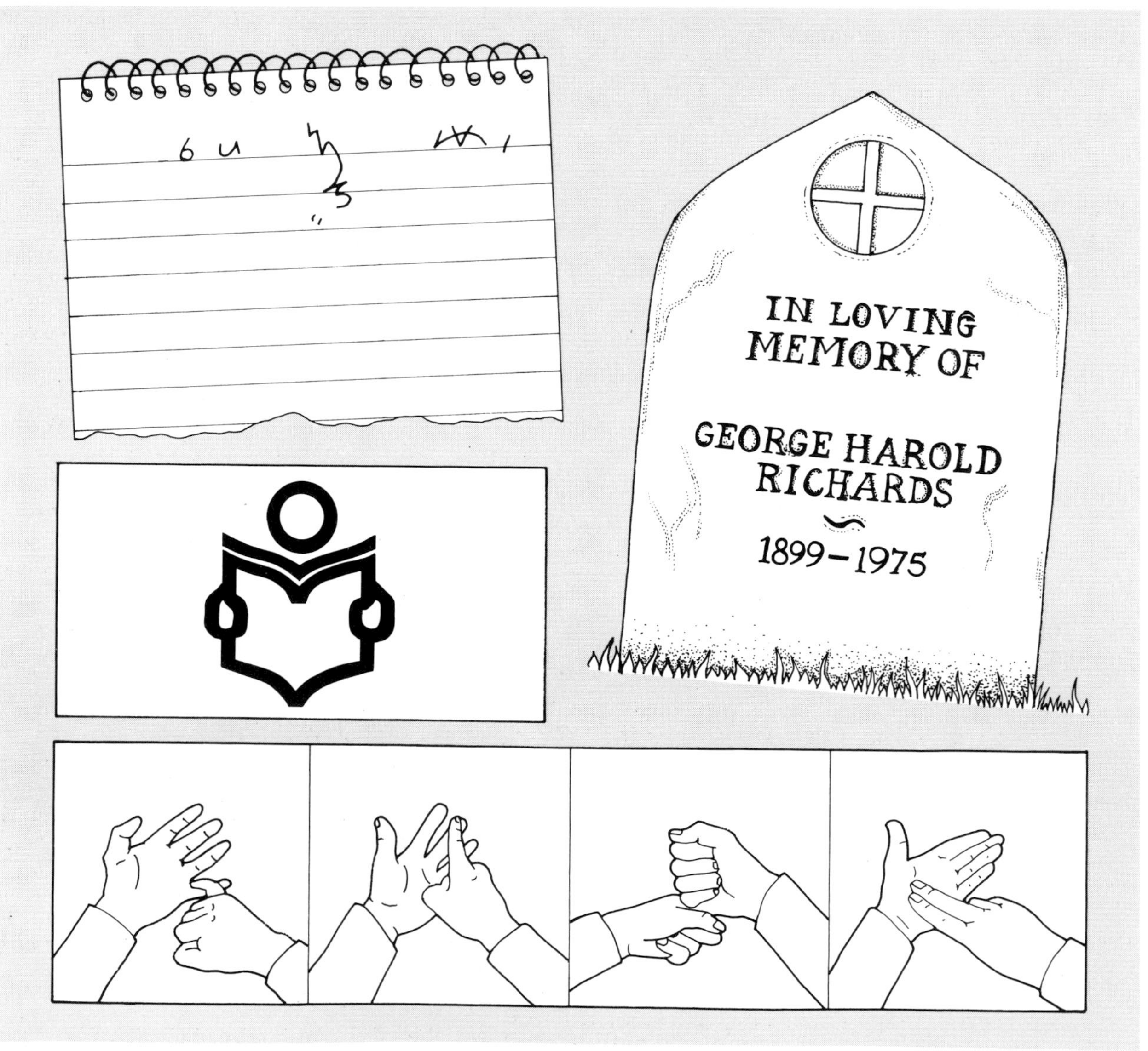

C Look at the four extracts from letters that follow, and, with a partner, discuss the following points:

Who is writing to whom?

What is the relationship between the two people?

What is the letter really about?

What words best describe the tone of the letter?

Are there any letters that you think were not written at the end of the twentieth century? If so, can you say why?

a

We were impressed by the very strong field of applicants that presented themselves. However, on this particular occasion, we regret that we will not be including your name on the short list..

c

Seven years, my Lord, have now passed, since I waited in your outward rooms, or was repulsed from your door; during which time I have been pushing on my work through difficulties, of which it is useless to complain, and have brought it, at last to the verge of publication, without one act of assistance, one word of encouragement, or one smile of favour. Such treatment I did not expect, for I never had a Patron before.

Is not a Patron, my Lord, one who looks with unconcern on a man struggling for life in the water, and, when he has reached ground, encumbers him with help? The notice which you have been pleased to take of my labours, had it been early, had been kind; but it has been delayed until I am indifferent, and cannot enjoy it; till I am solitary, and cannot impart it; till I am known, and do not want it.

b

Sam was such a very kind man, and a very dear friend. There are just so many occasions Tom and I can recall when he went out of his way to help us. Do you remember the Christmas in 1982, after Tom had had his accident and when we were snowed up? Sam came round and dug a path to our front door, and when he had finished, didn't even stop to have a drink because he wanted to help the Smiths down the hill.

d

I think it is better if I write to you about your report rather than coming to see you. It isn't entirely bad, but it isn't very good either.
You know how important I think it is that at your age you enjoy what you are doing and that you get the most out of life. So when you go out and play football or enjoy yourself at parties I don't raise any objections. But you've just got to realise you won't get any satisfaction from your life in the future if you don't decide now when it's more important to make an effort, and when you can just sit back and enjoy yourself. Which brings me to the report.

Match the beginnings of the letters (*1–4*) with their endings (*a–d*). Then match each pair with one of the extracts above.

1 *My Lord*
2 *Dear Stephen*
3 *Dear Mr Thompson*
4 *My Dearest Gertrude*

a *Yours sincerely*
John Smith
Personnel Manager

b *Love,*
Dad

c *With heartfelt wishes at this difficult time,*
Sarah

d *Your Lordship's most humble, most obedient servant,*
Samuel Johnson

D Complete each sentence with one of the words or phrases given.

bill stickers	newscasters	logo	cartoonists
correspondent	image	stereotypes	punch line
body language	bias	mismatch	channel
assertiveness training	commentators	sensationalism	distortion
breakdown	censorship	commercials	
soap operas	slogans	tuned in	

1 Whenever foreign visitors come into Mrs Jones's shop she can't help judging them according to national ....

2 A successful businessman has learnt how to project a positive ....

3 .... can be a useful asset to people whose self-esteem is low or who are reluctant to speak up for themselves.

4 The most popular TV programmes in Britain are the .... such as *Dallas*, *EastEnders* and *Neighbours*.

5 TV programmes on the ITV network are interrupted at regular intervals for ....

6 If you get bored watching what's on one TV ...., you can always switch over to another.

7 John's hopeless at telling jokes. He gets to the end and then forgets the ....

8 'Drinka Pinta Milka Day', 'Go to Work on an Egg': these are two examples of highly successful advertising ....

9 An estimated eight and a half million viewers .... to BBC coverage of the Olympic Games.

10 Companies are now so design conscious that they employ specialists to find them an eye-catching ....

11 .... will be prosecuted, so don't put up any advertising here.

12 ...., whose faces are seen every night as they read the news, frequently become celebrities.

13 The newspaper's .... in Bangladesh sent back harrowing reports of the devastation caused by floods.

14 While many newspaper editors try to guard against the .... of facts in their news reports, it is inevitable that some .... will creep into the way events are reported.

15 However unpalatable it seems, governments throughout the world resort to .... when it comes to the publication of politically sensitive reports.

16 The .... of the popular press, for example in the reporting of sex scandals, is one explanation for its success.

17 The guest of honour at the luncheon said how interesting everything was but his .... gave a different message.

18 I could see that relationship was not going to last long – Robin and Sarah were an obvious ....

19 Gerald Scarfe is one of Britain's most respected ...., his satirical sketches of political figures have frequently been more scathing than the criticisms of political ....

20 Many parents and their children go through the difficulties of a(n) .... in communication when the children reach their teens.

E Complete the text using the words and phrases given.

target	profitability	boost	handled
feature	in-depth	exposing	classified
coverage	readership	mass market	sales gimmicks
cover price	circulation figures	published	views
distributed	reviews	market share	personal finances

The Press in Britain

A wide variety of newspapers is .... *(1)* in Britain, and newspaper readers are generally loyal to the newspaper of their choice, tending to buy the same newspaper every day. The papers themselves vary from .... *(2)* dailies and Sunday papers .... *(3)* nationwide to regional, evening and weekly papers catering for the needs of people in a particular geographical area.

The papers with the highest .... *(4)* are the national tabloids which try to maintain their .... *(5)* by publishing sensational stories and .... *(6)* the private lives of people in the public eye. Readership of the tabloids is concentrated among less affluent social groups, and .... *(7)* is an important aspect of newspaper choice in this sector. .... *(8)* such as competitions with spectacular prizes are a common means of attempting to .... *(9)* sales.

For more extensive news .... *(10)*, readers may turn to the broadsheets, where in the best cases there is an attempt at .... *(11)* analysis of the current situation both at home and abroad. As in the case of tabloids, the editor has an important role to play in determining how a story is .... *(12)*, but more and more frequently the .... *(13)* of the newspaper proprietor have a role to play.

Both tabloids and broadsheets provide .... *(14)* articles and .... *(15)* of current books, films, plays and so forth. Sport also receives substantial coverage. Many newspapers now provide advice on how to handle .... *(16)*, as well as a more traditional business section.

Advertising revenue is an essential element in a newspaper's .... *(17)*, and advertisers take account of the social characteristics of a particular newspaper's .... *(18)* when determining at which group to .... *(19)* a particular sales promotion .... *(20)* advertising is also a valuable source of income.

Theme one: Getting the Message Across

Publicising the Circus

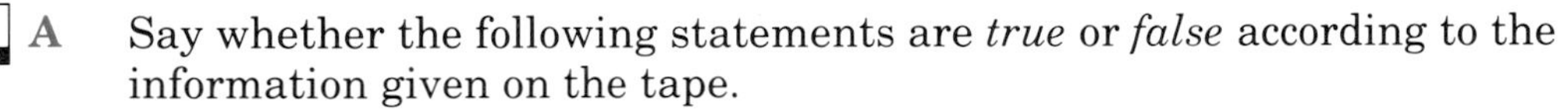

A Say whether the following statements are *true* or *false* according to the information given on the tape.

1 They spend less money on publicity if the circus is in a city.

2 You're likely to see fewer posters if the site for the circus is in a field on the edge of a town.

3 Posters are given out free.

4 Every school visited gets half-price tickets for each student.

5 TV adverts are used in special circumstances.

6 The circus is not keen on parades because of the danger of animals escaping.

7 Parades take place whenever the police agree.

8 They always put advertisements on local radio.

B In your society, can you think of any images that are especially powerful?

What areas of activity do these images come from?

Now quickly scan the text. Which images make the most impact on you? Can you say why?

You Too Could Become A Communications Expert In Just 15 Minutes.

Ever wished you were better at getting your message across? You know, spreading the word, disseminating stuff... communicating!

Like a true professional? Well, read on. Here are some of the all time, definitive, classics of communication.

Headlines that really gotcha. Posters that made you scared to go back in the water. Advertisements that made a man of you. Slogans that fed the world. Graffiti that really [illegible]ed you. Plus! A word from our sponsor on how you too could become a great communicator...

You too can have a body like a gorilla.

Advertising: "The rattling of a stick inside a swill bucket." George Orwell.

Whatever your opinion of advertising as a means of communication, there's no doubt the good stuff works.

And lasts. Probably the most successful and longest running ad ever was this one:

Orwell, more than most, might have benefitted from a spot of Dynamic Tension — the secret that Charles Atlas promised countless thousands would make them a new man in just 15 minutes a day. The ad first ran in the U.S. in the 1930's and Charles, (actually Angelo Siciliano, who died in 1972) continued to clench his buttocks and look tense for a good 40 years.

Big Brother is watching you.

"There is no nonsense so arrant that it cannot be made the creed of the vast majority by adequate governmental action." Bertrand Russell.

Some of the best communication has been pure propaganda.

The most memorable examples were created during the last two World Wars.

The messages were simple, direct and bore constant repetition — an essential ingredient of any propaganda. Thus:

The cartoon style of Fougasse, (pseudonym of the humourous artist, Cyril Kenneth Bird) added immensely to the power of posters such as 'Careless Talk Costs Lives.'

I ♡ sign language.

Great communication doesn't have to rely on words. Signs and symbols have long been powerful, silent communicators.

CND's famous peace symbol was introduced to Britain in 1958 by Bertrand Russell on the Aldermaston March. The original design by Gerard Holtom was adopted by CND and is thought to have come from the international semaphore alphabet, viz:

N (for nuclear) + D (for disarmament) + O (for total, complete, worldwide).

Whatever its origins, you won't wear your badge upside down again, will you?

The great thing about signs is that many of them are international. Some are known to a particular group only. For instance, unless you're a hobo or a gypsy, you won't know that + scrawled on a post or a fence means 'religious talk gets free meal', but you might guess that means 'man with a gun lives here'.

Signs have been used for hundreds of years by shops to inform the ignorant or illiterate of what they sold. Things like , , and are obvious.

But the Medici's balls take a bit of explaining. The three balls formed part of the crest of the Medici family who were great money lenders.

Some signs mean different things to different people. So think a skull and crossbones means pirates, whereas we all know it means poison.

Leaving your mark.

Logos are the orphans of the advertising world, shoved out on the streets to sell their hearts out. And of all the logos that surround us, none have got closer to ruling the world than Coca-Cola.

Frank M. Robinson, a bookkeeper, named and designed the logo of Coke back in 1886. He took the names of two of the ingredients, coca leaf and kola nut, spelt the kola with a 'c' (it looked better in advertisements), then wrote out the trademark in his own hand, virtually as it appears today.

And it may be Clicknology now, but a hundred years ago when George Eastman put roll film in a box camera and called it Kodak, he began the happy snaps business with the line, "you push the button, we do the rest".

Nipper the dog did a similar job for HMV in 1901 and he's still going strong – must be thanks to

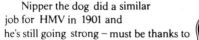

Graffiti and ~~toilet~~ humour.

For some reason we haven't room to speculate on, most graffiti is smutty and most is written, daubed, scratched or sprayed by men. But recently, women have taken up the challenge:

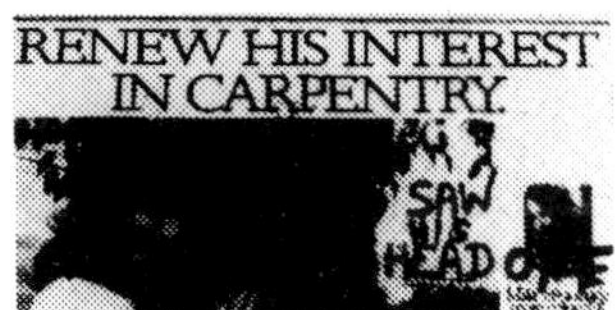

Know your !!! Slogan!

Slogans are a form of shorthand — rallying points for people who want to change the world, to keep it as it is, or to sell more soap.

The prize for the shortest slogan must go to this man: NON!

Charles De Gaulle's complex argument against Britain's entry into the Common Market.

And the prize for one of the best loved goes to Baden Powell.

More recently, 'Feed the World' became a youthful rallying cry which makes one of the 'sixties best known youth protests,'Make Love Not War' seem positively indulgent.

'Be Prepared'

FEED THE WORLD.

Stop me and bu~~y~~ EPS on~~e~~.

"It's not what you say, it's the way that you say it".

OK. This is it. The bit you've been waiting for.

Find out how you too could become a great communicator in just fifteen minutes today, by writing to Epson (U.K.) Limited, Freepost, Birmingham B37 5BR. Or in five seconds by calling up Prestel *280#; or ring 0800 289622 free of charge.

We can't guarantee the Epson will make you as successful as Charles Atlas of course, but at least looking your best won't be such hard work any more.

C Now look at the text again. How many different kinds of communication can you find referred to in the text?
Now answer these questions.

1. What did Charles Atlas advertise?
2. What are the key ingredients of effective propaganda?
3. Explain the origin of the CND symbol.
4. What two interpretations are there of the skull and crossbones symbol?
5. What is the origin of the Coca-Cola logo?
6. Look at the advertisement as a whole. What is being advertised?
7. How successful is this advertisement? Justify your answer.

D Using not more than 100 words, summarise the chief characteristics of effective written communication.

Living in Portugal

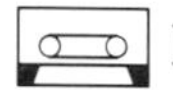

E Listen to Jean talking about her experience of moving to a foreign country.

1. List three consequences of Jean's not being able to speak Portuguese when she first went to live in Portugal.
2. Now listen to the tape again and pick out three areas where life in Portugal improved for Jean after she had been there for some time. Indicate the nature of the change.

Grammar: *modal verbs*

Ought to, should

A Like many modal verbs in English *ought to* expresses more than one meaning. Can you divide these sentences into two groups of five each, and say how the two groups differ?

1. You ought to visit your sick grandmother.
2. You ought not to leave the washing-up until the next day.
3. Here's £10. That ought to be enough.
4. Pam really ought to tidy up her bedroom.
5. Give it another shot. That ought to finish it off.
6. If you catch the 8.22, you ought to get there in time.
7. Oughtn't you to be in the classroom?
8. I think you ought to put that back where you found it.
9. The painters ought to have finished by now.
10. Ten plants ought to be enough to give you a good crop.

In how many of the above sentences can we use *should*?

B Can you use *ought* to in these sentences?

1. If I were you, I should confess the truth.
2. Should Peter be late, we'll start without him.
3. I suggest that you should offer to pay the minimum amount.
4. There is no reason why we should invite him.
5. I was staying in the cottage with Harriet one weekend when who should knock on the door but Jeremy Forsythe!
6. I shouldn't think they'll be coming now. It's quite late.
7. Do you think he'll let me borrow the books? I should think not!

Can you rewrite the sentences in Exercise B without using *should*?

(The changes are quite small, apart from no.*5* which needs a lot of changing.)

Must

C All the sentences below contain the word *must*. Can you divide them into two groups of six, and say what the difference in meaning is?

1 That must be the man Fiona was complaining about.

2 In this recipe you must use double cream – single cream won't give the right consistency.

3 You must be Dr Livingstone.

4 Applicants must have at least two years experience of teaching overseas.

5 You must be the youngest, aren't you?

6 You must be thinking that I was very rude to them, but ...

7 The heating system must be checked thoroughly before the house is put on the market.

8 They must clean the offices at night since we never see any cleaners there during the day.

9 Mr and Mrs MacFarquar don't look very happy. They must be wishing they had chosen a different hotel.

10 It must be a success – the future of the company depends on it.

11 I must get the engine tuned before winter begins.

12 You must come and see us next time you are in Edinburgh.

Which sentences can be re-written using *must have + past participle*, without changing the meaning (except that the sentence will refer to the past)?

Need

D *1* You needn't come every day.

2 I don't need to come to the meeting, do I?

3 Do we need to bring a packed lunch?

4 I needn't acknowledge the letter, need I?

5 He needs as much help as we can give him.

6 He need only pay back the money he borrowed, not the interest.

7 Need we wait any longer?

8 They need to get a lot fitter, don't they?

Now complete the answers to these questions.

1 Need I come for further treatment, doctor?
Yes, you ....
No, you ....

2 Must I come for further treatment, doctor?
Yes, you ....
No, you ....

E Look at these two sentences:

We didn't need to make our own beds – so we didn't.

We didn't need to make our own beds – but we did anyway.

(Did we know it wasn't necessary to make our beds?
Are both ways of finishing the sentence correct?
Which meaning is more common?)

Comment on these sentences using *didn't need to*.

1 A resident cook was included in the rent for the holiday villa.

2 We knew we could get fresh water from the frequent mountain streams along our route.

3 The previous owners had left a huge pile of logs ready for the fire.

4 Before he returned my car he put a full tank of petrol in.

5 The letters had all been rubber-stamped with my signature.

F *We needn't have changed our travellers cheques into cash because all the shops took travellers cheques.*

(Did we know this when we changed them? Do we know now? Was it necessary to change them?)

1 I took several books to read on the voyage but the ship had a very well-stocked library.

2 We loaded the car with logs for our weekend cottage but found we could buy them more cheaply locally.

3 We carried our tent with us but the nights were so warm we slept under the stars.

4 I prepared enough food for six but only Henry and Caroline came.

5 I ran off ten copies but only six people attended the meeting.

Theme two: First Impressions

A Discuss with a partner the following questions.

When you meet someone for the first time, what are the characteristics of that person that create the first impression?

Are these impressions based on aspects of the individual or on stereotypes?

How far do you think that the way individuals are perceived by other people is influenced by:
– sex stereotyping?
– education, upbringing and cultural norms?
– the role they are playing?

Now read **Text a** quickly and pick out three points that the author makes about self-presentation.

Text a

The Presentation of Self in Everyday Life

When an individual enters the presence of others, they commonly seek to acquire information about him or to bring into play information about him already possessed. They will be interested in his general socio-economic status, his conception of self, his attitude towards them, his competence, his trustworthiness, etc. Although some of this information seems to be sought almost as an end in itself, there are usually quite practical reasons for acquiring it. Information about the individual helps to define the situation, enabling others to know in advance what he will expect of them and what they may expect of him. Informed in these ways, the others will know how best to act in order to call forth a desired response from him.

For those present, many sources of information become accessible and many carriers (or 'sign-vehicles') become available for conveying this information. If unacquainted with the individual, observers can glean clues from his conduct and appearance which allow them to apply their previous experience with individuals roughly similar to the one before them or, more important, to apply untested stereotypes to him. They can also assume from past experience that only individuals of a particular kind are likely to be found in a given social setting. They can rely on what the individual says about himself or on documentary evidence he provides as to who and what he is. If prior to the interaction, they can rely on assumptions as to the persistence and generality of psychological traits as a means of predicting his present and future behaviour.

However, during the period in which the individual is in the immediate presence of the others, few events may occur which directly provide the others with the conclusive information they will need if they are to direct wisely their own activity. Many crucial facts lie beyond the time and place of interaction or lie concealed within it. For example, 'true' or 'real' attitudes, beliefs and emotions of the individual can be ascertained only indirectly, through his avowals or through what appears to be involuntary expressive behaviour. Similarly, if the individual offers the others a product or service, they will often find that during the interaction there will be no time and place immediately available for eating the pudding that the proof can be found in. They will be forced to accept some events as conventional or natural signs of something not directly available to the senses.

(*The Presentation of Self in Everyday Life* by Irving Goffman)

B Find a word or phrase in the text which, in context, is similar in meaning to the following.

Paragraph 1
1 to apply
2 position in society
3 for its own sake
4 with this knowledge

Paragraph 2
5 different sorts of information are available
6 if you don't know the person
7 pick up bits of information
8 pre-conceived ideas
9 mental characteristics

Paragraph 3
10 clear evidence
11 essential bits of information
12 can only be guessed at

C According to the text:

1 What do people generally want to find out when they meet someone?

2 Why?

3 How do they find out this information?

4 How can people find out about another person's beliefs and attitudes?

Clothes

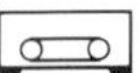

D Listen to the two men talking about clothes, and complete the table with the relevant information, using notes.

	Speaker 1	Speaker 2
1 What kind of clothes do they wear for work?		
2 What job do they do?		
3 What kind of clothes do they wear when they are not working?		
4 What attitudes do they have to clothes?		
5 How do they buy clothes?		
6 What do they now think of clothes they wore in the past?		

E Now read **Text b** quickly and find out:

1. what image of herself Lisa Ford projects

2. what the reporter's attitude is to Lisa Ford

Text b

Girl Talk – Where You Can Buy Success in the Coffee Break

The lights are relaxedly dimmed and lime juice cordial and iced water sparkle invitingly on green baize. Lisa Ford makes her entrance. She is expensively but discreetly dressed: the right suit with the right hemline, low-heeled shoes, high-necked blouse, the minimum of good jewellery. She hails from Atlanta, Georgia, and she's as fresh as if she'd just stepped out of the shower.

Close on two hundred women in business, government, and the professions have come to learn how to project themselves. By four o'clock today, I shall have crystallised my self-knowledge, dramatised my commitment goals, and eliminated the credibility robbers in my speech patterns. My body language will speak volumes.

'Excuse me, Joe,' I shall be able to say, when interrupted by a male colleague. Men interrupt women 76 per cent more often than they interrupt men. It is just another symptom of their sublime arrogance. 'Excuse me, Joe,' – clear and direct, not submissive, my hand up, but close to the body without aggression, the gesture that says subliminally: Stop. 'I would like to finish making this point.'

Note that I did not say, tentatively, 'Er, Joe, I'm sorry, but would you, – er – kind of mind if I – er – added some-thing? I mean, you probably won't think this is at all important, and of course, do feel free to sort of, well, criticise it if you like, but I'd just like to say …' And when Joe congratulates me on my profundity, I shall swallow the good British instinct that might lead me to say, self-effacingly, 'Gosh. It was nothing!' and say, as a man would, 'Thank you. When you are as talented as I am, it comes naturally.'

The lights are gleaming now on a glossy video held aloft: Success and Self-Programming. We can buy it during the coffee break. We should share our knowledge because knowledge is power. Okay, let's get down to counteracting our stereotypes. Women, as we all know, are seen as too emotional, lacking the ability to handle criticism. Women are seen as having nothing important to say. Women make it worse for themselves by voicing their anxieties. I must avoid power-robbing appearance mistakes and mannerisms that say I am a lightweight. 'Powerless people smile to please,' warns Lisa. Women are expected to smile, where men aren't. I must develop a strategy for investing in my own image: promote myself for positive visibility. Being decisive is a power skill – I must breeze into the office on Monday morning full of positive thoughts and ready to defuse unwarranted criticism.

Like toothpaste, it's the inner ring of confidence that counts because as Lisa says, 'The scary thing is, around 80 per cent of our internal dialogue is negative.' That's okay as far as it goes. I'm not knocking assertiveness training or the teaching of techniques to combat sexism. But isn't it frightfully un-British? I've got this uneasy feeling that if we all package ourselves as the selfprojectionists advocate, we'll produce a race of all-American clones.

Please, may I hang on to my occasional bursts of temper or bouts of moodiness? Do you mind my crooked teeth? On the way to school, I used to take out my hated brace as soon as I was out of sight of the house. When the dentist expressed mystification that the treatment wasn't working, and I had to defend myself by saying that I found it difficult to splutter German through all the metalwork, he told me sternly that I would later regret my vanity. My teeth are not perfect. But I can speak German.

Now an American miss would not have done this. American misses know that confidence is engendered through a flashing smile. It is engendered, too, through a high school and college education which positively encourages self-promotion and self-analysis. American misses would have no reservations about writing a 'Dear Boss' letter as advocated by this seminar in order to increase value and visibility. It would not stick in their throat to say, 'Thanks for approving my attendance at the Image and Self-projection Workshop. I learned a lot! Here are some of the highlights.'

No, allow me a bit of un-predictability, please. Woman, after all, is at best a contradiction still. Sorry, Joe. You wanted to say something?

(Pat Ashworth, *The Guardian*)

F Read the text again and find the word or phrase which, in context, is similar in meaning to:

Paragraph 1
1 comes from

Paragraph 2
2 nearly
3 removed negative ways of speaking

Paragraph 3
4 modestly

Paragraph 4
5 at an unconscious level

Paragraph 5
6 giving time and attention to my appearance
7 walk confidently and happily into the office

Paragraph 6
8 the frightening thing is
9 criticising

Paragraph 7
10 periods of bad temper
11 not straight

Paragraph 8
12 they would have no misgivings about saying

G Which phrases in the text appear to be quotations from Lisa Ford rather than the writer's own words? Find at least six.

H Now choose the best answer to the following questions.

1 What is the writer's view of Lisa Ford?
A She admires her self-presentation.
B She likes the way she is dressed.
C She sees her as a stereotype.
D She would like to see beyond the image.

2 The purpose of the seminar is to
A improve women's body language.
B eliminate irritating mannerisms.
C train women how to interrupt.
D teach the art of self-presentation.

3 The best way to handle interruptions is to
A go on talking as if nothing had happened.
B stop and listen to what the person interrupting has to say.
C raise your hand forcefully in the air.
D acknowledge the interruption and carry on talking.

4 What does the writer think about the seminar?
A She learned a number of new practical skills.
B She discovered that she would benefit from adopting a more positive approach to work.
C She disapproves of the approach put forward.
D She felt she had wasted her time by attending.

Language awareness: the language of newspapers

Special vocabulary

A Headlines make use of a number of particular words that have a special meaning in the newspaper context.

Match the word underlined in the headline to the explanation given on the list on the right.

1	**AID** FOR FAMINE VICTIMS INCREASED	*a*	surprise
2	FREE SCHOOL MEALS **AXED**	*b*	connected
3	**BAN** ON FOOTBALL HOOLIGANS	*c*	bad experience
4	TAKEOVER **BID** FOR BP	*d*	reduction
5	BOMB **BLAST** KILLS 9	*e*	question
6	HIGH STREET SPENDING **BOOM**	*f*	caused to suffer adverse effects
7	MPS **CLASH** ON GREEN POLICY	*g*	increase
8	**CUT** IN ARMS SPENDING	*h*	extreme danger
9	FUGITIVES **FLEE** FIGHTING	*i*	attempts to persuade
10	DRUGS **HAUL** AT AIRPORT	*j*	something seized or stolen
11	TEST MATCH **HIT** BY PROTEST	*k*	marries
12	DRINKING WATER **LINKED** TO DISEASE	*l*	try/attempt
13	RAIL STRIKE **LOOMS**	*m*	leaves
14	KIDKNAP VICTIMS **ORDEAL**	*n*	fall sharply
15	**PERIL** ON OILRIG	*o*	run away
16	PM'S **PLEDGE** ON POLLUTION	*p*	number of people killed
17	SHARES **PLUNGE**	*q*	assistance
18	FOOTBALL MANAGER **QUITS**	*r*	stopped
19	POLICE **QUIZ** STAR	*s*	approaches in a threatening way
20	POLICE **SEEK** RAPIST	*t*	disagree
21	PUBLIC SPENDING **SHOCK**	*u*	explosion
22	**THREAT** TO CUP FINAL	*v*	potential danger
23	DEATH **TOLL** NOW 28	*w*	look for
24	MP **WEDS** ACTRESS	*x*	prohibition
25	CANDIDATE **WOOS** VOTERS	*y*	undertaking/commitment

Grammar in newspapers

B Just as newspaper headlines use special vocabulary, they also use particular grammatical forms. Look at the headlines below, paying special attention to the verbs (underlined). When do the events take place, in the past, present or future?

1 GOVERNMENT TO **AXE** AID TO DISABLED

2 SMOKING **BANNED** ON LONDON UNDERGROUND

3 POP STAR **WEDS** IN SECRET

4 RAPE VICTIM **SEEKS** COMPENSATION

5 MP **QUIZZED** ON DEFENCE LEAK

6 QUEEN **TO VISIT** FRANCE

What three grammatical forms are used in the examples? When is it appropriate to use each form?

Now explain the meaning of the headlines.

C Another characteristic, also found in the text itself as well as in the headline, is the piling up of words in front of the subject. Look at these examples:

Whitehall spy scandal leaks split cabinet

Commuter blaze fear as underground enquiry reports safety risks

Shapely vivacious shop assistant, Tracey Thomas, 22, ...

Lean bronzed Brighton lifeguard, Terry Smith, 24, ...

Boyfriend, sprightly silver-haired retired park-keeper, Fred Glugg, 72, ...

D Another characteristic of headlines is the treatment of certain classes of word. On the basis of what you already know about headlines, how would you say the following are handled?

1 definite and indefinite articles
2 auxiliary verbs
3 prepositions

Predicting from headlines

E Look at the following examples of news headlines and predict what you think is the likely story.

1 SCHEME TO CRACK DOWN ON CREDIT FRAUD
2 TEACHERS AXED IN CASH CRISIS
3 NOTTINGHAM OUSTS TORIES
4 POST OFFICE WATCHDOG PLANNED
5 CRUNCH TIME FOR BREAKFAST TV
6 BUILDERS STILL BUOYANT
7 PM SNUBS CALL FOR DEBATE
8 SHARES FALL AS LOSSES MOUNT
9 HEROIN EPIDEMIC SWEEPS THROUGH PAKISTAN
10 ROCKET LAUNCHER SHINES IN ARMY EXERCISE

Style in the tabloids

F The language of the tabloid newspapers is unlike any encountered in other contexts (e.g. conversation or other forms of writing).

Look at this example and with a partner, see what features of tabloid style reporting you can identify.

Shapely starlet and fun-loving former convent girl Diane Fox, 19, dropped a bombshell yesterday. Her whirlwind romance with lean, bronzed lorry-driver, Bert Ford, 26, is *off*. In an exclusive interview at her hideaway love-nest, Diane said, ‘He vowed to wed me, but we were living a lie.’

Unsung hero of the M6 motorway madness pile-up, Bert swept Diane off her feet during a long, hot summer on the sun-kissed beaches of the island paradise of San Serife, where she had fled amid mounting speculation that her film career had reached rock-bottom. ‘My anguish turned to joy. It was like a dream come true. He made me feel like a princess,’ said Diane, fighting back the tears.

But the dream soon turned into a nightmare when Bert moved into Diane’s luxury mansion in leafy Surrey. ‘He quaffed all my whisky and spent all my crisp banknotes,’ she said. She knew the writing was on the wall when Bert’s mother, battling granny Ena Ford, 61, moved in too. That set the alarm bells ringing. It was a recipe for disaster and soon the feathers were really flying.

The moment of truth came when Bert’s credit card bill dropped with a sickening thud through Diane’s letter box. After a lovers’ tiff, Bert stormed out. ‘I’ll never be the same again,’ sobbed Diane. The rest is history.

Speaking from his sleazy, suburban home in Catford, with a mystery girl by his side, Bert was tight-lipped and ashen-faced. ‘I’m as sick as a parrot,’ was his exclusive comment to this newspaper.

Now rewrite the piece in your own words to indicate what the story was.

Theme three: The Media

A Before reading the text discuss the following questions.

How popular is newspaper reading in your country?

What different types of newspaper are there?

Has TV had any influence on reading habits?

The unpopular press

The decline of the British newspaper empire

Fewer British people today read papers than five years ago; far fewer buy papers than at any time over the past 30 years. This phenomenon, though more evident in the mass market dailies, can also be witnessed in regional, evening and weekly papers, where sales have been dropping alarmingly over the past decade. Nor is Britain alone: readership of newspapers in the US has been decreasing for several years, particularly among that most vital of groups, the young.

In August 1992, the total daily sales of the six tabloid titles available in Britain stood at just over 11 million, representing almost a 25 per cent loss of more than 3.5 million newspaper sales over 33 years. This decline cannot be accounted for by suggesting there has been a significant switch by tabloid readers to the serious broadsheets. We ought to note the very different trend of magazine readership. New magazines tend to aim for smaller specialist audiences. This trend might appear healthy but it also suggests that people are defining the narrowest of targets in their reading, setting limits on their intake of knowledge about the world.

So the problem remains one of dramatically decreased interest in the reading of newspapers by an increasing number of people who were formerly buyers of tabloid newspapers. But what is the reason? In a developed society with a growing population and with supposedly better educational standards, why are fewer people reading newspapers?

The Lost Readers

Work is closely bound up with the newspaper-reading habit; many people read on their way to the factory or office, or, traditionally, during their breaks. Once they stop working then newspaper buying, if not reading, gradually ceases too. The contents of a newspaper once formed part of the common currency of everyday talk and everyone needed to know what a newspaper was saying to take an active part. But old-style working patterns with tea-breaks taken in groups at regular intervals have broken down and where they remain, television has become people's major discussion topic. Over the past 20 years the numbers of people in work have fallen as a proportion of the population. Significantly, more young people are unemployed so they do not start the newspaper habit.

Retirement and unemployment also mean there is little money for newspaper buying, a serious matter when considering another factor: cover price inflation. Since 1969, the four leading tabloids have increased their prices on at least 17 separate occasions. Given that tabloids sell mostly to those who tend to be worst off, it is strange that managements have increased prices with little regard for their buyers. There are two more effects of high prices: firstly, cost discourages people from buying more than one title. Many newsagents report a decline in multiple purchase over the past couple of years. Secondly, cost has played a part in breaking the six-day-a-week buying habit. Readers often buy a paper on only three days, and some sellers claim more people are now likely to swap titles. However, most people asked to explain why fewer and fewer people are reading tabloid newspapers offer the same single reason: television.

It is the simple answer which is difficult to fault. Indeed, it may be such a truism that there is a danger in believing it to be the only factor worth considering. Certainly, news-papers defied the predictions of a quick death after the birth of national television. Instead, it has been a gradual strangulation. TV viewing in Britain is already the heaviest in Europe. Virtually every home has at least one set, and, on average, everyone watches television for about 24 hours a week. Significantly, the audience is drawn mainly from those below the age of 35, in the social groups that form the readership base of tabloids. Television, in its various forms, is therefore the dominant leisure activity, providing millions with their only form of entertainment. More significantly, it is now considered by most people to be their main news source. By last year, 70 per cent regarded television as their main source of world news. By 'most people' I mean, of course, that mass of the mass market which have been the traditional buyers of tabloid newspapers.

Tabloids depend not only on certain social classes for their readerships. Their other pre-occupation is with attracting the young, since the creation of habit is extremely important to building future sales. Yet children are drawn to television rather than newspapers for leisure and information. From all these statistics it is clear that tabloid newspapers are facing powerful competition for the attentions of their traditional audience. However, TV may be having a more sinister effect than merely stealing readers. It is not too farfetched to suggest it may be helping to deprive the potential tabloid readership of the enthusiasm to read newspapers. A TV viewer does not need to read. Yet there is no sign of any positive action among national tabloids to build the reading habit among potential new readers. They depend instead on games and promotional gimmicks to boost circulation. Most games are played only by older readers so the gimmicks have not so far attracted that crucial audience of young readers.

(Roy Greenslade, *The Guardian*)

B Now answer the following questions.

1. What does the text say has happened to newspaper sales in the last 30 years?
2. Describe developments in newspaper and magazine publishing.
3. What two factors make the change in newspaper reading habits surprising?
4. What explanation is given for the popularity of newspapers twenty years and more ago?
5. What three factors are put forward to explain the fall in newspaper sales?
6. Apart from the effect on newspaper sales, what danger is referred to following the dominance of TV?

The Press at Work

C Terry, a schoolboy, talks about how the Press handled coverage of an incident at his school. Answer the following questions using information provided on the tape.

1. Which men were at the school when Terry got there?
2. What were they trying to do?
3. How were they trying to do this?
4. Were they successful?
5. Did the true story emerge in the papers?
6. What is Terry's opinion of the press reports?

Talking points

A Look at these pictures. What can you tell about these people from their physical appearance?

B Read this extract, and answer the questions which follow.

Like all other fashion editors in the land, I get enough hate mail and takings-to-task at parties to be in no doubt that, as a nation, our attitudes to clothes are particularly and often violently screwed up.

Confused, uncomfortable, or ambivalent might be kinder words for it, but whatever the trouble, the expression of it always comes out in a boiling stream of anger. Why do fashion editors only use young, slim models? Why do we show expensive designer clothes? How can we print frivolous articles on fashion when children are starving in Ethiopia?

It is useless to argue that the British fashion industry is the fourth largest in the country and deserves coverage and support on the grounds of the employment it generates. Fashion is a moral minefield spiked with all kinds of nameless dangers, temptations and vices. The dread seduction of clothes touches terrible British sensitiveness to do with class, snobbery, puritanism, parsimony, sex and Right and Wrong.

(Sarah Mower, *The Guardian*)

What do you learn from this piece about:

1 British attitudes to clothes?

2 The British fashion industry?

C Discuss in groups:

What kind of clothes do you prefer to wear?

Are you influenced by the social occasion?

What is your image?

Are you happy with the image you think you project?

How different is the real you from the image?

Writing

Descriptions of people

A Select a person you know, and write a description of that person, taking care to emphasise those particular aspects of the person that you think most typical and most revealing of character.

Hints
When you describe people there are two major ways of writing about them. The first is to describe their physical characteristics; the second is to indicate key aspects of their character, as revealed by the way they behave.

Look at these two extracts from novels. Which tells you more about the people described?

Extract a

He was a young man of five-and-twenty, well-built, though a trifle meagre, and of pale complexion. He had hair that was nearly black, and a clean-shaven face, best described, perhaps, as of bureaucratic type. The clothes he wore were of expensive material, but had seen a great deal of service. His stand-up collar was lilac-sprigged.
(*New Grub Street* by George Gissing)

Extract b

Sir Walter Elliot, of Kellynch Hall, in Somersetshire, was a man, who, for his own amusement, never took up any book but the *Baronetage*; there he found occupation for an idle hour, and consolation in a distressed one; there his faculties were roused into admiration and respect; there any unwelcome sensations, arising from domestic affairs, changed naturally into pity and contempt, as he turned over the almost endless creations of the last century – there, if every other leaf were powerless, he could read his own history with an interest which never failed – this was the page at which the favourite volume always opened: *Elliot of Kellynch Hall*
(*Persuasion* by Jane Austen)

Which of the two people do we know more about? Why?

Job application

B You are Lesley Smith, aged 17, and you are thinking of applying to university. You have seen the following advertisement in *The Post* newspaper.

Department of Industry

Are you hoping to begin a science or engineering degree in the next academic year? Are you interested in financial and career sponsorship?

The Department of Industry could offer you sponsorship for the whole of your degree, with additional opportunities of vacation employment and the prospect of full employment at the end of your course.

Write to us at:

Department of Industry
10th Floor West
Barchester Towers
6 Framley Street
London SE1 9TT

telling us why we should consider you for our sponsorship scheme.

These are some notes you have made about yourself.

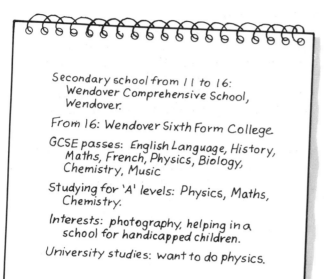

Secondary school from 11 to 16: Wendover Comprehensive School, Wendover.

From 16: Wendover Sixth Form College.

GCSE passes: English Language, History, Maths, French, Physics, Biology, Chemistry, Music

Studying for 'A' levels: Physics, Maths, Chemistry.

Interests: photography, helping in a school for handicapped children.

University studies: want to do physics.

Write a letter to the Department of Industry indicating why you would be a suitable candidate for their sponsorship scheme.

Hints

1 *Information:*
Give full details of your schooling and examinations taken or to be taken.

Talk about your interests and activities out of school, where these show you in a positive way.

2 *Style:*
Be formal, but informative and positive.

3 *Presentation:*
Make sure you present yourself and the information about you in the best possible way.

Literary approaches

What is unusual about the way in which the mirror is treated in the poem?

What picture emerges of the woman who looks in the mirror?

Are there any similarities between the mirror and the woman?

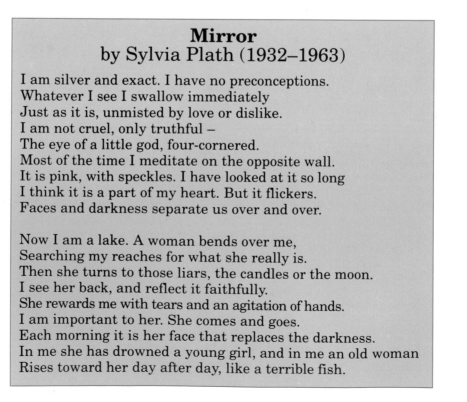

Mirror
by Sylvia Plath (1932–1963)

I am silver and exact. I have no preconceptions.
Whatever I see I swallow immediately
Just as it is, unmisted by love or dislike.
I am not cruel, only truthful –
The eye of a little god, four-cornered.
Most of the time I meditate on the opposite wall.
It is pink, with speckles. I have looked at it so long
I think it is a part of my heart. But it flickers.
Faces and darkness separate us over and over.

Now I am a lake. A woman bends over me,
Searching my reaches for what she really is.
Then she turns to those liars, the candles or the moon.
I see her back, and reflect it faithfully.
She rewards me with tears and an agitation of hands.
I am important to her. She comes and goes.
Each morning it is her face that replaces the darkness.
In me she has drowned a young girl, and in me an old woman
Rises toward her day after day, like a terrible fish.

Follow-up

A Fill each of the numbered blanks in the following passage with one suitable word.

The Steadily Shrinking Boundaries of Press Freedom

Among the conditions which a free and effective press requires are an absence of prior restraint and the ability to protect the anonymity of certain informants. The first of .... *(1)* is summed .... *(2)* in the Duke of Wellington's phrase: 'publish and be damned.' It .... *(3)* that while editors may publish whatever they .... *(4)*, unfettered by prohibitions of .... *(5)* kind, they must afterwards justify themselves in the courts .... *(6)* it is alleged that they have .... *(7)* the law by, say, libelling someone, or by compromising state security, or by breaching copyright or by prejudicing .... *(8)* fair trial.

It is not a licence .... *(9)* irresponsibility; errant editors .... *(10)* their publications can be harshly punished. In the United States, 'publish and be damned' is the almost invariable rule, and .... *(11)* works. By contrast, gagging injunctions of the kind which the Government .... *(12)* recently had imposed on many newspapers and broadcasting organisations, ... *(13)* an exercise in prior restraint. In effect, a wide exclusion zone for journalists writing about MI5 and MI6 is .... *(14)* established.

At the .... *(15)* time the Government is seeking to limit the extent to .... *(16)* reporters may protect their sources. Following yesterday's decision to dismiss his appeal, the Business Correspondent of The Independent, Jeremy Warner, ... *(17)* now return to the High Court, to be punished, ... *(18)* by a fine or prison sentence, for his refusal to say .... *(19)* had supplied him .... *(20)* accurate information about the progress of a take-over bid.

B Finish each of the following sentences in such a way that it is as similar as possible in meaning to the sentence printed before it.

1 Very few people are willing to do this job.
Hardly ....
....

2 'I'm sorry I was angry with you yesterday, Kate,' said Paul.
Paul apologised ....
....

3 She likes presenting seminars on self-promotion more than anything else.
What ....
....

4 Sally was never at a loss for words.
At no time ....
....

5 He did not hesitate to write a letter of complaint.
He had ....
....

6 Unless we use a special crane we cannot move these containers.
Only by ....
....

C Fill each of the blanks with a suitable word or phrase.

1 I wonder .... if I dealt with that point later.

2 When I was learning Finnish, I .... in mastering the pronunciation of the vowel sounds.

3 This story is not .... any documentary evidence.

4 They looked after us until the ambulance arrived, ... we were very grateful.

5 Try ...., I could not understand the new alarm system.

6 We .... by the high standard of performance of this orchestra.

D For each of the sentences below, write a new sentence as similar as possible in meaning to the original sentence, but using the word given. The word must not be altered in any way.

1 I don't think that Mary is able to accept criticism.
lacks
....
....

2 Work done before 9 a.m. isn't overtime.
count
....
....

3 He was forced to accept a transfer to another office.
choice
....
....

4 We can be confident that Rita will perform well in the games.
rely
....
....

5 His conviction for theft was not known to us.
aware
....
....

6 Are we likely to get this contract?
chances
....
....

E Choose the word or phrase (*A*, *B*, *C* or *D*) which best completes each sentence.

1 He made money not as a(n) .... in itself but in order to carry out his philanthropic schemes.
A purpose *B* end *C* result *D* ambition

2 .... to becoming Professor of Law at Oxford she spent five years at Harvard.
A Prior *B* Before
C Previously *D* Preceding

3 The bomb disposal team .... the bomb with only seconds to spare.
A defused *B* pacified *C* rendered *D* saved

4 Patricia bought some .... magazines to read on the train.
A flashy *B* glossy *C* bright *D* sparkling

5 To attend the seminar you must pay a .... of £120.
A price *B* cost *C* charge *D* fee

6 His colleagues got very annoyed with his frequent .... of temper.
A outbreaks *B* losses
C outbursts *D* extremes

7 Sally put into practice some of the techniques .... in the seminar.
A supported *B* expressed
C performed *D* advocated

8 Despite all indications .... the contrary, the island was in fact inhabited.
A to *B* on *C* or *D* by

9 In his fiftieth year he was .... down by a mysterious illness.
A hit *B* struck *C* knocked *D* done

10 The performance of Beethoven's fifth symphony was .... by a weak violin section.
A marred *B* harmed *C* reduced *D* lessened

11 The bank will lend you money according to your ....
A status *B* role *C* position *D* presentation

12 His appearance gave no .... as to her social class.
A characteristics *B* clues
C suggestions *D* signs

13 He is now .... to having to live in exile.
A submitted *B* accepted
C reconciled *D* agreed

14 She was .... by the prospect of facing such a large audience.
A unafraid *B* uncertain
C undaunted *D* unguided

15 He is not .... of taking on such responsibility.
A competent *B* able *C* ready *D* capable

Unit six

Revenge and Retribution

Lead-in

A Which of the following examples of wrongdoing is the most serious? Working with a partner, discuss the implications of each and see if you can put them in order with the most serious first and the least serious last.

a A child kicks a ball through a neighbour's window, breaking it.

b A driver has too much to drink and still drives his car. He runs into six people waiting at a bus stop.

c A financial advisor gives such poor advice that some of his clients lose all their savings.

d A person who knows he/she has a dangerous infectious disease deliberately risks infecting other people.

e A worker at a water reservoir unwittingly allows poison to enter the water supply and some of the customers need hospital treatment.

f A teacher preparing students for a public examination follows the wrong syllabus and the students fail.

g A farmer pollutes a river flowing through his land and all the fish in the river die.

h A property developer develops a site, knowingly destroying important archaeological remains.

i A man walks into the National Gallery and fires a shotgun at a painting by Leonardo da Vinci.

B Complete each sentence with one of the words or phrases given.

just deserts	deters	feud	cheek
get his own back	reprisals	retaliated	amends
tooth for a tooth	mitigating	settle	fit
into his own hands			

1 The two branches of the family have no contact with each other, because of a family .... dating back fifty years.

2 Stephen doesn't believe in taking things lying down. If someone does something against him, his first thought is how to ....

3 When, after a decade of violent crime, Adam Smith was shot by the police, people said he had got no more than his ....

4 Whenever one of their soldiers was killed the occupying army carried out .... against the civilian population.

5 'I don't believe in turning the other ....,' said Uncle Tobias. 'I believe in an eye for an eye, a(n) ....'

6 Those who argue for the re-introduction of the death penalty believe it .... potential murderers.

7 The jury believed the accused's statement that he killed his wife in a(n) .... of jealousy after learning of her affair with another man.

8 To make .... for the damage he had caused when he drove his father's car into a tree, Jonathan agreed to pay for the repairs and to clean the car every week for a year.

9 When the Security Forces killed a demonstrator taking part in a protest march, the guerrillas .... with a series of attacks on army barracks.

10 The judge considered that although the crime of which the defendant was accused was horrific there was sufficient evidence of .... circumstances to justify a light sentence.

11 In cowboy films, the hero often takes the law .... when he feels that the forces of law and order cannot help him.

12 Gang warfare broke out as the rival gangs decided to .... old scores once and for all.

C Complete the text using the words and phrases given.

reach a verdict	judge	Crown	represented
charged	witnesses	determine	stand
under oath	plead	prison	defendant
pass sentence	offence	convicted	
dock	acquitted	conviction	
summed up	discretion	committing	

Criminal Trials in Britain

Under the British judicial system, if a person is .... *(1)* with a serious offence, he/she has to .... *(2)* trial. This means he/she has to appear in court before a(n) .... *(3)* and jury. The role of the jury is to .... *(4)* whether the accused is guilty or not guilty. During the trial, the accused, also known as the .... *(5)*, has the right to be .... *(6)* by a lawyer, the Counsel for the Defence, who must present the best possible case for the accused. Another lawyer, the Counsel for the Prosecution, acting for the .... *(7)* (as the State is known during legal proceedings in Britain) is there to try to secure a(n) .... *(8)*.

At the start of the trial, the accused stands in the .... *(9)* and is asked 'How do you .... *(10)*?' If the plea is 'Not guilty', the trial proceeds. .... *(11)* are called to give evidence and are cross-examined by the lawyers. All evidence is given .... *(12)*. When all the evidence has been heard, and the judge has .... *(13)*, the jury retires to .... *(14)*. At least ten of the jury must be of the same opinion.

If the jury finds the accused not guilty, he/she is .... *(15)*. If, on the other hand, the accused is found guilty, it is up to the judge to .... *(16)*. Depending on the seriousness of the .... *(17)* this may be a fine, a suspended sentence or a(n) .... *(18)* term. British courts do not sentence people to death. All judges exercise .... *(19)* in the severity of the sentences they pass, but it is not unknown for a judge to make an example of the .... *(20)* prisoner in order to deter others from .... *(21)* similar offences.

Theme one: *What is Justice?*

A Before you consider in turn each of the two texts in this section, discuss in groups the following questions:

What is your idea of justice?

What do you consider to be a suitable punishment for murder?

Does the suitability of the punishment depend on the society in which the crime occurs, or is there a single answer, independent of the setting or the time?

B **Text a** is about the Bedu people of Southern Arabia, before the discovery of oil changed the region and destroyed the old way of life.

Text b is about contemporary western society. Both texts describe similar tragedies and their very different consequences.

Now read **Text a**. What idea of justice is revealed in this piece?

Text a

Revenge Killing, Arabia, November 1946

We left Shisur on 9 November in the chill of dawn; the sun was resting on the desert's rim, a red ball without heat. We walked as usual till it grew warm, the camels striding in front of us, a moving mass of legs and necks. Then one by one, as the inclination took us, we climbed up their shoulders and settled in our seats for the long hours which lay ahead. The Arabs sang, 'the full-throated roaring of the tribes'; the shuffling camels quickened their pace, thrusting forward across the level ground, for we had left the hill behind us and were on the steppes which border on the Sands. We noticed the stale tracks of oryx, saw gazelle bounding stiff-legged across the plain, and flushed occasional hares from withered salt bushes in shallow watercourses …

Bin Mautlauq spoke of the raid in which young Sahail was killed. He and fourteen companions had surprised a small herd of Saar camels. The herdsman had fired two shots at them before escaping on the fastest of his camels, and one of these shots had hit Sahail in the chest. Bakhit held his dying son in his arms as they rode back across the plain with the seven captured camels. It was late in the morning when Sahail was wounded, and he lived till nearly sunset, begging for water which they had not got. They rode all night to escape inevitable pursuit. At sunrise they saw some goats, and a small Saar encampment under a tree in a shallow valley. A woman was churning butter in a skin, and a boy and a girl were milking the goats. Some small children sat under the tree. The boy saw them first and tried to escape but they cornered him against a low cliff. He was about fourteen years old, a little younger than Sahail, and he was unarmed. When they surrounded him he put his thumbs in his mouth as a sign of surrender, and asked for mercy. No one answered him. Bakhit slipped down off his camel, drew his dagger, and drove it into the boy's ribs. The boy collapsed at his feet, moaning, 'Oh my father! Oh my father!' and Bakhit stood over him till he died. He then climbed back into his saddle, his grief a little soothed by the murder he had just committed. As Bin Mautlauq spoke, staring across the level plain with his hot, rather bloodshot eyes, I pictured the scene with horrible distinctness. The small long-haired figure, in white loincloth, crumpled on the ground, the spreading pool of blood, the avid clustering flies, the frantic wailing of the dark-clad women, the terrified children, the shrill insistent screaming of a small baby.

(*Arabian Sands* by Wilfred Thesiger)

C Find a word or phrase in the text which, in context, is similar in meaning to the following.

Paragraph 1

1 feeling
2 went faster
3 old
4 leaping
5 surprised

Paragraph 2

6 attack
7 being followed
8 pulled out
9 pushed
10 groaning
11 calmed
12 gathering

D Now say whether the following sentences are *true* or *false*. Justify your answers by reference to the text.

1 Sahail had been a deliberate target.

2 Bakhit stayed at the place where the attack happened until his son died.

3 The writer took part in the raid.

4 The camels were wandering freely without supervision.

5 The group of raiders travelled all night to avoid being attacked.

6 When they approached the village, their arrival produced no effect.

7 The Saar boy was killed because he refused to surrender.

8 Bakhit enjoyed killing the boy.

9 The effect of the boys death on Bakhit made up for the death of his son.

E Discuss with a partner whether the tone of the piece is:
A sensationalist.
B uncritical of the behaviour of those involved.
C biased in favour of certain of the characters.
D hostile to the killing.

F Before reading **Text b**, consider these questions in the light of what you said about **Text a**.

Is it more important to rehabilitate the criminal than to punish him?

Should the victims of crime have a say in the punishment of the criminal?

Now read the text.

Text b

Crimes and Punishments

'No punishment has ever possessed enough power of deterrence to prevent the commission of crimes. On the contrary, whatever the punishments, once a specific crime has appeared for the first time, its reappearance is more likely than its initial emergence could have been.' (Hannah Arendt)

'The severity of the punishment must also be in keeping with the kind of obligation which has been violated, and not (only) with the interests of public security.' (Simone Weil)

On the television screen, a middle-aged woman is telling a reporter about the death of her daughter; her voice and facial expression oscillate between tremulous grief and controlled rage. Three years ago, on a spring evening, her twenty-year-old daughter was walking home from the bus stop after a day of college classes. A young man stopped her at knife point and demanded her purse; she gave it to him and then started to scream. He stabbed her in the chest. She was dead on arrival at the nearest hospital emergency room. Because there were several witnesses, the police were able to arrest the killer on the same night. Six months later, he pleaded guilty to a reduced charge of manslaughter and received a sentence of zero-to-seven years. In just thirty months, he was released from prison for good behaviour.

'I just can't get over this,' says the slain girl's mother. 'I will never get over this. To know that the price of my child's life was less than three years, that this man is free now to do the same thing to someone else – I can't reconcile myself to it. I can't believe any more that there is such a thing as justice in the world. Everything I tried to live by, everything I brought up my children to respect: things just don't work that way.' The woman tells the reporter she is active in an organisation for crime victims and their relatives. 'We all know we have to get on with our lives,' she says, 'but that isn't easy to do under the circumstances. I felt as though my girl was killed twice – once by that scum, and once by the judge who said, *well, you only have to go to jail for a few years*. They killed her memory, saying that was all her life was worth.' The outraged mother spoke of justice, not revenge, but revenge was obviously one element in an ideal of justice to which she had adhered, without giving the matter much conscious thought, until the day when the issue was transformed from an abstraction into a painful personal reality. This sense of justice is so fundamental to our psychological well-being that it rarely intrudes upon our consciousness; like many basic assumptions, it remains largely unexamined unless and until it is sorely violated. The symbolic 'scales of justice' have a real meaning for most citizens, who believe that the legal system exists to maintain a moral and social equilibrium, and to restore the equilibrium when it has been violently disturbed.

There is, of course, a wide range of opinion on what constitutes appropriate redress. For those whose concept of justice is concerned primarily with the criminal's rights and prospects for rehabilitation, any extended punishment is simply another crime. For those focused totally on the victim's rights, only executions or other severe penalties will suffice to restore a sense of moral balance. Between these extremes lies a broad concept of justice that demands a greater measure of retribution than the American legal system currently dispenses, a spectrum of retribution that excludes both execution and the release of a killer from prison in less than three years. This intermediate sense of justice – one that is, I believe, shared by the largest proportion of the public – has been outraged by the inadequate response of the legal system to the rising incidence of violent crime during the past twenty years. Such outrage is unquestionably the single most important factor in the emotional resurgence of support for capital punishment today; it must be addressed by those who refuse, as I do, to include death in their concept of retributive justice.

It is true that a measure of popular enthusiasm for the death penalty exists independently of the general level of crime and violence in society. Otherwise, there would be no support for capital punishment in Western Europe, England, and Canada, whose crime rates make them appear as near-pastoral realms in comparison to the United States. In view of the relatively greater personal safety they enjoy, it's not surprising that those Europeans who favor capital punishment expend less passion on the issue than the Americans do.

A significant exception to this lack of passion is apparent when Europeans begin to talk about the need to 'get tough' with perpetrators of political violence. The United States has been relatively unaffected by the kind of highly visible terrorist acts that have influenced public opinion in England, France, Italy and Germany. Even our most traumatic political assassinations have generally been perceived as isolated acts rather than as full-scale ruptures in the fabric of society. This perception of violence as a phenomenon for which the instigators are *personally* and *individually* accountable reflects a characteristically American attitude that extends far beyond issues of crime and punishment.

(*Wild Justice* by Susan Jacoby)

G Now answer the following questions.

1 Express briefly in your own words Hannah Arendt's view of punishment.

2 How does the quotation from Simone Weil contrast with Arendt's view?

3 What was the young man sentenced for?

4 How long did he serve in prison?

5 What was the reaction of the victim's mother to the young man's release?

6 According to the text, what is the meaning behind the symbolic 'scales of justice'?

7 What is the difficulty about the idea of 'appropriate redress'?

8 In the writer's opinion, what view of justice is shared by most people?

9 What has happened in the last twenty years to this view?

10 And what has given rise to it?

11 Compare the incidence of crime in North America and Europe, and the attitude to the death penalty in these different areas.

12 In Europe, what area of activity changes the basic attitude to punishment?

H Write a summary contrasting the different attitudes to justice revealed in **Text a** and **Text b**. Use 120–150 words.

A Judge Speaks

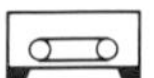

I Listen to a judge talk about sentencing and complete the gaps in the text. Use one or two words in each gap.

> The most difficult task for a judge is .... *(1)*. Another problem is ruling on points of law. Although these do not often occur in .... *(2)* courts, which deal mainly with .... *(3)*, when they do arise they can be .... *(4)* to deal with and he has to decide .... *(5)*. When he has to .... *(6)* for the jury, he tries not to .... *(7)* them by being too long. It is important that a judge does not .... *(8)* the jury one way or the other. He wishes he was able to comment on the .... *(9)* of the accused.
>
> Before sentencing he is able to look at information about the prisoner's background, including any .... *(10)*. It seems to him that many criminals that he sees have been dealt with .... *(11)* in the past. He listens to reports from Probation Officers but sometimes it is difficult to judge if a particular officer is .... *(12)*. He often deals with people arrested for carrying drugs and feels that often they have been tricked or even .... *(13)* by other criminals. Because of this he did not always follow the .... *(14)* on minimum terms of imprisonment.

Language awareness: *proverbs*

A English has many proverbs, common sayings that are familiar to all those who grow up speaking the language. Look at the proverbs on the right. Can you explain what they mean?

1 While the cat's away, the mice will play.
2 Too many cooks spoil the broth.
3 A bird in the hand is worth two in the bush.
4 A stitch in the time saves nine.
5 Make hay while the sun shines.

B Proverbs often fall naturally into two parts. Match the beginning of the proverb on the list on the left with its appropriate ending on the right. Then compare your answer with a partner. Again, can you say what the proverb means?

1	There's many a slip	*a*	repent at leisure.
2	Every cloud	*b*	catches the worm.
3	It never rains	*c*	shouldn't throw stones.
4	Marry in haste	*d*	want not.
5	Spare the rod	*e*	by its cover.
6	You can't judge a book	*f*	has a silver lining.
7	The early bird	*g*	laughs longest.
8	He who laughs last	*h*	'twixt cup and lip.
9	Waste not	*i*	and spoil the child.
10	People who live in glasshouses	*j*	but it pours.

C Because of the fact that proverbs often fall into two natural parts, people often say the first part of the proverb and don't bother to complete it, because their listeners know what is coming. Can you think of a suitable ending for these proverbs?

1 Don't count your chickens …
2 A fool and his money …
3 Warm hands, …
4 If you don't like the heat …
5 As you make your bed …

Theme two: Retribution

A Read the following text about Andy Gibb and answer these questions:

Where would you expect to find a text of this sort and when? What is a piece of this nature called?

Andy Gibb

Andy Gibb, who died yesterday at the age of 30, had a meteoric career as a pop singer in the 1970's, and at one time seemed likely to achieve a popularity to rival that of his brothers, the Bee Gees. But this triumphant progress, and the millions of dollars that came with it, ended in drug addition, bankruptcy, and finally death, in hospital, in Oxford.

Andy Gibb was born in Manchester on March 5, 1958, but grew up in Australia where his parents moved when he was six months old. The family returned to England in 1967, and Gibb finished his education, such as it was, in Britain, drifting out of school at 13. He was later to return to Australia where he was the opening act on a Bay City Rollers tour, in 1976.

Creating an identity for himself, in the shadow of the immense success of the Bee Gees was always bound to be difficult, but Andy Gibb got a big break into the charts in 1978 with *Shadow Dancing*, the title single of an album of that name.

Reaching Number One, the song stayed in the charts for weeks, riding on the back of a teenage craze for disco music which John Travolta had stoked to fever pitch, through the films *Grease* and *Saturday Night Fever*, in the second of which Gibb's brothers participated.

Andy Gibb's voice was recognisably from the Bee Gee's stable, but his immense success could hardly have been founded on vocal qualities alone. What sent the young fans wild was his pretty face, flowing blond locks and his lithe figure, which radiated the healthy, tanned sex-appeal of a male Farrah Fawcett-Majors.

He was especially big in America, where he and his brothers settled towards the end of the Seventies, basing themselves in Miami.

A string of Number One hits followed *Shadow Dancing*, including *Love is Thicker than Water* and *I Just Want to be Your Everything*. Almost overnight Gibb became a millionaire. He spent frenetically, buying boats, renting limousines for the most trifling journeys, hiring private jets for longer trips.

But nemesis was at hand. After only two and a half years the hit records suddenly stopped coming. Following the break-up of Gibb's relationship with *Dallas* star, Victoria Principal, he began to rely on drugs and was soon spending $1000 a day on cocaine. Two sojourns in Betty Ford's famous detox clinic failed to halt his decline. He squandered his fortune and was reduced to living on an allowance from his brothers which paid for life's necessities, heating, lighting and food.

At the time of his death he had filed for bankruptcy in Miami, and was reduced to penury, though he was thought to be facing up to the realities of his situation, and trying to make a new start.

Gibb leaves a daughter, Peta, by his former wife, Kim, from whom he was divorced in 1978.

(The Times)

B Find a word or phrase in the text which, in context, is similar in meaning to:

Paragraph 1
1 very rapid

Paragraph 3
2 chance
3 the hit parade

Paragraph 4
4 developed intensively

Paragraph 5
5 hair
6 supple and athletic

Paragraph 7
7 wildly
8 insignificant

Paragraph 8
9 retribution
10 stays
11 wasted

Paragraph 9
12 extreme poverty

C Now choose the best answer to the following questions.

1 Andy Gibb's brothers were
- *A* responsible for his success.
- *B* a source of inspiration to him.
- *C* supportive of him in good and bad times.
- *D* keen to make him suffer for his excesses.

2 Andy Gibb's appeal was due to
- *A* his singing voice.
- *B* the professionalism he exhibited on stage.
- *C* his brothers' influence.
- *D* his good looks.

3 Andy Gibb became a big star
A by spending a number of years following other good singers around.
B overnight.
C by exploiting his brothers' association with John Travolta.
D by being able to exploit an existing craze.

4 Andy Gibb enjoyed a lifestyle that
A was typical of pop stars.
B seems excessive even for pop stars.
C was the same as that of his brothers.
D inevitably led to his early death.

5 Andy Gibb's misfortunes began when he
A failed to break the drugs habit.
B broke up with Victoria Principal.
C stopped making successful records.
D squandered his money.

A Story with a Moral

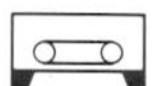

D Listen to the story on the tape and give brief answers to the following questions.

1 Describe the man's appearance.

2 What did he buy?

3 What did he ask the manageress?

4 How did she react?

5 How did the man pay for his goods?

6 What was the real motive for the man's coming into the shop a second time?

7 Why did the police become interested?

8 What information was the woman able to give the police?

9 How did the policeman feel when he received the information?

10 Why did the woman remember the man so well?

11 What is the moral of the story?

Grammar: conditionals

The sentences, *a*, *b* and *c* are fully acceptable and correct, but differ from the *three types* of conditional, *d*, *e* and *f* with which you are probably familiar.

However, this three type classification (*d*, *e* and *f*) is intended to facilitate your understanding of conditional sentences, not to hinder your understanding of sentences that do not comply with it.

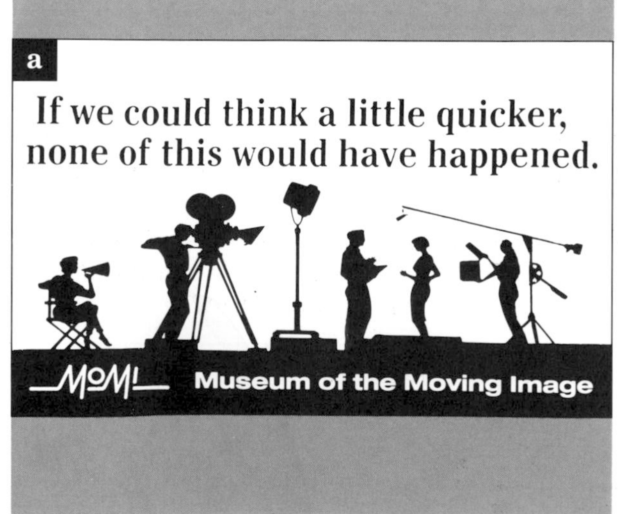

Sentences like the following are quite common:

BRITISH RAIL SEASON TICKETS: if you're using Access or Barclaycard, remember we need two working days' notice for tickets longer than six months.

If you don't like it, don't eat it.

If you should see Martin, tell him the inspectors have arrived.

If they liked your face, you got the job.

If it was too hot, we stayed indoors.

If all the money had been spent by Tuesday, we just starved for two days until father got paid again on Friday.

If you can raise £5,000, I guarantee to double it.

In the exercises that follow, bear in mind the following points.

1. We can express conditional meaning without using *if*.
2. *If* doesn't always express a conditional meaning.
3. The *if*-clause and the main clause of a sentence may not refer to the same time.
4. Don't try and force conditional sentences into a rigid pattern. Consider the meaning of each part of the sentence separately.
5. Modal, progressive, perfect and passive forms are all found in conditional sentences.

A What *time* is referred to in each part of these sentences?

1 If you don't like shellfish, why didn't you say so before we ordered the meal?

2 If I speak to them, they just ignore me.

3 If I speak to them, they will take no notice.

4 If I knew the answer, I would have told you.

5 If I had known then what I know now, I would have told you.

6 If the firemen had better equipment, they would have put out the fire more quickly.

7 If they had bothered to look at the notice-board, they would know what today's programme is.

8 If you're going to take those boxes, then I'm going to call the police.

9 If you missed with the first shot, it just charged straight at you and you'd had it.

10 If you don't want to do this job, why haven't you said so before?

B Rewrite these sentences using the word *if* and making whatever changes are necessary to keep the same meaning:

1 With a bit of luck, we'll be finished by Friday.

2 But for the prompt arrival of the police, there would have been a serious riot.

3 Given four more staff, I could have the orders packed and despatched within twenty-four hours.

4 I would visit her, but I don't think she would be pleased to see me.

5 Say you get lost? What would you do then?

6 Gregory's report may not be ready by then, in which case we will postpone the meeting for another week.

7 But for a penalty goal in the last minute, Chelsea would have beaten Liverpool 1–0.

8 Assuming the engine has been repaired by then, we can use the van.

9 Unless we hear from him soon, we must conclude that he is no longer interested.

10 Touch the money and I'll pull the trigger!

11 Post your application today. Otherwise it will be too late.

12 Spray this on your roses and forget about greenfly.

C Rewrite these sentences without using the word *if* and making whatever changes are necessary to keep the same meaning:

1 If you heat lead, it melts.

2 As if it matters what you wear!

3 It is a good composition, if rather short.

4 I wonder if Henry will come or not.

5 If you are keen on horse-riding, Exmoor is the place for you.

D Why does *would* occur in both parts of this sentence?

We would appreciate it if passengers would report any suspicious packages to the duty officer.

How many of these are acceptable English sentences?

1 If you won't take the medicine, you shouldn't complain about feeling unwell.

2 If you would agree to buy at this price, we would guarantee the goods for twelve months.

3 I would be grateful if you would reply as soon as possible.

4 We would go to the seaside if John wouldn't be so ill.

5 If you won't work, you won't get paid.

E Complete these sentences.

1. The animals could have escaped if ....
 ....
2. If you will insist on leaving early ....
 ....
3. It would be very much appreciated if ....
 ....
4. We might get there on time if ....
 ....
5. If you won't sign the contract ....
 ....
6. If you like bird-watching ....
 ....
7. If we had realised what he wanted ....
 ....
8. If the aircraft engine had been properly ......
 maintained ....
9. If he hadn't been looking out of the window
 ....
10. If you couldn't afford to buy winter clothing
 ....

Theme three: Getting Even

The Rolls Royce

A Listen to the first story about revenge and answer the questions briefly.

1. What was the selling price of the car?
2. How did the man feel when he saw the advertisement in the paper?
3. What did he do?
4. What was the value of the car?
5. What condition was it in?
6. Was the offer genuine?
7. Why was the woman selling the car at such a price?
8. How did she justify her action?

The Landlord

B Now listen to the second story and say whether the following statements are *true* or *false* according to the information on the tape.

1. The woman was a tenant and wanted to buy the house where she was living.
2. Her landlord was harassing her.
3. She was being very calm and rational.
4. The landlord burgled the flat.
5. The landlord cut the telephone wires.
6. The woman left the flat so that it could be redecorated.
7. The woman got legal help.
8. The woman herself thought up the egg idea.
9. The clever thing about using the egg was that it would not be easy to locate.
10. The narrator approved of this form of revenge

The Department Store

C Now listen to the third story and choose the best answer according to the information on the tape.

1. For this particular department store, which was the worst?
 A Objects being stolen from the store.
 B Adverse publicity.
 C Losing money unnecessarily.
 D Breaches of security.
2. When the customer indicated how he intended to pay, the assistant
 A didn't react in any special way.
 B was suitably impressed.
 C grumbled.
 D was so overwhelmed he fell down.

3 When the assistant heard that the buyer wanted to take the piano with him he

A accepted it as normal.
B was slightly surprised.
C was rather suspicious.
D hurriedly made the necessary arrangements.

4 How did the store actually get the money for the piano?

A They traced the man with the Mercedes.
B They alerted the police.
C They held a press conference.
D They billed a number of their customers.

5 How much money did the store receive?

A £44,000.
B £33,000.
C £260,000.
D £11,000.

Talking points

A How do you get your own back?

Discuss in groups of three. Draw up a list, then report these to the class.

B If the following things happened to you, what would you want to do?

1 You were wrongly accused of stealing.

2 Your best friend was killed in a terrorist bomb explosion.

3 A person in authority tried to damage your reputation.

4 Someone made derogatory remarks about you on the basis of where you come from.

5 Someone was rude about your physical appearance.

6 A neighbour kept waking you up at night with loud music.

C Look at the following quotes. Do you agree with them?

1 *'Don't get mad, get even.'*

2 *'Hell hath no fury like a woman scorned.'*

3 *'Revenge is a dish best tasted cold.'*

4 *'Kiss and make up.'*

5 *'Forgive and forget.'*

6 *'He that is without sin amongst you, let him first cast a stone.'*

7 *'Revenge, at first though sweet.*

Bitter ere long back on itself recoils.'

8 *'Resist not evil: but whosoever shall smite thee on thy right cheek, turn to him the other also.'*

D Look at the following list of bad behaviour, misdemeanours and crimes.
What punishment would you consider suitable?

1 A girl finds out that her boyfriend of six months is seeing someone else.

2 A man stole £10,000 from a bank and gave it all to charity.

3 A lorry driver fell asleep at the wheel and crashed into a mini-bus, killing seven people.

4 A girl of six hit another six-year-old with a stone, killing her.

5 A surgeon was supposed to cut off a patient's right leg. Instead, he cut off the left leg.

6 A teacher had inside information about examination questions. He told his students and the examining board found out.

7 A man obtained an airline steward's uniform and travelled around the world by just walking onto the aeroplane and offering to help.

8 An unemployed man used his credit card to take his family on a round-the-world trip. He was back home before the credit card company realised he couldn't pay.

Writing

Narrative essay

A Re-tell, in English, a story of revenge. You can either tell a story that is well known in your country or write from your own experience.

Hints

1 Provide all the relevant details, and present them in an order that makes the most impact on the reader.

2 Elaborate the character and behaviour of the people involved.

3 Pay attention to the pace of the story and keep your readers interested by maintaining this.

4 Devote considerable time to planning the final paragraph so that you bring out the moral or key point of the story.

Argument

B *'Capital punishment should be imposed for terrorist killings.'* Discuss.

Hints

1 Consider the following questions:

Should capital punishment be the penalty for any crime?

What is the nature of terrorism and the reasons for it?

Is all politically-motivated violence terrorism? Are terrorists like other criminals?

Is violence carried out by the state to be judged differently from violence carried out by individuals?

2 When you are sure of your point of view, organise your composition with the main paragraphs framed by an introduction and conclusion.

Literary approaches

In this extract Jane Eyre, the heroine and narrator of the story, is left alone with her guardian and uncle's wife, Mrs Reed. She has just been given a pamphlet by Mr Brocklehurst, the person who runs the school to which she is to be sent.

What do Mrs Reed and Jane Eyre think of each other? Why?

What picture emerges of Jane's character?

Jane Eyre by Charlotte Bronte (1816-1855)

Sitting on a low stool, a few yards from her arm-chair, I examined her figure, I perused her features. In my hand I held the tract containing the sudden death of the Liar: to which narrative my attention had been pointed as to an appropriate warning. What had just passed; what Mrs Reed had said concerning me to Mr Brocklehurst; the whole tenor of their conversation, was recent, raw, and stinging in my mind; I had felt every word as acutely as I had heard it plainly, and a passion of resentment formented now within me.

Mrs Reed looked up from her work: her eyes settled on mine, her fingers at the same time suspended their nimble movements. 'Go out of the room; return to the nursery,' was her mandate. My look or something else must have struck her as offensive, for she spoke with extreme though suppressed irritation. I got up; I went to the door. I came back again; I walked to the window across the room, then close up to her.

Speak I must: I had been trodden on severely, and must turn; but how? What strength had I to dart retaliation at my antagonist? I gathered my energies and launched them in this blunt sentence –

'I am not deceitful; if I were, I should say I loved *you*; but I declare I do not love you: I dislike you the worst of anybody in the world except John Reed: and this book about the Liar, you may give to your girl, Georgiana, for it is she who tells lies, and not I.'

Mrs Reed's hands lay still on her work, inactive: her eye of ice continued to dwell freezingly on mine.

'What more have you to say?' she asked, rather in the tone in which a person might address an opponent of adult age than such as is ordinarily used to a child.

That eye of hers, that voice, stirred every antipathy I had. Shaking from head to foot, thrilled with ungovernable excitement, I continued –

'I am glad you are no relation of mine. I will never call you aunt again as long as I live. I will never come to see you when I am grown up; and if anyone asks me how I liked you, and how you treated me, I will say the very thought of you makes me sick, and that you treated me with miserable cruelty.'

'How dare you affirm that, Jane Eye?'

'How dare I, Mrs Reed? How dare I? Because it is the *truth*. You think I have no feelings, and that I can do without one bit of love or kindness; but I cannot live so; and you have no pity. I shall remember how you thrust me back – roughly and violently thrust me back – into the red-room, and locked me up there, to my dying day, though I was in agony, though I cried out, while suffocating with distress, "Have mercy! Have mercy, Aunt Reed!" And that punishment you made me suffer because your wicked boy struck me – knocked me down for nothing. I will tell anybody who asks me questions this exact tale. People think you a good woman, but you are bad, hard-hearted. *You* are deceitful!'

Ere I had finished this reply, my soul had begun to expand, to exult, with the strangest sense of freedom, of triumph, I ever felt. It seemed as if an invisible bond had burst, and that I had struggled out into unhoped-for-liberty. Not without cause was this sentiment; Mrs Reed looked frightened; her work had slipped from her knee; she was lifting up her hands, rocking herself to and fro, and even twisting her face as if she would cry.

'Jane, you are under a mistake: what is the matter with you? Why do you tremble so violently? Would you like to drink some water?'

'No, Mrs Reed.'

'Is there anything else you wish for, Jane? I assure you, I desire to be your friend.'

'Not you. You told Mr Brocklehurst I had a bad character, a deceitful disposition; and I'll let everybody at Lowood know what you are, and what you have done.'

'Jane, you don't understand these things: children must be corrected in their faults.'

'Deceit is not my fault!' I cried out in a savage, high voice.

'But you are passionate, Jane, that you must allow; and now return to the nursery – there's a dear – and lie down a little.'

'I am not your dear; I cannot lie down. Send me to school soon, Mrs Reed, for I hate to live here.'

'I will indeed send her to school soon,' murmured Mrs Reed, sotto voce; and gathering up her work, she abruptly quitted the apartment.

I was left there alone – winner of the field. It was the hardest battle I had fought, and the first victory I had gained. I stood awhile on the rug, where Mr Brocklehurst had stood, and I enjoyed my conqueror's solitude. First, I smiled to myself and felt elated; but this fierce pleasure subsided in me as fast as did the accelerated throb of my pulses. A child cannot quarrel with its elders, as I had done – cannot give its furious feelings uncontrolled play, as I had given mine – without experiencing afterwards the pang of remorse and the chill of reaction. A ridge of lighted heath, alive, glancing, devouring, would have been a great emblem of my mind when I accused and menaced Mrs Reed; the same ridge, black and blasted after the flames are dead, would have represented as meetly my subsequent condition, when half an hour's silence and reflection had shown me the madness of my conduct, and the dreariness of my hated and hating position.

Something of vengeance I had tasted for the first time. An aromatic wine it seemed, on swallowing, warm and racy; its after-flavour, metallic and corroding, gave me a sensation as if I had been poisoned. Willingly would I now have gone and asked Mrs Reed's pardon; but I knew, partly from experience and partly from instinct, that was the way to make her repulse me with double scorn, thereby re-exciting every turbulent impulse of my nature.

Follow-up

A Fill each of the numbered blanks in the following passage with one suitable word.

Hanging: When the Debate is Just a Gloss on Gut Reactions

When the House of Commons debates capital punishment next Tuesday, each side will accuse the other of dishonesty, and each side will be right. It is human nature – sophisticated, educated human nature – to deny the emotional origin of our .... *(1)*, to present them in empirical terms .... *(2)* than admit .... *(3)* we rationalise what we first instinctively believe. It is more honest .... *(4)* admit that we are most of us either hangers or abolitionists .... *(5)* nature and that subsequent argument is often intellectually dubious.

In the course .... *(6)* what claims to be a rational discussion, each side has its specialism in dishonesty. Both kinds turn on .... *(7)* question of deterrence. Again and again in the debates on capital punishment .... *(8)* led to .... *(9)* final abolition in 1969, and thereafter also, abolitionists have argued that capital punishment .... *(10)* a negligible deterrent effect. This flies in the face of all common sense and observation. .... *(11)* if many passionate or domestic murders are committed .... *(12)* a thought to the consequence, it .... *(13)* be conceded that capital punishment has *some* deterrent value.

For their part, the hangers are shifty about their motives. Retribution is .... *(14)* of fashion, and so they stress the level of murder since abolition. In .... *(15)*, retribution is more respectable than .... *(16)* side may realise, perhaps more respectable than deterrence .... *(17)* a justification for punishment, certainly more so than rehabilitation (not that that comes .... *(18)* into the hanging debate). It can be argued that the .... *(19)* of punishment is not to reform someone – which grossly interferes with his personal autonomy – but rather to punish, to uphold and objectify the law, to reward those who obey the law .... *(20)* chastising those who break it.

B Finish each of the following sentences in such a way that it is as similar as possible in meaning to the sentence printed before it.

1 He would do anything to get revenge.
There's ....
....

2 John said that he disapproved of capital punishment.
John expressed ....
....

3 It's more of an art than a science.
It's not ....
....

4 The crime rate has risen sharply in the last ten years.
There has ....
....

5 Whatever your personal opinions, you must carry out your duty.
No matter ....
....

6 The police officers never mistreated the prisoner.
At no time ....
....

C Fill each of the blanks with a suitable word or phrase.

1 He described the battle .... he had been wounded.

2 It's up to you to .... to deal with the situation.

3 Now you have to put .... all the theory you have learnt.

4 The Minister declared that .... resigning.

5 The driver took .... of the 120 km per hour speed limit.

6 The punishment must be in .... with the crime.

D For each of the sentences below, write a new sentence as similar as possible in meaning to the original sentence, but using the word given. The word must not be altered in any way.

1 A high standard of customer service is the reason for the company's success.
founded
....
....

2 He decided to make Edinburgh his permanent home.
settle
....
....

3 She felt unable to accept the court's decision.
reconcile
....
....

4 He became a very popular singer.
achieved
....
....

5 There is no evidence at all to connect my client with this crime.
lack
....
....

6 Christopher was determined to get revenge.
back
....
....

E Choose the word or phrase (*A*, *B*, *C* or *D*) which best completes each sentence.

1 We'd better eat the bread now. It will be .... by tomorrow.
A stale *B* old *C* inedible *D* bad

2 This cream will have a(n) .... effect on sunburnt skin.
A soothing *B* calming
C antiseptic *D* Healthy

3 Several .... came forward to give details of the crime to the police.
A observers *B* onlookers
C passers-by *D* witnesses

4 He .... guilty to the crime.
A admitted *B* pleaded *C* said *D* confessed

5 In the .... of an average day he attends four meetings.
A course *B* length *C* hours *D* work

6 A serious .... of foot-and-mouth disease caused hundreds of cattle to be destroyed.
A outbreak *B* attack *C* incident *D* sickness

7 The police officers, though armed, tried to avoid a(n) .... with the gunman.
A meeting *B* confrontation
C encounter *D* attack

8 The government introduced some unpopular .... to control inflation.
A steps *B* rules
C actions *D* measures

9 He had a(n) .... for singing popular songs.
A talent *B* skill *C* trick *D* ability

10 Everyone was surprised .... how quickly he became successful.
A to *B* a *C* with *D* on

11 His main claim to .... is his best-selling first novel.
A reputation *B* fame *C* name *D* success

12 Mrs Jones .... four foster children as well as six of her own.
A educated *B* raised
C bore *D* brought

13 He will be .... from prison in six months' time.
A sent out *B* let go
C released *D* discharged

14 His .... for murder lasted nine days.
A trial *B* proceedings
C process *D* condemnation

15 The police .... him with armed robbery.
A arrested *B* charged
C penalised *D* accused

Unit seven

Reputation

Lead-in

A Who are these people?

What are they famous for?

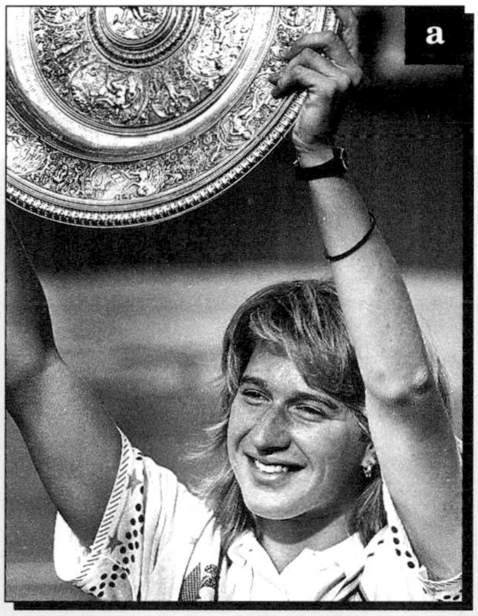

a

b

c

d

e

f

g

h

Famous People

Now listen to the tape and match each description with one of the photographs of famous people.

B Complete each sentence with one of the words or phrases given.

publicity	figures	posthumous	legendary
popularity	cowardice	recognition	best-seller
defeats	villain	notorious	status
champion	whizz-kid	renowned	
failure	outstanding	illustrious	
prodigy	beating	eminence	

1 Ned Kelly was a(n) .... nineteenth-century Australian bandit.

2 Having become a millionaire at the age of twenty-one, Michael is regarded as a(n) .... in financial circles.

3 Membership of the Royal Society is restricted to scientists who have achieved .... in their chosen field.

4 Jerez in southern Spain is .... for sherry, and Kalamata in Greece for olives.

5 Winston Churchill came from a(n) .... family, being descended from John Churchill, Duke of Marlborough.

6 Robert Browning had to wait many years for .... as a major poet, whereas his contemporary, Alfred Tennyson, achieved .... with the public and critics early in his career.

7 Mozart was an infant .... who continued to demonstrate his genius as he grew up.

8 Admiral Byng was accused of .... in the face of the enemy, court-martialled, and executed in 1757.

9 Politicians are regarded as public .... and can expect their private lives to be subject to scrutiny.

10 Emily Dickinson was virtually unpublished in her lifetime. Her fame as a poet is entirely ....

11 The researchers used a questionnaire to discover their interviewees' social ....

12 In Shakespeare's play *Othello*, much of the interest is focused on the ...., Iago, whose lies and malice lead to tragedy.

13 The famous novelist, Jeffrey Archer, made a fortune by writing a(n) ....

14 Simon Bolivar suffered several .... before his great victory at Carabobo in 1821.

15 He won the Wimbledon final by .... last year's winner.

16 The World Chess .... retained his title against all challengers.

17 Most film stars regard it as natural to spend their lives in the glare of ....

18 Although Eddie 'The Eagle' Edwards always came last in the ski-jump competitions, nobody regarded him as a(n) ....

19 Even in her lifetime, Maria Callas was a(n) .... figure, because of a unique combination of acting and vocal skills.

20 He gave a(n) .... performance at the Olympics, winning more medals than any other athlete.

C Complete the text using the words and phrases given.

aspiring	pressure	rewards	craft
fans	agent	stardom	talented
drop out	lured	achieve	in the public eye
invasion	dedicated	precarious	a big break
autograph	role	ruthless	negative aspects

Fame

Fame is a very successful American TV series. Set in a New York theatre school, it charts the ups and downs in the daily lives of a group of .... *(1)* performers as they learn about their .... *(2)*. All are .... *(3)* and ambitious, ... *(4)* to their future profession. A few are ....*(5)* and will go to any lengths to............................*(6)* their ambitions.

We see the students rehearsing, preparing for auditions, putting on their own shows. Occasionally, one of the lucky ones gets .... *(7)* – is spotted by a leading .... *(8)* or is offered a(n) .... *(9)* in a film. Some students find the .... *(10)* too much and .... *(11)*. But the majority are .... *(12)* by the bright lights, and complete the course, ready to enter a(n) .... *(13)* profession where the .... *(14)* can be great – wealth, glamour, ... *(15)*, a life .... *(16)*. Few at this time think of failure, or even of the .... *(17)* of success – .... *(18)* of privacy, constant recognition and mobbing by .... *(19)* hunters and .... *(20)* and every action under public scrutiny. It's a time of hope.

Theme one: Fame or Notoriety?

A Fill in the labels from the list of words given.

1 jockey
2 silks
3 thoroughbred horse
4 whip
5 grandstand
6 saddle
7 stirrups
8 bridle
9 reins
10 bit
11 bookmaker
12 odds

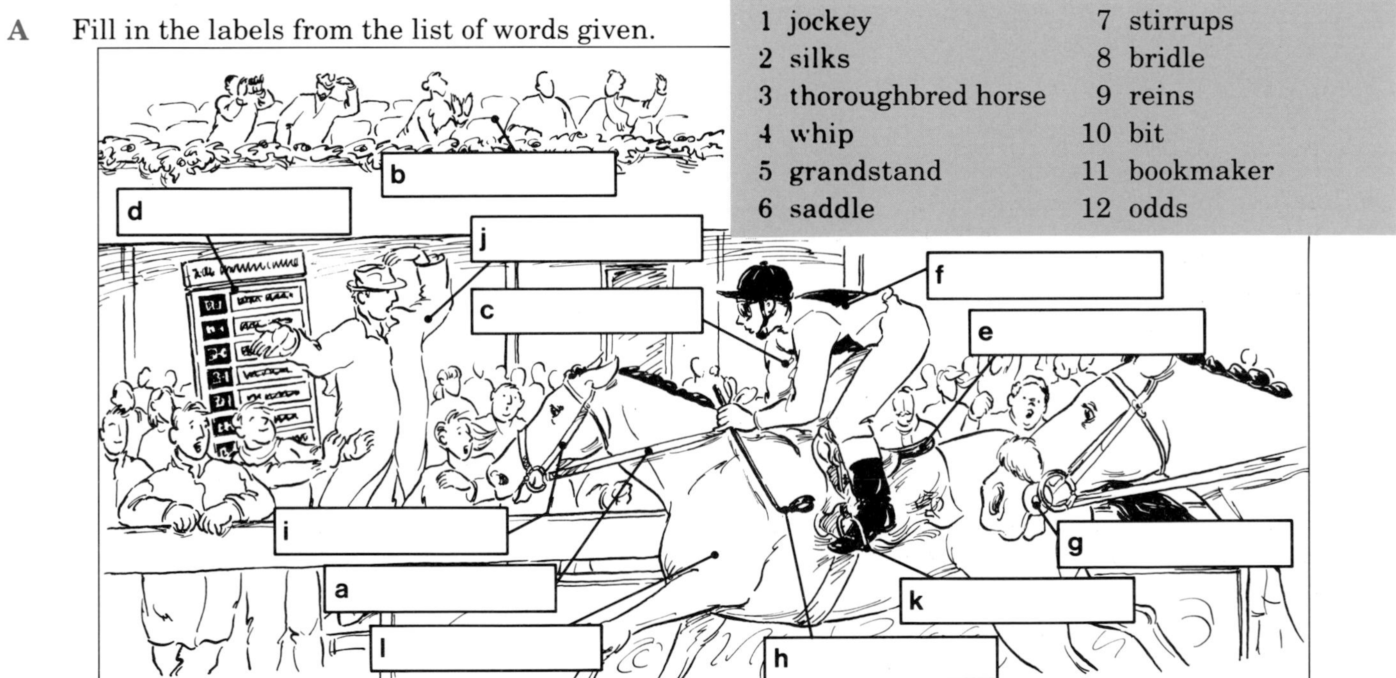

B What do you know about horse-racing?

Do you know the names of any internationally famous jockeys?

What rules are there about this sport in your country?

Now read the text and answer the questions which follow.

Three-year Sentence for Tax Evasion

Fall from Grace of a Man Who Rode his Luck Too Far

Lester Piggott has been hounded by controversy in and out of the saddle since he began riding forty years ago.

Eleven times champion jockey, Piggott gained a record twenty-nine classic wins before retiring to take up training two years ago. He rode his first Derby winner, *Never Say Die*, at the age of eighteen.

However, the exceptionally talented youngster showed an increasing tendency to recklessness and, a fortnight after his Derby win, he was suspended for the rest of the season, as a result of his riding of the same horse at Royal Ascot. The stewards of the Jockey Club, racing's ruling body, told him that 'in spite of continuous warnings he continued to show complete disregard for the rules and the safety of other jockeys'.

Piggott's unique empathy with highly-strung thoroughbreds led him to be recognised as the world's best jockey, and the most sought after. But, not even his greatest admirers would say he was the easiest man to get on with, and his association with two top trainers, Sir Noel Murless and Vincent O'Brien, for whom he rode many of his biggest winners, ended in deep bitterness.

As a freelance in the autumn of his professional life, he was frequently criticised for 'jocking off' other riders. That is to say, he would use his reputation and his relationship with leading owners and trainers to get himself a coveted ride in a big race at the expense of a colleague.

A prime example was his eleventh-hour substitution for the great Australian jockey, Bill Williamson on *Roberto*, before the 1972 Derby. The racing world showed what it thought of Piggott's behaviour when his victory, one of a record nine Derby wins, was greeted with an unprecedented silence.

Such ruthlessness may have contributed to his unpopularity within the sport itself, but his singular will to win at all costs undoubtedly helped him to become Britain's highest paid sportsman. His personal fortune has been estimated at £20 million, at least.

Off the track, Piggott's indiscretions have often cost him dear in financial terms and kudos. In 1968, he was fined £750 for attempting to export currency. Last year, he was fined £1,000 for possessing guns and ammunition without a licence. Along with England's current leading jockey, Steve Cauthen, he also lost nearly £100,000 earlier this year when they invested in a scheme intended to reap large profits on the world oil market.

Piggott received an OBE* in 1975, but the revelation of his tax and VAT* offences are thought to have cost him a knighthood last year. His conviction yesterday and his jail sentence will mean the loss of his trainer's licence, although his wife, Susan, is being allowed to take over the running of his Newmarket stables.

Piggott could face further disciplinary measures by the Jockey Club over allegations in *The People* newspaper that he bet against himself in races.

The constant brushes with authority, together with Piggott's 'loner' image, have served to imbue him with something of a film star quality in the eyes of the public. His gaunt, deeply-etched face has been ravaged by continual excesses of dieting to keep his body weight down to at least a stone below its natural minimum.

His natural reticence, almost certainly born out of the fact that he has a speech impediment and is partly deaf, has made Piggott appear aloof – and he certainly did nothing to dispel this perception of him.

Once, after riding a typically brilliant race to get home in front on a favourite, 'Old Stoneface', as he is often known, remained as impassive as ever as the crowd cheered him. The trainer suggested that he might at least consider giving them a smile. To which Piggott replied: 'Why should I? They'd be throwing things at me if I lost.'

Most informed judges believe that he was certainly the greatest post-war rider, if not the best ever. At the same time, many of them questioned his unique riding style, perched high above his mount with his bottom thrust in the air. Clad in flamboyant jockeys' silks he looked like one of those exotic African birds that cheekily hitch a ride on the back of a hippo.

Piggott could be unbelievably subtle on a horse, bringing him with a perfectly timed run to pop his nose in front on the line and thus give him as easy a race as possible. Conversely, there was no stronger finisher in the game. You could almost hear the merciless cracking of his whip up in the grandstand as he drove *Roberto* to the narrowest of Derby wins.

The accumulation of Piggott stories, many of them apocryphal, would fill several bookshelves. A good many concern his much-publicised meanness and obsession with all things financial. Of all the stories, a personal favourite is the incident that occurred when Piggott was riding in a race at Deauville a few years ago. He dropped his whip at a crucial moment, but leaned across and grabbed the whip of a fellow rider. Piggott duly won the race and in that famous nasal monotone said of the incident afterwards: 'Well, he had no chance of winning anyway!'

That, in a nutshell, is Piggott – unique, outrageous, a one-off. Few would argue that he deserved his punishment yesterday, but his departure will leave a cloud hanging over the racing world that will take a long time to dispel.

(John Karter, *The Independent*)

* *OBE*: Order of the British Empire (an honour awarded by the Queen)

* VAT: Value Added Tax

C Find a word or phrase in the text which, in context, is similar in meaning to:

Paragraph 3
1 inclination
2 disregard for danger

Paragraph 4
3 feeling for
4 in demand

Paragraph 5
5 a skilled working person without a regular employer

Paragraph 6
6 last-minute
7 had not happened before

Paragraph 8
8 obtain

Paragraph 10
9 claims

Paragraph 12
10 distant

Paragraph 14
11 wearing

Paragraph 15
12 on the other hand

Paragraph 16
13 not necessarily true but widely believed
14 of the utmost importance

Paragraph 17
15 briefly

D Without quoting sentences from the passage, answer the following questions.

1 How was Lester Piggott earning his living at the time of his arrest?

2 What do you learn about Piggott's riding style in the first three paragraphs?

3 Explain what is meant by the expression *'jocking off'*.

4 What example of *'jocking off'* is given in Piggott's career?

5 What was the reaction to Piggott's win following this incident?

6 How successful has Piggott been in financial terms?

7 What examples are given of Piggott's financial indiscretions?

8 What two factors give Piggott a film star image?

9 What is Piggott's reputation as a rider?

10 Describe the incident at Deauville and Piggott's attitude to it.

E In a summary of 100–120 words describe the character of Lester Piggott as it emerges from the piece you have read.

Language awareness: eponyms

An eponym is a word that is derived from a person's name. Something a person has done, or invented, or discovered, or been associated with, has made them so famous that their name has become part of the English language. For example, from the name of Franz Mesmer (1734-1815), an early practitioner of hypnotism, we get the verb *to mesmerise*, which means 'to be so fascinated by something you see that you cannot move or speak':

He was mesmerised by the thousands of multi-coloured butterflies that fluttered around him.

Many eponyms have lost their obvious personal associations, are not written with capital letters and are used as nouns, verbs and adjectives just like other words. Examples of such words are *to boycott* (from Charles Boycott 1832– 97) and *to galvanise* (from Luigi Galvani 1737–1798). But other eponyms remain closely associated with something invented by the eponymist. For example, a *bowie knife,* a *Geiger counter*, a *diesel engine* (from Colonel James Bowie 1796– 1836, Hans Geiger 1882– 1945 and Rudolf Diesel 1858– 1913).

A Which words are derived from the names of the people on the list below?

1	Laszlo Biro	*7*	Patrick Hooligan
2	The Earl of Cardigan	*8*	Joseph McCarthy
3	Sir George Everest	*9*	Samuel Morse
4	Giuseppe Garibaldi	*10*	The Marquis de Sade
5	Thomas Hobson	*11*	The Earl of Sandwich
6	Charles Mackintosh	*12*	The Duke of Wellington

B Can you match the people on the list in Exercise A with these things and ideas?

a	a raincoat	*g*	slices of bread with a filling
b	rubber boots	*h*	a mountain
c	hounding innocent people for political reasons	*i*	giving the customer no choice
d	a ball point pen	*j*	a dot-dash alphabet
e	a currant biscuit	*k*	violent behaviour
f	pleasure in inflicting pain	*l*	a long-sleeved woollen garment which buttons at the front

C Do you think these people would be pleased, displeased or indifferent at the way their names have become part of the language?

Can you think of any other eponyms?

Theme two: Public Image

Circus People

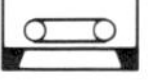

A Barbara talks about working in a circus. Are the following statements *true* or *false* summaries of what Barbara says?

1	Circus people are commonly thought to be dishonest.	*4*	Most of the people in her circus were born to that way of life.
2	Many actors and film stars have worked in circuses.	*5*	Circus people are in no way connected to gypsies.
3	Shopkeepers are sometimes reluctant to serve circus people.	*6*	A lot of circus people are well-educated.

7 Travelling with the circus is a very romantic life.

8 Many people join the circus and then leave after only a few weeks.

9 To adapt successfully to circus life, you have to be very committed.

B Read the following passage in two minutes and then:

– state four things that Terry Venables has done

– outline two problems that are currently facing Tottenham Hotspur Football Club.

The Cockney Hero with a Difference

Given that professional football has become a branch of show business, an unscripted soap, the appointment of Terry Venables as manager of Tottenham Hotspur Football Club can be compared to an incident in *Dallas* or *Dynasty*. When he takes over officially next month, he will be entering the most critical phrase of an already remarkable career.

Cockney hero comes home to the club he supported as a boy and whose colours he wore in an FA Cup final is a neat enough summary but, on its own, not sufficiently appealing to justify the attention Mr Venables commands in the popular Press. To understand this it is necessary to understand the man rather than his role, not his achievements but his personality: quick-witted, articulate, flamboyant, independent, generous, cunning, shrewd and ambitious, Mr Venables is, above all else, different. As a teenager, he dared to sing with the Joe Loss Band. Later he co-scripted a television series and helped write a novel. He does not conform.

The circumstances which prevailed when he was first approached by Irvin Scholar, the Tottenham chairman, were those of the boardroom rather than the barrow. Mr Scholar acquired a controlling interest at White Hart Lane four years ago and was seeking a replacement for David Pleat who had resigned. Conveniently, Mr Venables was unemployed after spending three years with Barcelona, the biggest club in world football, where, despite winning the Spanish champion-ship and reaching the European Cup final, he failed to survive a poor start to this season.

The tale, at this point, takes an unusual twist. Mr Venables, on holiday in Florida, accepted the Tottenham job, but only after establishing guidelines that are possibly unique in the history of football management. Financially independent (he is thought to have earned £750,000 in Spain) and fully aware of Tottenham's predicament, Mr Venables sought more than a substantial salary and bonuses. He will get shares in the club and a say in its overall running.

This is important in view of the great changes that have occurred at White Hart Lane since Mr Scholar took control. Tottenham has become a thriving commercial enterprise, a public company engaged in marketing and promotion, to the detriment, some say, of the game.

'There used to be a football club over there,' said Keith Burkinshaw, a former manager, sadly on the day he left. 'There was a time when we were important,' a player said, 'now we come second to those people knocking back booze in the executive boxes on match days. Of course, they would like a winning team, but they will never get one because the people who are responsible for running the club are obsessed with making money.'

However ambitious, the majority of managers might think twice before submitting themselves to such an atmosphere, but not Mr Venables. If it was his destiny to manage the team he once cheered from the terraces, he has also been given an opportunity to satisfy his restless nature.

Mr Venables was born in 1943 and became a professional footballer in 1960. He described his reaction to finding himself in the same team as his childhood hero, Johnny Brookes. 'Not only was Johnny a great player, but also a great bloke. But for all his ability, he was one of the least confident players I ever met. At half-time, we were winning 2-1. I looked up and saw Johnny Brookes make for me. This was my big moment. Brookes with two hundred-and-odd league games and three international caps behind him, my idol. I waited in anticipation for words of wisdom. Do you know what he said? He asked me how I thought he was playing. I couldn't help it. I had to laugh.'

John Hollins, who knew Mr Venables as a young player, said, 'He was so sharp and clever, particularly when it came to talking about the game. Even then you knew he would become an outstanding coach and manager.' Cliff Jones, the former Welsh international said, 'Terry probably realised that he fell a bit short of becoming a truly outstanding footballer. He had tremendous ability and a real mind for the game but he lacked pace, which is ironic because he sees that as the most important element. But there was never any doubt in my mind that Terry would establish himself as an exceptional coach. I haven't come across many who talk as much sense about football.'

In May 1984, after a successful career in English football as player, coach and manager, Mr Venables agreed to join Barcelona. The pressure in Spain could have cost him his marriage. His wife, Christine, who has remained loyally tight-lipped, stayed at their English home in Essex, while Mr Venables went to Barcelona. He achieved much there, but football is always about tomorrow. If his time at White Hart Lane is successful, Mr Venables hopes it will lead to management of the English national team.

(Geoffrey Wheatcroft, *The Independent*)

C Find a word or phrase in the text which, in context, is similar in meaning to:

Paragraph 4
1 an unexpected development in the story
2 knew all about Tottenham's problems

Paragraph 5
3 having a harmful effect

Paragraph 6
4 drinking a lot of alcohol

Paragraph 8
5 profound advice

Paragraph 9
6 not quite good enough
7 couldn't keep up with a fast game

Paragraph 10
8 said nothing

D Now read the text again and choose the best answer to the following questions.

1 The Press has given Mr Venables a lot of coverage because
A he used to be a very successful player.
B he has a very persuasive personality.
C he is a skilful manager.
D he behaves in an unpredictable way.

2 Mr Venables's first connection with Tottenham was as a
A player.
B coach.
C fan.
D manager.

3 Mr Venables accepted the Tottenham job on condition that
A he would have a voice in policy decisions.
B his pay would be higher than it had been in Spain.
C he had overall control of the club.
D his bonus payments would be in the form of shares.

4 Some former supporters of Tottenham are hostile to the current set-up on the grounds that
A there is too much drinking.
B the game is not the first priority.
C the management does not appreciate the players.
D making money won't help the club.

5 When Johnny Brookes spoke to him, Mr Venables expected to hear
A some advice.
B a joke.
C some critical remarks.
D a question.

6 When Mr Venables was a young player people were very impressed by
A his speed as a player.
B his sense of humour.
C his ability to talk about football.
D his self-confidence.

7 Mr Venables ambition now is
A to be reconciled with his wife.
B for his club to win a major championship.
C to impose his ideas on Tottenham.
D to be appointed manager of England.

Robert Browning

E Choose the best answer to the following questions (*1–7*), according to the information on the tape.

1 The narrator first read poems by Robert Browning

A at school.
B when she discovered him for herself.
C when a schoolfriend lent her a book.
D when her mother gave her some to read.

2 The message of the lecturer was that

A ambition led to social advancement.
B hard work was necessary for successful studying.
C time should not be wasted.
D human beings should strive for excellence.

3 Browning's poem about the grammarian puts forward the view that

A knowledge is power.
B too much studying leads to ill health.
C intellectual pursuits can't bring pleasure.
D people must work to achieve their aims.

4 A characteristic of Browning's that the narrator admires is

A his inexhaustible thirst for knowledge.
B his description of physical objects.
C his studies of the insane.
D his shrewd judgements.

5 One problem of biographers of Browning is that

A they get the facts wrong.
B they are dull.
C they are less subtle than Browning himself.
D they don't provide a balanced picture.

6 From the text we learn that Browning was married to

A a feminist.
B a writer.
C a literary critic.
D a complicated woman.

7 Which word best fits the narrator's view of Browning? He was

A understanding.
B dedicated.
C sociable.
D demanding.

Grammar: *perfect tenses, simple past*

Present perfect

A How many of these sentences are unacceptable? Can you change the unacceptable ones?

1 Tom is unemployed since he lost his job as a painter.

2 William has often been invited to speak at the annual conferences.

3 This is the first time I've driven this car.

4 I never saw him before.

5 These paintings always belonged to my family.

6 These dinosaur bones have been here for 200 million years.

7 Have you renewed your library books yet?

8 The new security system is in operation since last Monday.

9 William Shakespeare has written Othello.

10 I've visited York four times this year.

11 Wine is produced in this region since Roman times.

12 They have been to Stockholm four years ago.

13 Are you now or have you ever been a member of a political party?

14 Did you ever meet Sheila?

15 Has he told you the news?

Present perfect, past simple

B Complete these sentences with either a present perfect form or a past simple form. Some sentences can be completed with both forms.

1 .... earlier this year.

2 ....every day for the last six weeks.

3 .... already.

4 .... since last year.

5 .... recently?

6 .... at ten o'clock. ....

7 .... this morning.

8 .... for three days.

9 .... since we were at college together.

10 .... all her life.

11 .... last month.

12 .... for the last week.

13 .... since he got a new job.

14 .... throughout this century.

15 .... at the end of last week.

Present perfect continuous

C 1 Which of these sentences makes it clear that the job is finished? Which one explains why your hands are scratched (whether the job is finished or not)?

I've been pruning the roses.
I've pruned the roses.

2 Which of these sentences would you choose to express the idea of repetition?

I have tried to contact her by phone.
I have been trying to contact her by phone.

3 Which of these two sentences is more likely to mean that she is a pilot?

She has trained to be pilot.
She has been training to be a pilot.

4 Which of these sentences is more likely to mean that Henry's victories will continue?

Henry has won a lot of races.
Henry has been winning a lot of races.

5 Which sentence would you be more likely to say if you are looking at a sleeping baby?

The baby has slept for two hours.
The baby has been sleeping for two hours.

6 Is there any significant difference between these sentences?

I have lived in Kingston for five years.
I have been living in Kingston for five years.

Theme three: Two Women

A On 3 January 1988 Mrs Margaret Thatcher became the longest-serving Prime Minister of the United Kingdom this century. She was forced to resign two years later, after acting as Prime Minister for a period of eleven years.

Read through the texts to find out the attitude of various people towards her.

BRIEF BIOGRAPHY

Born Margaret Hilda Roberts 13 October 1925 in Grantham, Lincolnshire – daughter of a shopkeeper

Educated: Kesteven and Grantham Girls' School
Somerville College Oxford

Research Chemist 1947–1951

Married Denis Thatcher 1951

Twins, Mark and Carol, born 1953

Called to the Bar, Lincoln's Inn, 1954

Member of Parliament for Finchley 1959 –1992

Secretary of State for Education and Science 1970 –1974

Leader of the Opposition 1975 –1979

Prime Minister 1979 –1990

Led the Conservative Party to election victory in 1979, 1983 and 1987

Led Britain into the Falklands War, 1982

Survived a bomb explosion at her hotel in Brighton during the 1985 Tory Party Conference

Created Baroness Thatcher of Kesteven in the County of Lincolnshire, 1992

Text a

One of Us

Her style was built on domination. None of her colleagues had ever experienced a more assertive, even overbearing, leader. That had always been her way of doing business, and it became much more pronounced when, having defeated all her male rivals in 1975 (when she was elected leader of the party), she needed to establish a dependable ascendancy over them. With her command of facts and figures and her reluctance ever to lose an argument, she seemed so damnably sure of herself that nobody could suppose there lurked much uncertainty anywhere in her make-up. Certitude was her stock-in-trade. It was what got most of her ministers down, fainthearts that they were. It was also what the country most noticed about her. Whenever perceptions of her character were tested in opinion polls, she always scored heavily in the assertive virtues of firmness and clarity. Mirroring this, hardly anyone said they didn't know what they thought about her. There were supporters and opponents, and almost no one in between. To an important extent, this clarity and sureness were deceptive. Her manner had become habitual. But in part it was an act, put on to convince herself and others that she really was the boss, and a cover for deeper apprehensions.

. . . . .

She maintained her domination partly by sheer forensic competence. She was not an inspiring orator, possessing no natural felicity of phrase or command of the unexpected thrust. Throughout her time as Prime Minister she did not make a single speech which anyone would place in an anthology of great parliamentary occasions, or even a speech that would stand out in the memories of those who heard it. But she was rarely, if ever, embarrassed, and never for want of thorough briefing on the facts. She made her mark not by elegance but by combat. She was a fighting speaker who always wanted to win, preferably leaving a corpse rather than taking hostages.

(*One of Us* by Hugo Young)

Text b

A style of her own but it left us cold

Although she was feted and adored by male politicians and commentators the world over, there was little love lost between Britain's first woman Prime Minister and the rest of her sex, writes **Valerie Grove**.

Thatcher managed to develop and sustain an image of womanhood which will be every bit as lasting as the images we cherish of Queen Elizabeth 1, Boudicca and Queen Victoria. The latest in a line of commanding women: in a blue suit, with padded shoulders, upswept fair hair, a thrusting arm and a pointed finger, saying not just: 'No, no and no,' but 'I'm enjoying this!' On this wave of admiration we might let the Thatcher image rest. The first woman Prime Minister, around whom male political columnists danced attendance for a decade. But here is the confusion: on women she has had a quite different effect. We were not immune to the fierce pride she invoked. But much of the time her style also made us cringe. Yes, it was time we had a woman Prime Minister. She proved that it could be done, she could play a man's game, outwit men and cause them to smile boyishly even when she ticked them off. But the response among women included few instinctive fellow-feelings. She enshrined a workplace image; a woman making her mark in a masculine environment; a suit with a skirt in the midst of a sea of suits with grey trousers. She has always been a working mother; so in the abstract, it is supposed that she must have opened up possibilities for other women. Did she? It might seem so: by simply being up there, by not making a song and dance about *rights*; by her daunting five-hour nights and nineteen-hour days. The sheer organisation of it: the red boxes at midnight, the getting up at 5 a.m. and putting on a silk suit that remained immaculate all day.

And yet – did her great achievement make any impact on the lives of working women? Frankly, no. The real, practical benefits for women – equal pay, and the right to maternity leave – were established in the mid-1970s. Thatcher extolled housewifely virtues without ever having to be one; and as for motherhood, she told Miriam Stoppard that when she first beheld her twin babies, her first thought was: 'I am not going to be overcome by this.' A thoroughly feminist sentiment. But it was the men in her cabinet who claimed to wish to spend more time with their families.

When I met Thatcher in November 1968 – she was the newly appointed Shadow Minister of Transport – I found her 'rather beautiful in a fine-boned, regal way, with a soft gentle voice.' There was still a sweet, fair prettiness about her; the hectoring came later. Maureen Lipman, who did a half-hour television imperson-ation of her, said that at the end of the day's filming she found herself feeling unloved. 'It was all that studied insincerity.' No woman listening to that voice could ever take it seriously. Only susceptible males – in which group we must include the world's statesmen – ever would.

Above all, Thatcher has not exhibited that common female trait: real curiosity about others' lives. Everyone ushered into her presence has said the same. For women in search of role models the first woman Prime Minister proved a contradiction: so impressive, but so very unlike what most women would like to be – loved and happy. A hard act to follow, and harder still to emulate.

(Valerie Grove, *The Sunday Times*)

Quotes

1 *'Mrs T loathed the sort of businessman that I am ... she liked the flashy and the trashy. She didn't like the solid and she didn't like being told her policies were unhelpful, which of course they were ... She thought that unless you earned an enormous amount of money and had a lot of money you weren't anybody at all. You might actually be Mother Teresa but the fact that you hadn't got the money meant you didn't rate ...'*

(John Harvey-Jones, businessman and former Chairman of ICI)

2 *'She's the most disastrous politician ever to come to power in this country. She lacked compassion, one of the most important things in the world.'*

(Jeffrey Barnard, columnist)

3 *'Anyone who's been in a hospital or school in the last eleven years knows something's gone very wrong. But I was amazed by her resignation. It was the final U-turn. As*

Enoch Powell said, all political careers end in disaster. Her only option is to become a US citizen and stand for President.'

(Ian Hislop, Editor of Private Eye)

4 *'She's a great woman. I'm sure she feels relieved: she can go home, get on with her housework and look after Denis. What's happened is a tragedy.'*

(Bernard Manning, Comedian)

5 *'A brilliant tyrant surrounded by mediocrities.'*

(Harold MacMillan, former Conservative Prime Minister)

Text a

B Find a word or phrase in the texts, which, in context, is similar in meaning to:

Paragraph 1

1 expressing opinions forcefully
2 unwillingness
3 was highly rated
4 worries

Paragraph 2

5 inspiring public speaker
6 elegance of phrasing
7 achieved an impact

Text b

Paragraph 2

8 impressive
9 untouched by
10 feel embarrassed
11 reprimanded
12 embodied
13 a big fuss

Paragraph 3

14 saw
15 feeling

C Now read all the texts again and answer the following questions.

1 Describe Mrs Thatcher's career before she became a politician.

2 What political experience had Mrs Thatcher had before she became Prime Minister?

3 Describe Mrs Thatcher's leadership style.

4 What were Mrs Thatcher's abilities as a public speaker?

5 What were the physical characteristics of Mrs Thatcher's style?

6 What aspects about her did women admire?

7 What did they dislike?

8 In the opinion of John Harvey-Jones, how did the qualities Mrs Thatcher admired in businessmen clash with those *he* admired?

D Work in groups of three. Using the information available, write three paragraphs of about 50 words each.

Your first paragraph should be in praise of Mrs Thatcher.

Your second paragraph should express a critical view of her.

Your third paragraph should give a balanced account, with both good and bad points.

Mother Teresa

E Choose the best answer to the following questions, according to the information on the tape.

1 Helen describes Mother Teresa as 'good' for a variety of reasons. Which of the following does she *not* give? Mother Teresa

A uses the media in a skilful way.
B overcomes obstacles.
C does what she thinks is right.
D is brave.

2 According to Helen, Mother Teresa has become a mythical figure

A and does everything she can to perpetuate this image.
B through media attention.
C and has altered her behaviour as a result.
D but would prefer to have remained a private person.

3 The media has a useful role to play for Mother Teresa because

A Mother Teresa's reputation is enhanced.
B it informs the world of Mother Teresa's latest activities.
C Mother Teresa is paid by TV companies who film her.
D it brings publicity and consequently financial aid.

4 Helen considered that the encounter with the sick child was

A an intrusion into a private moment.
B specially staged for TV.
C not significant.
D an example of Mother Teresa's special quality.

Talking points

A Why do people want to collect relics of the famous?

What is your view about the prices paid for memorabilia?

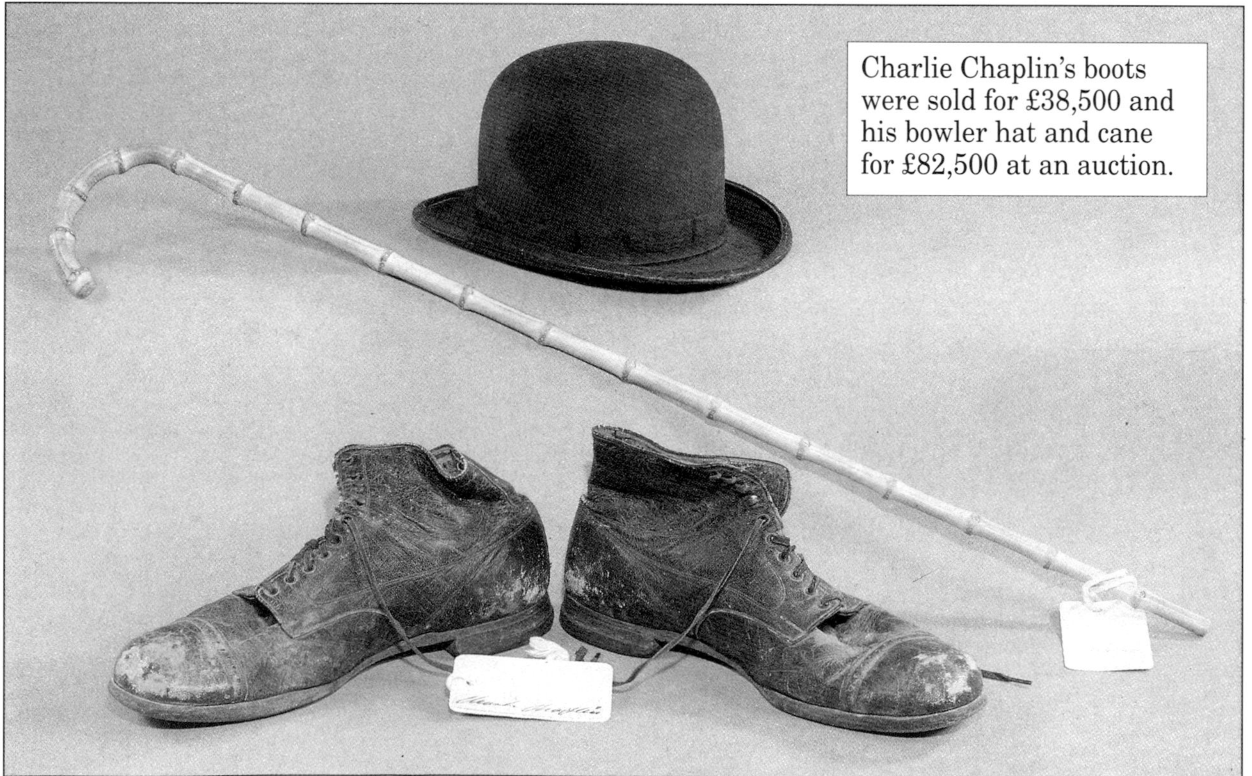

Charlie Chaplin's boots were sold for £38,500 and his bowler hat and cane for £82,500 at an auction.

B Read through the following quotations.

Which particularly appeal to you, and why?

Can you think of any people to whom any of these quotations apply?

1 *'Successful crimes alone are justified.'* (John Dryden)

2 *'It is not enough to succeed: others must fail.'* (Gore Vidal)

3 *'Some are born great; some achieve greatness; some have greatness thrust upon them.'* (William Shakespeare)

4 *'All great men make mistakes.'* (Winston Churchill)

5 *'If you become a star, you don't change; everybody else does.'* (Kirk Douglas)

6 *'The secret of success is sincerity; once you can fake that you've got it made.'* (Arthur Bloch)

7 *'Is it possible to succeed without any act of betrayal?'* (Jean Renoir)

8 *'A celebrity is someone who is known for being famous.'* (Studs Terkel)

9 *'In the future, everyone will be famous for fifteen minutes.'* (Andy Warhol)

10 *'Those who tell you it's tough at the top have never been at the bottom.'* (John Harvey)

11 *'The banalities of a great man pass for wit.'* (A Chase)

12 *'Skill is fine and genius is splendid, but the right contacts are more valuable than either'.* (Sir Archibald McIndoe)

C Read this text and answer the questions that follow.

Hounding of the Princess

Scotland Yard chiefs are to review security surrounding the Royal Family amid growing concern about the 'persecution' of the Princess of Wales.

Buckingham Palace is increasingly alarmed at the activities of money-grabbing photographers with motor bikes and two-way radios who are accused of making the Princess's life a misery.

The concern has been highlighted by an incident reported in Sunday newspapers, which claimed that Diana broke down in tears when she was photographed leaving a private dinner engagement last week.

Confronted

An unnamed photographer 'spotted' the Princess with friends in a Kensington mews. He took some pictures but handed over his film when allegedly being confronted by a royal detective with Diana herself intervening. She was claimed to have 'begged' for the film.

Today Yard chiefs will study a report on the incident which will highlight the fears of the Royalty Protection Squad about freelance photographers who hound Diana day and night.

Quite apart from the distress they are causing the Princess, their continued presence is becoming a security nightmare.

Whenever Diana moves from her London home at Kensington Palace the paparazzi go too. They pool their resources and watch every exit. They know every royal limousine and when Diana's is seen they make their move.

Linked by walkie-talkies and on powerful motor bikes to weave through London's traffic, they have no difficulty in keeping up.

They have a detailed knowledge of Diana's 'off-duty' habits, her favourite restaurants and shops and the homes of friends and confidantes.

After many years in the most public gilded cage in the world, Diana still finds it a harrowing existence.

(Richard Kay, *Daily Mail*)

1 According to the article what was causing Diana distress?

2 What is your view about what was happening to Diana?

3 Is this the price she should have to pay for being famous?

Writing

Composition

A Choose one quotation from Exercise B in the *Talking points* section of this unit. Write a composition of about 300–350 words on it.

Hints
Before you start your composition compare and contrast these two compositions with the title:

'Some are born great, some achieve greatness and some have greatness thrust upon them.' (William Shakespeare 1564–1616).

What are their good and bad points? Try to bear these in mind when you plan and write your composition.

Composition a

This is a good quotation. I can think of lots of people who are famous. Pop stars, politicians, military leaders. They have all got something special. Though of course sometimes they just know the right people. I think that knowing the right people is more important than anything else in becoming famous - and Shakespeare doesn't talk about this at all.

My favourite popstar is Michael Jackson. He's an American star and he's made lot a lot of very good records. His clothes are very unusual - tight-fitting trousers, short jackets. He also wears make-up - so that he looks very special. He's often surrounded by women because he is so attractive. He comes from a famous musical family, but I don't really know much about them.

Someone else who is great as far as I'm concerned is the writer Jackie Collins. She writes books about men and women and there is lots of romance and changes of partner. And there's always something happening in her books. She writes about things I don't know about glamorous people like film-stars.

I don't know what Shakespeare means about people being born great, but my examples really are.

Composition b

Shakespeare is renowned for his aphorisms, and we can see why in this quotation taken from Twelfth Night. Shakespeare says there are three forms of greatness, although he does not define what greatness is. I am going to treat it as if it is similar to fame. The first form of greatness is that attained by being born into a high position: the second gained through one's own efforts and special talents: and the third achieved without any special effort, by an accident of fate. If we look at each category in turn, what examples can we find?

Traditionally, it is members of the aristocracy that are seen as being 'born great', and today we see members of royal families, at least in Britain, as being major public figures. If we look at Prince Charles, the heir to the British throne, we see a man, now in his forties, who all his life has been in the public eye. He hasn't actually done much, apart from making public appearences and speeches, but every word and act has been subjected to the minutest scrutiny. Now his wife and young sons are subjected to the same treatment.

When we look at the second group Shakespeare pinpointed, those who achieve greatness, we come perhaps to the most interesting group, those possessed of special talents and abilities, the great figures of the human race. We think of those who achieve intellectual and artistic distinction - the Galileos, Michelangelos and Mozarts - as well as political and military leaders, adventurers and sportsmen. Their personal qualties and deeds single them out among their contemporaries. Their careers are studied long after they are dead, as people try to dissect their lives and characters in order to determine where their greatness lay, trying perhaps to emulate it.

Shakespeare's final category refers to those who have 'greatness thrust upon them'. This group seems to be made up of those who became known through some sort of accident - by marriage, by demonstrating heroism in a terrible accident, by filling a political or military void. Some, in Andy Warhol's phrase are 'famous for fifteen minutes'. Some, like Winston Churchill, capitalise on their great good fortune and then fall into the second category.

Much more could be said about Shakespeare's quotation, and it would be very interesting to discuss the concept of 'greatness' and the overlap between the three categories. But that must be the subject of another essay.

Obituary

B In Unit 6 (page 107) you read the obituary written on the death of the pop singer Andy Gibb. Read through this again, and look at the details about his life that were picked out for mention.

Now choose a figure of your own (real or imaginary, ancient or modern) and write this person's obituary.

Hints

1 Pick out all the appropriate factual details such as:

- birth
- social background
- achievements
- professional and personal life.

2 Mention character traits.

3 Don't forget:

- an obituary is not just a recital of events, it is an evaluation of a person's life.
- pay attention to the tone in which things are written. Obituaries appear when people have just died and it is important not to offend surviving relatives, colleagues and friends.

Literary approaches

What idea of death emerges from this poem?

Death the Leveler

by James Shirley (1596–1666)

The glories of our blood and state
Are shadows, not substantial things;
There is no armour against fate;
Death lays his icy hand on kings:
Sceptre and Crown
Must tumble down
And in the dust be equal made
With the poor crooked scythe and spade.

Some men with swords may reap the field,
And plant fresh laurels where they kill:
But their strong nerves at last must yield;
They tame but one another still:
Early or late
They stoop to fate,
And must give up their murmuring breath
When they, pale captives, creep to death.

The garlands wither on your brow;
Then boast no more your mighty deeds!
Upon Death's purple altar now
See where the victor-victim bleeds.
Your heads must come
To the cold tomb:
Only the actions of the just
Smell sweet and blossom in their dust.

Follow-up

A Fill each of the numbered blanks in the following passage with one suitable word.

Richard Burton

Of all the actors of our time, Richard Burton was the one most likely to succeed in the theatre where others had failed .... *(1)* he had so wished. He plainly did .... *(2)* so wish or at least not strongly .... *(3)* to resist the financial temptations of the film studio. But it is on the stage .... *(4)* an actor realises his greatest potential and it seems a .... *(5)* that Burton did not realise .... *(6)*. The gift was always .... *(7)*.

At Stratford-upon-Avon in the 1951 season he played Prince Hal in Shakespeare's *Henry IV*. That role established him in the front .... *(8)* of the young players of his .... *(9)* but the sirens of Hollywood had already begun to sing. His greatest acting triumphs were in the Old Vic's 1955–56 season, but this was virtually the last London .... *(10)* of him on stage. Hollywood .... *(11)* claimed him. He himself never had any .... *(12)* about his decision to abandon the theatre .... *(13)* the glamour and money of films. .... *(14)* from his 1964 *Hamlet*, Burton never .... *(15)* played the great Shakespearean roles.

Where did Burton .... *(16)* wrong? Perhaps nowhere. It is tempting to .... *(17)* his marriages to Elizabeth Taylor or his hunger to make big .... *(18)*. It is just possible, however, that playing leading men .... *(19)* Shakespearian drama simply wasn't .... *(20)* his talents lay.

B Finish each of the following sentences in such a way that it is as similar as possible in meaning to the sentence printed before it.

1 Most teenagers think twice about a career on the stage, even if they are very keen.

However ....

....

2 Anna's mother is worried about her health, as well as being concerned about her career.

Quite apart ....

....

3 This jockey continued to break the rules, although he was officially warned about this behaviour.

Despite ....

....

4 Mr Taylor was sacked from his job as Minister of Defence when details of his private life were revealed.

Revelations ....

....

5 This letter guarantees that the boots are authentic.

The authenticity ....

....

6 Mary plans to finish her novel and then go abroad.

Mary will go abroad when ....

....

C Fill each of the blanks with a suitable word or phrase.

1 If he hadn't indulged in dubious financial schemes, he .... be in prison.

2 Diana could .... the consequences of her decision.

3 Mrs Collins came to Penley School in 1979, so if she is still teaching there in 1995, she .... at the school for sixteen years.

4 Surprising ...., Charlie Chaplin's origins were very humble.

5 That actress doesn't like doing her own make-up. She prefers .... by a professional.

6 The book was due to appear in April, and it is now June. It must .... by now.

D For each of the sentences below, write a new sentence as similar as possible in meaning to the original sentence, but using the words given. The words must not be altered in any way.

1 This drink is different from all the others.
difference
....
....

2 These events did not benefit Tom.
detriment
....
....

3 She's very proud of the way she keeps her house clean and tidy.
takes
....
....

4 He always took the best jobs for himself without thinking of the bad effect on his colleagues.
expense
....
....

5 The commentator decided to criticise particularly the council's housing policy.
singled out
....
....

6 This TV programme will not make any difference to the difficult situation that exists between these two organisations.
strained relations
....
....

E Choose the word or phrase (*A*, *B*, *C* or *D*) which best completes each sentence.

1 .... his outstanding talent, this runner should have no difficulty in qualifying for the national team.

A Given *B* Provided that
C Allowing for *D* By

2 The actors in the Amateur Dramatic Society decided to .... their resources in order to buy costumes for the new production.

A gather B pool
C join D amalgamate

3 She left her job with The Times in order to work as a(n) .... journalist.

A independent *B* liberated
C freelance *D* solo

4 The procession left the main street and .... its way through narrow streets to the church.

A strode *B* directed
C rambled *D* wove

5 The actress was so upset by the journalists' persistent questions that she .... in tears.

A broke off *B* burst out
C broke down *D* cried out

6 The show was broadcast during .... viewing time.

A prime *B* high *C* main *D* peak

7 Tom looked a depressing sight, ... in his oldest and dirtiest clothes.

A clad *B* wearing
C dressed up *D* clothed

8 Reading between the ...., I should say Maria is homesick.

A sentences *B* lines
C words *D* papers

9 Everyone wants to .... the rewards of hard work.

A harvest *B* collect
C gather *D* reap

10 As a young actor he got a number of interesting parts, but he ended his career in a soap ....

A series *B* opera
C commercial *D* company

11 The Press follows Diana's every move. She feels ....

A chased *B* dogged
C invaded *D* hounded

12 Despite persistent questioning from journalists about her private life the film star remained ....

A close-knit *B* stony-faced
C tight-lipped *D* tight-fisted

13 There was such .... between the two actors that the audience was spellbound.

A sympathy *B* empathy
C feeling *D* sentiment

14 Neil's rashness in the face of danger finally .... him his life.

A cost *B* lost
C took *D* deprived

15 That, in a ...., is it: he is brilliant.

A flash *B* nutshell
C phrase *D* brief

Unit eight

Survival and Endurance

Lead-in

A Look at these pictures. From the list on the right, decide which would be the three most serious problems that would be faced by the people in the different pictures:

cold	disease	anger
heat	fear	hunger
wind	loneliness	thirst
rain	ignorance	pain
exhaustion	panic	

For each picture choose the two best aids to survival from this list:

equipment	courage
pride and ambition	strength and fitness
the will to survive	comradeship
knowledge	

B Complete each sentence with one of the words or phrases given.

yearned	shelter	stunned	blunt
scanned	tracked	thrusting	hazards
cunning	wreckage	craved	stupor
weary	weapon	glimpsed	inhibitions
conserve	lose track	mental discipline	
fend off	terrain	stamina	

1 This mountainous .... is quite unsuitable for wheeled vehicles. Even on foot, it is hard going.

2 Oliver used his camera tripod to .... the baboons as they tried to climb in the Land Rover.

3 A sharp knife is the best survival tool. A(n) .... one would be worse than useless.

4 The survivors took as many useful things as they could find from the .... of the aircaft.

5 It is easy to .... of time if you are confined to the same prison cell for year after year.

6 Polar bears, blizzards and frostbite are just some of the .... you would face if you were lost in the Arctic.

7 Gordon stayed in the .... he had built from driftwood and palm tree leaves and moved as little as possible in order to .... energy.

8 As a(n) .... he recited all the poems he could remember.

9 He climbed to the top of the highest tree on the island and .... the horizon for any sign of a ship.

10 He discovered a bottle of rum in the first-aid box, drank it all and collapsed in a drunken ....

11 There were ten of us in a very small lifeboat and we had no choice but to overcome many of the .... we would have had in our normal lives.

12 Richard .... a deer in the bushes and threw his spear at it.

13 After forty days on a diet of nothing but fish, Miranda .... something sweet.

14 Jennifer fashioned a primitive .... from a stick and a sharp stone.

15 The sudden impact of the crash left him .... for a few minutes.

16 Carrying a rucksack weighing 40 kilograms made him feel very .... at the end of the day.

17 Andrew needed to use all his .... to avoid contact with the dangerous animals in that area.

18 Felicity .... the wounded deer for hours before catching up with it and finishing it off by .... her knife into its side.

19 You need a lot of .... to complete a marathon.

20 After six weeks at sea in his small boat, Francis .... for the comforts of home.

C Complete the text using the words or phrases given.

will	stung	swept	resourcefulness
ingenuity	skid	poisoned	bare
odds	fall-out	capsize	vertigo
robust	sunstroke	steel	stranded
improvise	frostbite	exposure	bitten
gored	unscrupulous	reluctance	
stave off	altitude sickness	thwart	

In Danger

Every year thousands of people find their normal, peaceful, humdrum lives transformed by sudden accidents and disasters. They are .... *(1)* on rocks at high tide, ... *(2)* away by avalanches and mudslides, trapped in pot-holes and kidnapped by hijackers. They suffer from .... *(3)* in extreme weather conditions, ... *(4)* in hot climates, ... *(5)* in sub-zero temperatures, ... *(6)* on high buildings, ... *(7)* on mountains. Cars .... *(8)* and crash, boats .... *(9)*, houses collapse in earthquakes and are blown away in hurricanes. Land and animals are contaminated by nuclear .... *(10)*. People are savaged by dogs, ... *(11)* by snakes, ... *(12)* by bulls, ... *(13)* by bees and wasps, and .... *(14)* by bacteria in food. Sometimes no amount of human strength and .... *(15)* is any use in the face of looming catastrophe; but for anyone who has to endure unusually stressful experiences, it is an advantage to be physically .... *(16)*, and to have plenty of .... *(17)* and initiative. In critical situations, people have to .... *(18)* methods for escape and rescue, for signalling and obtaining food, using whatever is to hand. To .... *(19)* hunger, they may have to overcome their .... (20) to eat certain types of food, and ....*(21)* themselves to kill animals with their .... *(22)* hands. To stay alive they may have to .... *(23)* malicious attempts to harm them and behave in ways that they would normally regard as .... *(24)*. In such situations the .... *(25)* are against you. To stand a chance of beating them, it is the .... *(26)* to survive which is the most important thing.

Theme one: *At the Mercy of the Elements*

Mayday Message

A You will hear a 'mayday' message from a ship which is in an emergency situation. Radio reception is very bad, with plenty of hiss, crackle and general distortion. You will hear it three times. Write down the complete message.

B Steven Callahan's yacht *Solo* sank in the middle of the Atlantic Ocean. He spent 76 days alone in a tiny rubber raft, travelling 1800 miles before reaching land.

Take two minutes to read these extracts from his story and then list the dangers faced by Steven.

Eleven Weeks Adrift

It is my 11th day in the raft. Each day passes as an endless age of despair. I spend hours evaluating my chances, my strength and my distance from the shipping lanes. The raft's condition seems generally good, although the tent leaks through the observation port when nearby waves break. One night we shot down the front of a big roller, for several seconds sliding upon its tumbling foam as if we had fallen over a waterfall. Then last night we nearly capsized again. Everything is soaked. Today though, a flat, hot sea surrounds me. The sun beats down on the wide expanse of this liquid frying pan and things begin to dry out once more …

Nagging, screaming thirst causes me to watch each minute pass, to wait for the next sip. I've only had one cup of water for each of the first nine days Daytime temperatures are in the eighties or nineties. Hours pass between single swallows of water. To keep cool and to reduce the seating, I pour seawater over myself …

The shaking of the raft jerks me from my stupor. I look down. A flat, grey round-headed beast scrapes its hide across the bottom as it lazily swings round for another bite. It's incredible that the dorados* and triggers* have not fled the shark at all! He slowly swims round to the stern and slides under. Rolling over, belly up, he bites one of the ballast pockets, quaking the raft with his convulsive ten foot torso. Bless the pockets. He might tear a hole in the floor, but that shouldn't damage the tubes, at least not yet. Should I take a shot and risk losing the spear? He cruises out in front of me just below the surface. I thrust, and the steel strikes his back. It is like hitting stone. With one quick stroke he slithers away, not in any particular hurry. I watch for a long time before collapsing, craving water more than ever …

Quick, hard punches batter my back and legs. It is not a shark, but a dorado. Their nudging has grown more confident, almost violent, like a boxer's jab. Time and again they hit where any weight indents the floors of the raft.

I have missed my targets so many times that I am slow to take aim. Punch, punch – it's a damned nuisance. The dorados circle in from ahead and take a wide sweep around the raft as if in a bombing pattern. They shoot out in front, to the side – too wide, too deep.

Casually I point the gun in the general direction of a swimming body. 'Take that!' Thump. The fish lies stunned in the water. I too am stunned. I hoist him aboard. Foam, water and blood erupt about his flailing tail. His clublike head twists spasmodically. All my strength goes into keeping the spear tip from ripping into my inflated ship as his heavy, thrashing body whips it about. I leap upon him and pin his head down on to the eighth of an inch-thick plywood square that serves as my cutting board. A big round eye stares into mine. I feel his pain. The book says press the eyes to paralyse the fish. My captive's fury increases. Hesitantly I plunge my knife into the socket – even more fury. He's thrusting loose. Watch the spear tip. There is no time for sympathy. I fumble with my knife, stick into his side, work it about, find the spine and crack it apart. His body quivers; his gaze dulls with death. I fall back; behold my catch. His body is no longer blue as when in the sea. Instead, my treasure has turned to silver.

Pandemonium now surrounds the raft. I have noticed that these fish often travel in pairs. My captive's mate strikes with unmitigated fury. I try to ignore the painful beatings for three hours while I clean my catch. I cut the flesh in one inch-square by six inch-long strips. These I poke holes through and thread on strings to dry. As evening approaches I throw the head and bones as far away as possible. Sharks can detect a single part of blood per million parts of water.

At least 30 fish gather for their nightly escort. They beat at the raft like a lynch mob buzzing with hatred. Silent murmurings reach my ears. 'You will pay for your murder, human.' I yell back, 'Leave me alone! Why can't you just leave me alone?' Time and time again I load my spear, jerk the powerful elastic, and blindly fire into their midst below the raft. My arms tire. The spot on my chest where I rest the butt of the gun while loading is sore. Still, one fish cannot be driven off. Mechanically I eat a slab of her mate as I watch her wheel around in the clear water to strike me again and again.

The flesh is not as delicious as I had anticipated. She continues to beat at me into the night ...

Whack! A tremendous blow to my back. Snapping slaps race across the floor of the raft like machine-gun fire. The raft lifts completely off the water with a twisted rubber squeal and crashes back down. Shark attack! I spring to the entrance with weapon in hand. The slapping was a dorado; the shark must have pinned it under the floor. Now he forgets the fish, grabs the raft, and jerks it about by one of the ballast pockets on the other side. I can't get to him without risking falling overboard. Wait, you must wait. A raspy blow comes from port. Wait, got to wait. It's as black as hell out, I can't see anything. There it is. I jab, – hit! He thrusts away, turns, attacks, Another blow knocks me off my knees. I wait – damn! He rakes across the bottom towards me. Jab – hit! Again the water swirls and explodes as he turns and knocks me down. Bastard! Wait ... Darkness, stillness. I'm trembling all over; I reach for my water bottle and take a few swigs. For an hour each little slap of water or groan of rubber causes me to jump, ready to fend off a new attack ...

I fight the vision of 1400 miles of wet desert separating me from the first oasis. I try to forget my fear of the attacks. I struggle with my weariness of pumping up the raft and divert my nerves from the caustic cuts on my back and knees. Exhausted, I find sleep for another hour.

(*Adrift: 76 Days Lost At Sea* by Steven Callahan)

* *dorados* and *triggers*: types of fish

C Look at these headings:

The sea
Parts of the raft
Parts of the fish
Movements of the hand or arm
Movements of the fish

Now classify the words on the right into five groups according to these headings.

a big roller	spine
fumble	stern
nudging	hoist
tumbling foam	swirls
poke	torso
ballast pocket	socket
hide	a boxer's jab
tubes	plunge
slither	flailing
liquid frying pan	tent

D Now read the text again and answer the following questions.

1. In what ways does the writer suffer because of the design and condition of the raft?
2. In the second paragraph the writer waits for *'the next sip'* of water, but at the end he takes *'a few swigs' (line 59)*. Explain the difference.
3. What can the writer do to defend himself against sharks?
4. In what way is the fish *'stunned' (line 28)* and in what way is the writer *'stunned' (line 28)*?
5. What is the writer's worst problem?
6. How does the writer interpret the behaviour of the fish? Why does he make this interpretation?
7. Why must the writer be patient when the shark attacks?

E In 100 words summarise the survival problems encountered by the writer and the means by which he overcame them.

Mount St Helens

F Listen to the first part of Joseph's story of an unusual experience and decide if the following statements are *true* or *false*.

1 They wanted to try out their new canoe.

2 There were three people in the party.

3 As soon as the weather started to worsen, they felt afraid.

4 They pulled the canoe out of the water when they couldn't see far ahead.

5 They thought that there had been a terrible accident at the Hanford Nuclear Reservation.

6 Although very frightened, they knew that they were not in serious danger.

7 While standing under the trees they could see and hear nothing.

8 They stayed on the river bank until a car came along.

9 Four cars went by without stopping.

10 When they were told about the volcano, they thought it was good news.

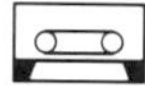

G Now listen to the second part of Joseph's story and choose the best answer to the following questions.

1 Which of the following statements about Mount St Helens is *not* true?

A It had been inactive for a long time.
B It is covered in snow.
C Some steam and ash had come out of the top.
D There was a big bulge in the side.

2 How did Joseph finally get to his car?

A The driver of a pick-up truck took him to it.
B The driver of a sports car took him to it.
C He walked to his car.
D He saw it when lightning lit up the area.

3 Why didn't they want to stay in Ellensburg?

A It was too near the volcano to be safe.
B It was not the sort of town they liked.
C The cowboys were rough and hostile.
D Nobody in the town understood what had happened.

4 What did they find most surprising when they reached Seattle?

A The baseball game had not been interrupted.
B Life was perfectly normal.
C People didn't know about the eruption.
D The weather had improved dramatically in a short time.

5 Which of the following phrases best describes them when they arrived home?

A still very frightened.
B annoyed that no one was interested in their story.
C confused about time and rather dirty.
D completely exhausted.

Language awareness: puns

English writers are fond of puns, plays on words that involve features of the language already covered in previous units, such as the fact that:

- words of different meaning have the same sound;
- certain words have a variety of different meanings;
- words and phrases are often used with a metaphorical as opposed to a literal meaning.

A Look at the following sentences and pick out the puns. Say what feature of the language they are based on. You may need to use your dictionary to help you.

1 *'Arctic ozone layer is slaying Santa's reindeer.'*
2 *' 500 000 miles on same engine – it's vantastic.'*
3 *'A new range of cheeses for the cheese bored.'*
4 *'Milk delivers bottle.'*
5 *'British Airways will stub out smoking.'*
6 *'Dying for a cigarette.'*
7 *'General flew back to front.'*
8 *'Buying the wrong computer could be terminal.'*
9 *'Butter: why waste your bread on anything else?'*
10 *'Ground coffee taste without the grind.'*

B Look at the following headlines from newspapers. What do you think the news story is likely to be?

1 CHRISTMAS SNOW ON THE CARDS
2 T-REX BONES HELD IN FEDERAL VAULT AS SIOUX SUE FOR SUE
3 TOWN WHERE CARS TAKE A BACK SEAT
4 BACON PRICES SLICED
5 IT'S SNOW JOKE BEING A GP
6 CUTS EAT INTO BRITISH APPLE CAMPAIGN
7 COUNCIL PULLS PLUG ON OPEN AIR POOL
8 HAYDN SEEK
9 HOUSEWIVES SHELL OUT FOR EGGS
10 PURRFECT PUSS GETS THE BOOT
11 BUTTER BATTLE SPREADS
12 BALLOON RACE: SIX DROP OUT

C Puns are frequently used in advertising. Look at the following examples and match the pun to the advertisement (on the next page) from which it is taken. Comment on the pun and its appropriateness.

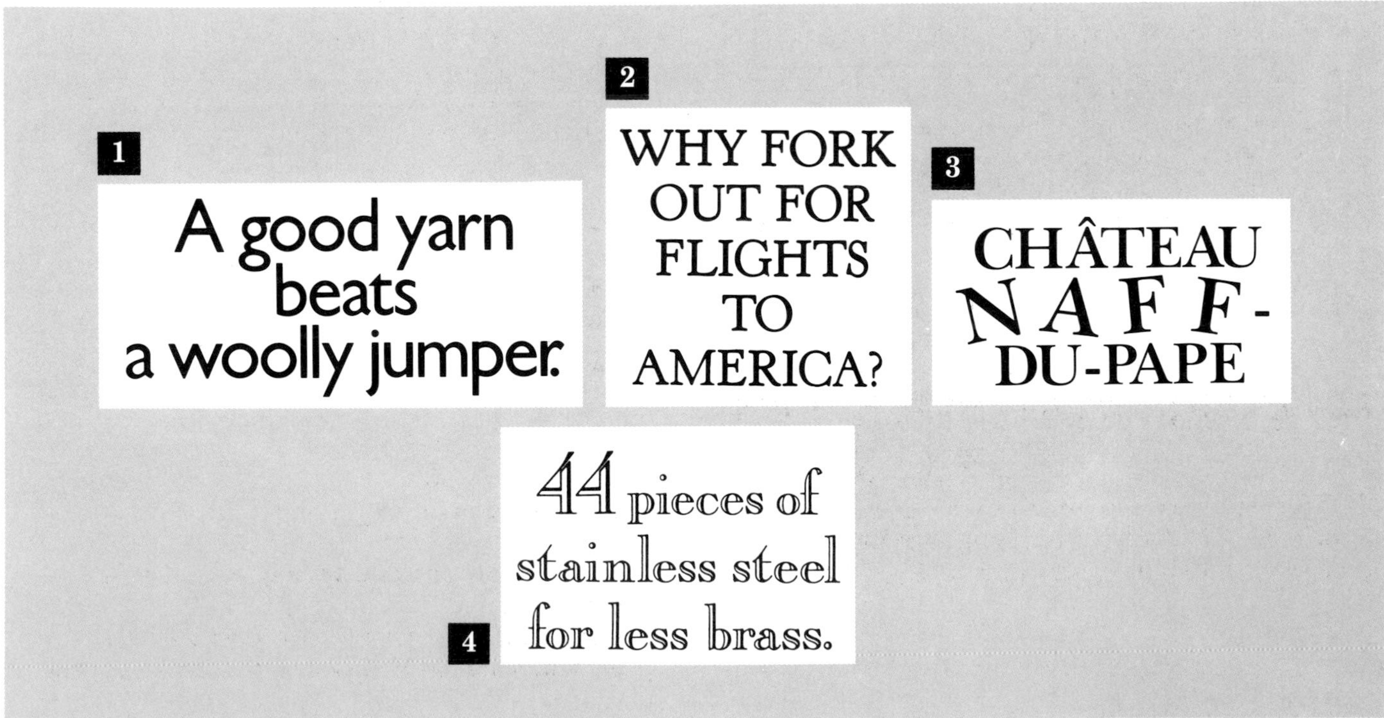
1
A good yarn beats a woolly jumper.
2
WHY FORK OUT FOR FLIGHTS TO AMERICA?
3
CHÂTEAU NAFF-DU-PAPE
4
44 pieces of stainless steel for less brass.

a

Spend £150 on Spear & Jackson hand or garden tools between now and the end of December, and we'll give you a return airline ticket to America absolutely free.

Spend just £200 and we'll give you two!

All you need to do is book and pay for two weeks accommodation in any Hyatt Hotel in America.*

For the complete low-down, pick up a leaflet at your nearest stockist when you buy your next Spear & Jackson hand or garden tool.

(Don't forget, they make terrific presents.) Then saw off into the blue.

PERFECT TOOLS FOR A PERFECT JOB.

James Neill Tools Ltd, Sheffield S13 9BR. *Offer excludes Hawaii.

b

In a black stained wooden box, the Berkley canteen of six table knives and forks, dessert knives, forks and spoons, soup spoons, teaspoons and two table spoons, has been reduced from £140 to £99.

So now you can fork out less for your cutlery.

habitat

Lakeside Retail Park, West Thurrock.

c

The pleasure that comes from a book is not just momentary. Take a look around Dillons this Christmas and you're sure to find a present, be it fiction or fact, that will bring lasting enjoyment to someone.

Europe's finest bookstore is at 82 Gower St, London WC1. Tel: 01-636 1577.

Also in Oxford, Cambridge, Nottingham, Liverpool, Manchester, Wolverhampton, Birmingham and stores nationwide.

A Pentos Company

d

Châteauneuf-du-pape, at its best, is rich in colour, slightly sweet and low in acidity. Consequently it matures quickly and should always be savoured at its peak.

But if your idea of storing the wine involves simply jamming the cork back in, your taste buds are in for an unpleasant surprise. One Châteauneuf – ruined.

However, with a Vacu-Vin Wine Saver your bottle can be opened, then sealed in seconds, any number of times. By extracting the air from the bottle, Vacu-Vin stops oxidation and the wine is kept in perfect condition – for days or even weeks.

And whether you have a humble vintage or an exceptional '83 or '84 to share out, Vacu-Vin makes sure that the last glass will taste as delicious as the first.

Around £7 at good stores and wine merchants (or telephone 0264 58036 for your nearest stockist).

Theme two: Hard Times

Growing Up in Occupied Territory

A Listen to the tape and choose the best answer to the following questions.

1 The speaker's most vivid memory of the war is

A being hungry.
B queuing for long periods.
C being afraid.
D lack of freedom.

2 When he started queuing at 6 a.m., what would he do at 7.45 a.m.?

A He would call his mother.
B He would be served.
C He would go to school.
D He would take a break and return later.

3 Why did he offer his potatoes to his father?

A He knew his father was hungry.
B He had eaten enough.
C It was customary for sons to do that.
D He had been impressed by a story in a book.

4 Why did he work on farms during the school holidays?

A He earned extra money to buy food.
B He and the other students were obliged to do so.
C It was safer in the countryside than in the town.
D The farmers provided free food.

5 During the summer camp by the sea, which of the following did he *not* eat?

A seaweed.
B dental soap.
C shellfish.
D octopuses.

6 During the summer camp by the sea, why did he feel more hungry than usual?

A He and his friends had to find their own food.
B They couldn't get enough carbohydrates.
C The food shortage was at its worst at that time.
D It was the effect of the sea air.

7 Which of the following experiences did the speaker *not* have?

A He discovered an arms cache.
B The police searched the flat where he lived.
C He often had to rush to air-raid shelters.
D A bomb fell on a shelter where he and his friends were.

B How would you cope if you had to spend two years completely alone?

What sort of people are kept in solitary confinement and why?

Now read the text and answer the questions which follow.

Solitary Confinement

A soldier took me by the arm and led me to the forecourt of the building, where a prison van was waiting. I was crammed into a compartment, and the van left at once. I tried to follow its course by feeling the turns, but being able to see nothing I was soon lost, and when we stopped again and I was rushed out of the van and into another large building, I had no idea where I was. I only realised that it was a prison, bleak and uncompromising, boding not temporary detention but an irrevocable end, where men wait powerless and destitute on *'the crowded arid margins of existence'* ...

The door slammed behind me with a crash, the double lock bolted with two heavy clicks, and I was alone. The numbness which had possessed me since morning was beginning to recede; disaster had heaved and shaken and had now subsided, and I could survey the wreckage with a slow beam of understanding. For the first time since my arrest I acted rationally, if hopelessly, going to the window and door to make sure that no one had been careless ...

A slight sound made me turn. In the middle of the door there was a peep-hole, which had been uncovered. Through it a cold blue eye, like slimy glass, was watching me. I looked vainly at the iron bed, the wooden table hinged to the wall and the stool chained to it, at the thin straw mattress, the ragged blankets and the dirty earthenware toilet in the corner. There was nothing even to throw. Then the shutter of the peep-hole slid back, and the eye disappeared, leaving me sick at heart and angry as a child.

Of the following days I remember little in particular, because nothing happened and the days in prison are distinguishable only by such rare incidents as from time to time make one of them memorable among its fellows. Although I never lost count of the day of the week or of the date, I followed them subconsciously, and life was divided into longer periods, limited by state of mind or a physical condition; and it was these more personal symbols than sun or moon which marked out the calendar of this period.

But I became an anchorite with almost the ease of inborn talent, as puppies learn to swim, and in the earliest days I had already established the routine by which I was to live, with little variation, for five hundred and twenty-six days.

Throughout the summer, while it was fine and warm, I slept bare between my two blankets, and when in the early morning I heard the trolley rattling round the floor with the 'coffee' (a euphemism, but it will serve) I put on my trousers and washed under the cold tap. This was an operation which required some skill, for the tap was of the push-button kind and had to be pressed with one hand while the water was scooped up with the other. And when I had done that, my active day was ended. As Economic Man my small doings were quite passive, and as *homo artifex* I was incapacitated by lack of the wherewithal to draw, write or make anything; nor could I even be a student, however poor, since I had nothing to read. The fourteen or more hours of daylight could be filled only by the aimless movement of my body in the cell or by the meandering of thoughts within my head.

To shorten the morning lap of this daily marathon, after I had washed, I used a series of pastimes which I regarded as ridiculous but useful. I started by manicuring myself with a sliver of wood which I managed to peel from the stool. I had never done such a thing before, at least with any but the most perfunctory attention, but now I made a great show of it, partly because the more care I took with it the longer it would last, and partly because I had sentimental memories of being chided for my ill-kept hands and thought that the least I could do now was to make myself as presentable as I might be.

But this was all I could do for my toilet except on one day a week when the guards brought shaving things round from cell to cell. The soap was bad, the brushes thin and the blades, by the time they reached me, so blunt that they pulled more bristles than they cut. Shaving was supposed to be strictly supervised by the guards, but often they were careless, having more than one prisoner to watch, and at these times I managed to cut my nails too. I had many scruples about this, thinking guiltily of my neighbour's beard, but I am afraid I overcame them and hoped that I would be forgiven. I hated to bite my nails. Yet I never thought to cut a vein.

When the manicure was finished, I sat on my stool and with what even then appeared ridiculous solemnity, forbade myself to rise again before I had catalogued the countries of England, Scotland, Wales and Ireland and after them the States of America and their capitals, as far as I could remember them. And if, after that, I still felt that I could sit on for a while, I invented other exercises, such as journeys from one place to another, naming the towns and peoples on the way and listing their languages and trades.

Once, when I was well trained in these austere ways, I managed to sit for a whole morning occupied with questions of geography, and I was pleased with myself for passing the time so diligently. I believed that I was not only conserving energy by sitting still but also that I was keeping my brain in working order by saving it from the sloth of dreaming which it more naturally sought.

When I could sit no longer, I did physical exercises, remembering a warning that one could never tell, even in prison, when fitness would be critical. But I performed them with a vigour much greater than the hope of escape which chiefly justified them, and there is doubt in my mind whether they did more good than harm.

The whole of this programme, which required great concentration and not a little insanity of a self-conscious kind, can normally have lasted little more than an hour. Rarely had the shadow on the opposite wall begun to show when I reached the end of my repertoire and was reduced to the chief stock-in-trade of all those in solitary confinement: pacing up and down the cell.

My abode was some ten feet long by five feet wide.*

(*Solitary Confinement* by Christopher Burney)

* *ten feet long by five feet wide* = 3.05 metres x 1.525 metres

C Find a word or phrase in the text which, in context, is similar in meaning to:

Paragraph 1
1 pushed into a small space

Paragraph 2
2 closed with a loud noise
3 lack of feeling
4 with no chance of success

Paragraph 5
5 a hermit

Paragraph 6
6 without clothes
7 resources
8 wandering

Paragraph 7
9 told off

Paragraph 8
10 not sharp
11 hairs

Paragraph 9
12 seriousness
13 prohibited

Paragraph 10
14 simple and severe
15 extreme laziness

Paragraph 11
16 energy

Paragraph 12
17 *walking*

Paragraph 13
18 a place to live

D Are the following statements *true or false?*

1 The writer did not know when he would be released.
2 He never made any serious plans to escape.
3 He tried to attack the guards.
4 Dressing and washing were the only two actions that he performed in a typical day.
5 He always managed to cut his nails once a week.
6 He never considered suicide.
7 He feared that he might become insane.
8 He spent a lot of time walking up and down.

Air Raids in Manchester

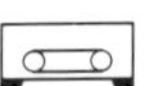

A Listen to the tape and answer the questions with short sentences.

1 What do you think *'bombed out'* means?

2 How many times was the speaker *'bombed out'*?

3 Name at least six things that your neighbours would offer you if you were *'bombed out'*?

4 What was it like inside the shelters?

5 Why did the speaker have to look after her two younger sisters?

6 What indicates that normal life went on despite the bombing?

Grammar: -ing *form, infinitive, clauses*

-ing form

A What different types of *-ing* forms can you find in the following sentences?

Can you classify them? On the right are some words you will need:

gerund	*passive*
present participle	*preposition*
subject	*possessive*
object	*followed by*
adjective	

1 Dancing is a particularly good form of exercise.

2 James hated ironing his shirts.

3 Digging the garden gave Tom a severe backache.

4 Sebastian hated being told what to do.

6 It's used for cleaning the barrel.

7 Not being given the correct instructions was very annoying.

8 We need some more typing paper.

9 Looking through his diary, he found some old letters.

10 Julian's not wanting to go on the trip was a great disappointment to us.

11 We were surprised at Michael's not having been offered the job.

12 Keep going!

13 NO EATING OR DRINKING IN THE CLASSROOM.

14 The policemen had observed flashing lights, which they thought came from a flying saucer.

15 Making working models of locomotives is his hobby.

B Complete these sentences in an appropriate way, using the *-ing* form of the verb.

1 Don't waste your time	*7* What's the point of ....
2 It's no good	*8* Is there any chance of ....
3 It's hardly worth	*9* We are not used to ....
4 There's no point in	*10* I strongly object to ....
5 It's not worthwhile	*11* In addition to ....
6 There's nothing worse than	*12* There's no excuse for ....

-ing form, infinitive

C Comment on the differences in meaning between the following pairs of sentences.

1 *I hate to phone him so late in the evening.* (What am I going to do?)
I hate phoning him so late in the evening. (Am I going to do anything?)

2 *I'd prefer to go by bus.* (Are we thinking about the future or the past?)
I prefer going by bus.

3 *I'd like to work overtime this evening.*
I don't like working overtime.

4 *I dread to think what will happen at the meeting.*
I really dread going to these meetings. (Have I been before?)

5 *Did you remember to speak to Mr Williams at the meeting?*
Yes, I did. I remembered to speak to him. (Which came first – the thought or the action?)
Do you remember seeing anyone else there?

6 *You really must try to keep up with the others.* (Is this going to be difficult?)
Try planting your seeds a few weeks later than usual. (Are we sure that this will lead to success? How would you describe this activity?)

7 *Later, I regretted speaking to him so harshly.* (Which came first – regretting or speaking?)
We regret to inform you that we have closed this account. (Is there a time difference between feeling regret and giving information – or not?)

8 *He went on to talk about his travels in China.* (Did he talk about anything else?)
He went on talking about his plans for reorganising the company. (Was that the only thing he talked about?)

9 *We stopped to admire the view.* (What did we stop?)
We stopped ordering goods from that firm. (What did we stop?)

10 *'You will forget doing these things,' said the hypnotist.* (Which is first – the actions or the act of forgetting?)
I forgot to buy some flowers. (Which was first – not remembering or not buying?)

D Complete these sentences in an appropriate way, using an infinitive or the -*ing* form of the verb. In some cases you will be able to use both forms, depending on what you choose to write.

1 I can hardly remember ....

2 I hope Sally hasn't forgotten ....

3 I always remember ....

4 I couldn't possibly have forgotten ....

5 There's no way John would forget ....

6 Do you remember ....

7 As long as I live I will never forget ....

8 I really dread ....

9 What would you prefer ....

10 The house needs ....

11 Please stop ....

12 It's 1 p.m., so let's stop ....

13 I would really hate ....

14 You needn't bother ....

15 I have always regretted ....

16 We regret ....

17 If you want to get fit, why don't you try ....

18 I'm sorry ....

19 That's the last time I'll try ....

20 She went on ....

Clauses

E Look at this sentence:

Despite the very high price, James decided to purchase the coins because they would complete his collection, which was one of the best in England.

The words *James decided to purchase the coins* form the main clause and can stand alone as a sentence. The other clauses *Despite the very high price, because they would complete his collection*, and *which was one of the best in England* are attached to the main clause with the linking words *despite, because* and *which* and cannot stand on their own as sentences.

In the following sentences (*1–7*), write down the words that form the main clause.

1 Much as he liked swimming, Tom hesitated to join his friends in their plan to swim across the lake at midnight, even though they encouraged him to come with them, because he thought that it was too cold in December for swimming in the open.

2 Whenever Jack visited Ludlow he went straight to the Red Dragon bookshop because he was sure he would find some bargains, providing, of course, that the eccentric owner had remembered to open the shop.

3 In case the jeep broke down on the treacherous mountain roads or, even worse, the way was blocked by a rockfall which might mean that, as he tried to clear it, he would be attacked by the bandits who were known to live in the mountains and prey on travellers, especially those who were forced to spend the night there, Martin always carried a small motor bike in the back of his vehicle so that he could use it as a rapid means of escape if he had to.

4 Every student had to complete a 4000 word essay, which had to be typed, with the exception of those students who had already completed at least one year at another university, providing that they could produce a certificate verifying their previous studies.

5 In order to reach as many potential customers as possible, the company decided to launch a television advertising campaign, in spite of the high cost.

6 Angela, whose elder brother, a national champion, had given her some coaching, hit the target every time, whereas her fellow students, who hadn't had any previous experience of archery, usually missed, even after many hours' practice, much to the frustration of the instructor, who was really doing his best to train them.

7 Bob, who had hardly even seen a mountain before coming on the course and, moreover, walked with a slight limp, was, according to the instructors, one of the best climbers that they had ever seen.

F Which of the following are not acceptable English sentences? Can you rewrite the unacceptable ones?

1 In order to climb the mountain, because it was very icy so the climbers wore special boots which enabled them to get a grip on the ice.

2 However much he practised, John couldn't reach the standard necessary to pass his grade eight piano examination, so he decided to stop taking lessons, even though he enjoyed them, and to devote much less time to piano-playing than in the past.

3 When he first bought the house, because he didn't like the way it was decorated, although it took a long time and was expensive until it was redecorated to his satisfaction.

4 They ran to the large tree, it was in the corner of the field, it sheltered them until the storm stopped.

5 In case you have a complaint, we want our customers to be satisfied so write to the address below, say where you purchased the product and when.

6 If your kitchen is planned by us, we will give you a computer print-out of the design, including measurements, and a free bottle of champagne, even if you do not make a purchase.

7 Immediately after finishing the five kilometre swim, the competitors mounted their bicycles who they rode one hundred kilometres, because many who retired through exhaustion, only three who completed the final part of the competition which it was a forty-two kilometre marathon.

Theme three: *In Pursuit*

A What is 'tracking'?

Can people be tracked over all types of terrain?

Is tracking a useful skill?

Now read the text and answer the questions which follow.

The Art Of Tracking

The art of tracking people or animals over different types of terrain is not only very skilful and requires lots of patience and a skilful eye, but it is very rewarding when you come up with the right results. With regular practice you are not only able to follow signs effectively, but you will be able to tell whether the signs are male or female, young or old, injured, sick or fit and even carrying something or indeed someone. It is also possible to tell if the person you are tracking is indeed trying to outwit you. Remember it is impossible for a man to move across any ground without leaving some kind of sign. Man cannot fly, so unless he is using some kind of aid to cross the ground, then it is impossible for him not to leave a sign of some sort.

Things that help the tracker are our age, sex, fitness and more often than not, cunning.

Normally, when man walks, he walks in what I call the 'heel toe pyramid' style. By this I mean the man's normal natural gait. In this he tends to put down his heel first making a very definite imprint, then rolling onto his toe, this being hardly visible as the man moves from foot to foot. At this stage he is transferring his weight evenly and regularly. This to the tracker tells him that the person he is tracking is fit, fresh and seems to have no worries or indeed any intimation that he is being followed in any way. Should the man's signs suddenly change into a more definite toe sign with the forward edge of the toe showing a good clean edge this tells the tracker that the person he is tracking has now changed into a hard, fast, running action and is still fresh in body and stamina and has possibly now suspected that he is being followed. Should the toe sign suddenly start to spurt sand or soil backwards then the person is trying to run as fast as he possibly can and in so doing he is unknowingly helping his tracker. To outwit your tracker effectively, try to remain as normal and as fresh as possible. Running on the sides of your feet or trying to run backwards, to outwit him, only helps him. For instance, trying to run on the outside of your feet tells the tracker that you are conscious of him being near, that you have shortened your stride and that you are now trying to beat him at his own game. This is fine, but remember, he as all the time in the world to find you, while you are the one who needs to put as much space between you as you can.

(*No Need to Die* by Eddie McGee)

B Match these words from the passage with the pictures:

1 *fit, fresh and seems to have no worries*

2 *has possibly now suspected that he is being followed*

3 *unknowingly helping his tracker*

4 *conscious of him (the tracker) being near*

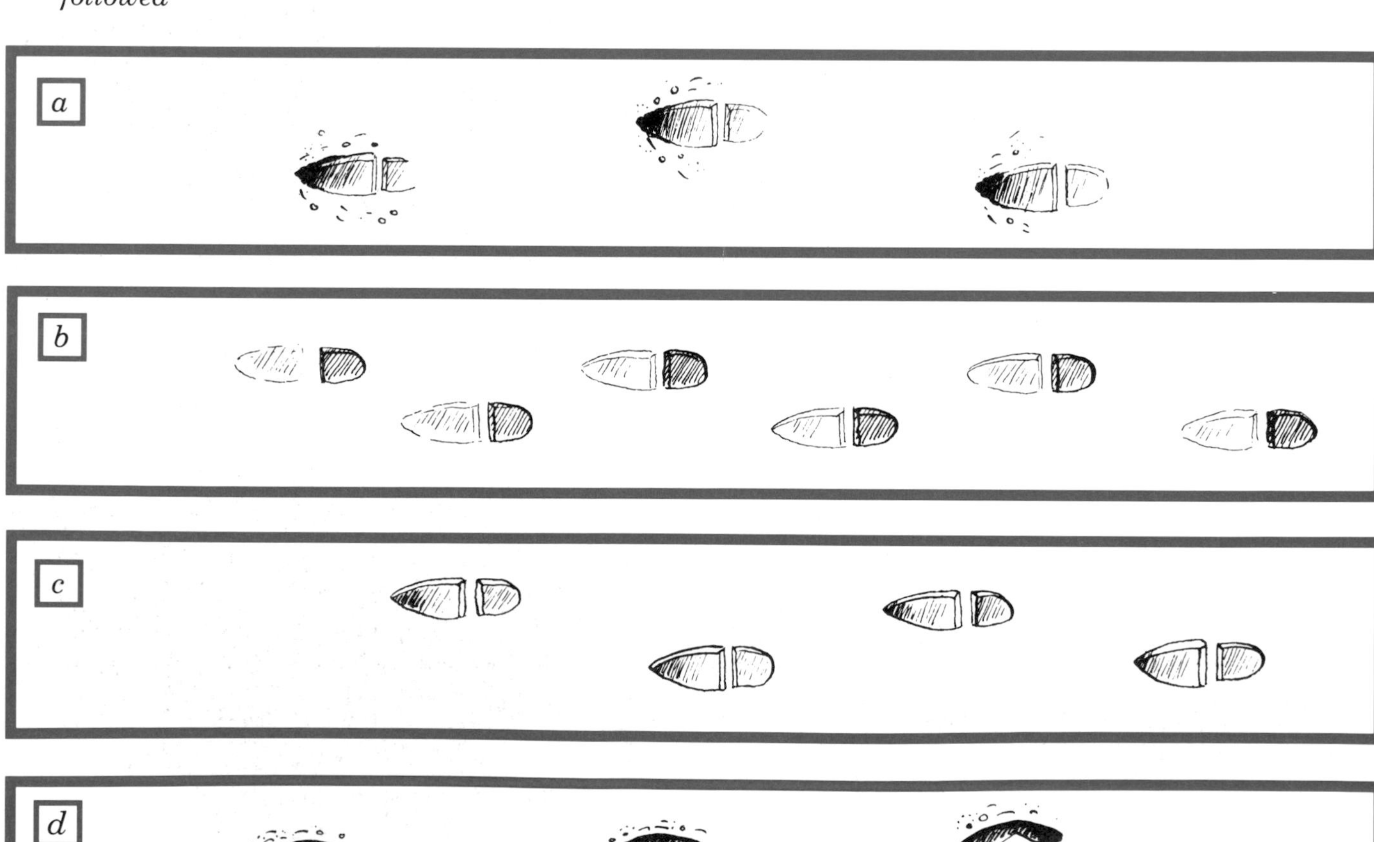

C Now answer the following questions.

1 How many of the following attributes are not particularly important to the tracker?

a skill
b youth
c patience
d physical fitness
e practice
f good eyesight

2 If you know you are being tracked you should:

a run on the sides of your feet.
b use some kind of aid to cross the ground.
c behave normally.
d lengthen your stride.

Talking points

A Describe these photographs.

B Describe the problems and difficulties, in each situation, of:

- dealing with survivors suffering from shock and injuries – and guilt
- co-ordinating emergency services
- planning for emergencies
- evacuation
- clearing wreckage and debris
- protecting the environment
- apportioning blame
- prosecuting the negligent and irresponsible
- compensation for loss, distress and injury.

Writing

Giving instructions

A You are a travel journalist writing a regular newspaper column for tourists and travellers. This week you want to deal with problems encountered by travellers abroad, such as what they should do if the car in which they are travelling breaks down, they run out of money or their passport is stolen.

Write the travel piece for your newspaper (about 350 words) giving the traveller clear instructions as to what to do.

Hints
Remember:

- to provide an introduction and conclusion
- to organise the travel piece into paragraphs covering each main idea
- to make your instructions clear, accurate and precise
- you need not necessarily write the whole of the piece of continuous prose. Some lists could be included.

Survival story

B Write the story of a survival from the survivor's point of view. You may choose any suitable subjects area (e.g. earthquake, shipwreck, etc.)

You can write this *either* in the form of a diary kept at the time *or* in the form of a memoir written later.

Hints
The survivor's personal story is the key here. It is this viewpoint that counts, so it's only necessary to give details of how the accident or disaster happened in so far as the survivor is immediately affected.

Literary approaches

Read this extract from a novel and consider these questions.

How does Crusoe react to his surprising discovery?

What feelings does he experience?

The Life and Adventures of Robinson Crusoe
by Daniel Defoe (1660-1731)

It happened one day about noon going towards my boat, I was exceedingly surprized with the print of a man's naked foot on the shore, which was very plain to be seen in the sand. I stood like one thunder-struck, or as if I had seen an apparition; I listened, I looked round me, I could hear nothing, nor see any thing; I went up to a rising ground to look farther; I went up the shore and down the shore, but it was all one, I could see no other impression but that one. I went to it again to see if there were any more, and to observe if it might not be my fancy; but there was no room for that, for there was exactly the very print of a foot, toes, heel and every part of a foot; how it came thither I knew not, nor could in the least imagine. But after innumerable fluttering thoughts, like a man perfectly confused and out of my self, I came home to my fortification, not feeling, as we say, the ground I sent on, by terrify'd to the last degree, looking behind me at every two or three steps, mistaking every bush and tree, and fancying every stump at a distance to be a man. nor is it possible to describe how many various shapes affrighted imagination represented things to me in, how many wild ideas were found every moment in my fancy, and what strange unaccountable whimsies into my thoughts by the way.

When I came to my castle, for so I think I called it ever after this, I fled into it like one pursued; whether I went over by the ladder as first contrived, or went in at the hole in the rock which I called a door. I cannot remember; no, nor could I remember; no, nor could I remember the next morning, for never frightened hare fled to cover, or fox to earth, with more terror of mind than I to this retreat.

I slept none that night; the farther I was from the occasion of my fright, the greater my apprehensions were, which is something contrary to the nature of such things, and especially to the usual practice of all creatures in fear: but I was so embarrassed with my own frightful ideas of the thing, that I formed nothing but dismal imaginations to my self, even tho' I was now a great way off of it. Sometimes I fancy'd it must be the devil; and reason joyned in with me upon this supposition; for how should any other thing in human shape come into the place? Where was the vessel that brought them? What marks was there of any other footsteps? And how was it possible a man should come there? But then to think that Satan should take human shape upon him in such a place where there could be no manner of occasion for it, but to leave the print of his foot behind him, and that even for no purpose too, for he could not be sure I should see it; this was an amusement the other way; I considered that the devil might have found out abundance of other ways to have terrify'd me than this of the single print of a foot; that as I lived quite on the other side of the island, he would never have been so simple to leave a mark in a place where 'twas ten thousand to one whether I should ever see it or not, and in the sand too, which the first surge of the sea upon a high wind would have defaced entirely. All this seemed inconsistent with the thing it self, and with all the notions we usually entertain of the subtilty of the devil.

Abundance of such things as these assisted to argue me out of all apprehensions of its being the devil; and I presently concluded then, that it must be some more dangerous creature, viz. that it must be some of the savages of the main land over-against me, who had wandered out to sea in their canoes, and, either driven by the currents or by contrary winds, had made the island; and had been on shore, but were gone away again to sea, being as loth, perhaps, to have stayed in this desolate island as I would have been to have had them.

Follow up

A Fill each of the numbered blanks in the following passage with one suitable word.

Kidnapped

Penelope Tremayne, an English woman in her sixties, ... *(1)* kidnapped in 1986 and spent five weeks .... *(2)* a hostage in the jungle.

She has now written a book, *Nor Iron Bars a Cage*, about her .... *(3)*. 'The uncertainty was the hardest to .... *(4)*,' she says. 'I was much more ready to be shot than to be kept for an .... *(5)* number of months or years.'

She .... *(6)* the individuals who guarded her with distant sympathy but makes it .... *(7)* that they were ignorant and brutal. She was questioned for gruelling hours, ... *(8)* her kidnappers were not well-schooled in the .... *(9)* of interrogation and their incompetence added touches of farce to the ordeal. They went .... *(10)* her address book insisting that respectable private citizens were spies, ... *(11)* she hid the only document that .... *(12)* have incriminated her inside her blouse.

After her first grilling, she was moved to a .... *(13)* of insanitary hovels and simply had to wait for her .... *(14)* to be decided. 'They kept on saying I was going to die,' she .... *(15)*, matter-of-factly. To keep herself .... *(16)*, she recited poetry. She also wrote, digging back into her past. Her religious belief was the .... *(17)* help of all.

Has her experience changed her? 'I came out ten years older. But I'm perfectly happy to say that .... *(18)* from what I was .... *(19)* my family through, it's something I wouldn't have missed for .... *(20)*.'

B Finish each of the following sentences in such a way that it is as similar as possible in meaning to the sentence printed before it.

1 The raft seems to be in good condition despite a leak in the observation port.

Although ....
....

2 I couldn't see out of the vehicle at all.

I was ....
....

3 I succeeded in beating him at chess on only one occasion.

Only ....
....

4 There was hardly ever enough work to keep me occupied for the whole morning.

Rarely ....
....

5 I am certain Stephen would leave some kind of sign before going away.

Surely Stephen wouldn't ....
....

6 'I think someone is following me,' said Ted.

Ted suspected he ....
....

C Fill each of the blanks with a suitable word or phrase.

1 Finding .... to understand his accent, I asked him to speak more slowly.

2 It was when I saw the bars on the windows .... I was in prison.

3 In prison I quickly established the routine .... to live for the whole period of my captivity.

4 We were .... to finish at 5.p.m. but usually left early.

5 I doubt .... the medicine did me good.

6 I wondered .... myself against the sharks .

D For each of the sentences below, write a new sentence as similar as possible in meaning to the original sentence, but using the word given. The word must not be altered in any way.

1 All the days seemed the same to me.

distinguish

....

....

2 The team of experts finally managed to get the right solution to the problem.

came

....

....

3 There was sufficient time for us to feel we had no need to hurry.

world

....

....

4 I spend all my energy trying to support my family.

goes

....

....

5 You have to be very clever to reach the end of the game in ten minutes.

skill

....

....

6 The number of people in the square must have exceeded 10 000.

least

....

....

E Choose the word or phrase (*A*, *B*, *C* or *D*) which best completes each sentence.

1 Conditions in the makeshift shelter were very ....

A crammed *B* limiting
C cramped *D* jammed

2 The hunters arrow hit the buffalo and blood .... from the wound.

A spurted *B* dropped
C dripped *D* hurled

3 The captain ordered his men to take .... and fire.

A target *B* direction
C aim *D* sight

4 The prisoner managed to beat the warders at their own ....

A match *B* game
C trade *D* profession

5 You can tell from that man's .... that he has an injured heel.

A step *B* pace
C gait *D* walking

6 The ambusher's victim walked .... into the trap.

A blindly *B* shortsightedly
C ignorantly *D* unconciously

7 If you're sailing a yacht you must be careful to avoid established shipping ....

A alleys *B* paths
C channels *D* lanes

8 It had been a long journey, and the last .... made all the soldiers feel weary.

A stretch *B* route
C trek *D* lap

9 The fugitives .... refuge in a hut on the mountainside.

A pursued *B* looked for
C sought *D* seized

10 The fisherman grabbed at the fish but it .... out of his grasp.

A heaved *B* slithered
C pushed *D* jerked

11 The attack came suddenly and the settlers were only able to .... it off by using all their resources.

A keep *B* push
C turn *D* fend

12 A brick thrown by a demonstrator hit the policeman and .... him.

A stunned *B* jabbed
C struck *D* amazed

13 The game warden .... his knife into the animal's belly and it fell down dead.

A hoist *B* nudged
C plunged *D* cut

14 There's no way the leader will change his mind. The decision is ....

A fixed *B* irrevocable
C resolute *D* tenacious

15 If the boat is unevenly loaded, there is a danger it will ....

A invert *B* somersault
C capitulate *D* capsize

Unit nine

Buying and Selling

Lead-in

For Sale

A Listen to the six extracts on the tape and try to guess what the people are selling.

B How are the following goods sold in your country?

ties	double-glazing	fitted kitchens	life insurance
plastic food containers	cosmetics	milk	

C Discuss with a partner:

1 What different forms of selling do you know?

2 What strategies are employed for the selling of different products?

3 What makes a successful salesman? Is the salesman's success related to the particular product he is selling?

4 What makes a successful product?

D Complete each sentence with one of the words or phrases given.

distribution network	launch	branches	consumer
sales technique	customers	discount	initiative
sales force	commission	gross	bids
spending power	marketing	targeted	products
street traders	monopoly	enterprise	middleman
purchase	net	aimed	
merchandise	range	wholesale	
chain	retail	warehouse	

1 Buying goods .... is much cheaper than obtaining them from a(n) .... outlet.

2 One of Britain's major travel companies has been able to make a considerable increase in profit by selling direct to the public, thus cutting out the ....

3 Marks and Spencer has a(n) .... of shops throughout Britain, Europe and North America.

4 Not all .... of Laura Ashley carry the same stock.

5 .... watchdog programmes have become common on radio and TV in Britain as dissatisfied .... give vent to their feelings of frustration and anger at being taken advantage of.

6 If a company is going to .... a new product on the market, then a committed .... will improve the chances of success.

7 This store stocks a wide .... of goods .... at people setting up home on a limited budget.

8 The goods are moved from the factory to a(n) .... and then transported to the retailer.

9 Clients booking their holiday before 31 December will be eligible for a(n) .... of 10%.

10 John showed considerable .... when he had to take over from the Chairman at short notice.

11 Our course is designed for those salesmen who believe that an improvement in .... will lead to better sales, and so to increased ....

12 The Art Department came up with a brilliant idea for promoting the client's goods but the .... Department tried it out on a sample population and gave it the thumbs down.

13 The .... in this shop is imported from India.

14 The .... of pensioners has increased so considerably in recent decades that this group is now being .... by advertisers.

15 The auctioneer was kept very busy taking .... from the floor and on the telephone. In the end, the painting was sold to a dealer from Bond Street.

16 Martin set up a successful .... importing goods from the Far East.

17 British Telecom's .... over the supply of telephones was ended in 1985 when other companies were allowed to market their ....

18 Most .... need to develop a sophisticated sales pitch in order to attract the attention of passers-by, who will then be encouraged to stop and make a(n) ....

19 When Simon took over as Managing Director, he was concerned about the time it took goods to be delivered, so his first priority was to improve the ....

20 The firm's .... profit of £20 million was reduced to £16 million .... when tax was taken into account.

E Complete the text using the words and phrases given.

survives	subsidies	day-to-day	running
reduces risks	under-financed	hallmark	sectors
long term	to the wall	techniques	aspects
profit margins	competitive	paperwork	unforeseen
niche	lack	profitably	estimate

Getting It Right

How many people would start a long car journey without a route map? How many would build a house extension without drawings and a detailed .... *(1)* of costs? .... *(2)* a business is infinitely more hazardous than the first and much more prolonged than the second – the uncertainties continue as long as the business .... *(3)* – yet many owner managers manage .... *(4)* with a few or no plans for the future.

An overall plan, however, not only .... *(5)* but makes the enterprise better able to cope with the .... *(6)*. Planning is also the .... *(7)* of the businesses which take off successfully and of the .... *(8)* survivors – those who dig themselves in .... *(9)* and survive the winds of insecurity year after year.

Planning in an appropriate form for a small firm means being especially conscious of certain .... *(10)* of the business and using some fairly simple and often inexpensive .... *(11)*. It also means .... *(12)* and some administration, the very things that many private business owners hoped to avoid by working for themselves.

The most commonly mentioned start-up problem is finance. Many firms are set up .... *(13)* and then overtrade. Some enter highly .... *(14)* areas because these are cheap to enter but .... *(15)* of initial finance and low ....*(16)* put the business under constant pressure and allow little time for planning.

This has sometimes been exacerbated by government .... *(17)* to new start-ups which simply push older businesses .... *(18)* in highly competitive, densely populated .... *(19)* such as retailing. This underlines rule number one – planning should start as early as possible. Find a market .... *(20)* where there is a real advantage over others in terms of product of service. New products or services, or some combination of these, are a key to successful start-up.

Theme one: *Business Ventures*

Starting your own Business

A Simon describes the stages by which he and a partner set up a business importing and selling wine. Complete the missing stages in the plan.

1 They drove to France and brought back wine in their car.

2 In response to demand from friends for wine, they decided to expand.

3 ....

4 ....

5 They presented the bank with a business plan, asked for and received a loan.

6 ....

7 They decided to use a transport company.

8 They produced and distributed a list.

9 ....

10 ....

11 ....

12 They expect to be self-financing by the end of the third year.

B Work in pairs with another student. Student A reads **Article a** (pages 162–163) and student B reads **Article b** (pages 163-164).

Then together answer the following questions.

1 How, when and where was Derwent Valley Foods founded?

2 What was the traditional industry in the area where the company was founded? What effect did this have?

3 Who are the directors?

4 What range of products do they market?

5 What are the special features of the product?

6 What features of their marketing have been unusual?

7 What was the initial advertising gimmick?

8 How was the company financed when it was set up?

9 How difficult was it for the product to establish a market niche?

10 What problem was encountered in 1984?

11 How many products are now marketed?

12 How big is the labour force?

13 What is the current turnover? And profits?

14 What has been the reaction to the company of the established leaders in their field?

15 How do sales of Phileas Fogg products compare with sales in the mainstream market?

16 What does the consumption of snacks tell you about British eating habits?

17 How healthy is it to eat snacks?

C Using the information you have gained from the texts and the questions, write a history of the company, Derwent Valley Foods, using not more than 150 words.

Article a

Guzzling on the hoof costs Britons £1 billion a year

We eat on the run, grazing through packet after packet of crisps, nuts, savouries. James Erlichman questions the move to 'healthier' snacks.

'I'm afraid gunk won,' she said. 'We tried to sell an additive-free range of snacks to children, but they just didn't like the taste. So we put the additives back and sales soared.'

The words were spoken by Ann Charlesworth of Derwent Valley Foods, – the perky little outfit from County Durham which launched the highly successful range of Phileas Fogg snacks six years ago.

Phileas Fogg broke all the rules. They came in exotic flavours, were aimed at adults, had no 'see-through' window on the packets, were backed by virtually no advertising and cost, by ordinary crisp standards, a ludicrous amount. Unlike the children's range, they contained no artificial ingredients.

Lines like Tortilla Chips and Shanghai Nuts were such a hit that the company, built at Consett in the shadow of the former British Steel works, has virtually doubled its employees to 180, and enjoys sales of £11 million a year. A perfect Thatcher tableau, some might say. Men who used to make steel for motor cars, now making garlic flavoured Mignons Morceaux for the coffee table.

But they still could not devise a natural snack pleasing to the jaded palate of the nation's junk-fed youth.

The mainstream snack market is enormous and still growing. This year Britons will munch their way through more than £1 billion worth of savoury snacks. That includes 5.1 billion packets of crisps – or nearly 100 for each man, woman and child. Next come the 2.2 billion packets of extruded and reconstituted hoops, rings and thingamajigs made from maize, wheat and potato flour. We will also consume nearly 79 million pounds of assorted nuts worth £120 million.

All this puts Phileas Fogg's sales in perspective. Indeed, the snacks industry is dominated by some very big companies.

The total sales figures come from KP, the division of United Biscuits, which claims to be the biggest player in the league with 24 per cent of the total UK snack market. But rival Nabisco, the US company, with its four separate divisions – Smiths, Walkers, Tudor and Planters – owns 35 per cent of the British market. The only other company in the big league is Golden Wonder, now owned by Dalgety, which is best known for crisps and has just under 13 per cent of the market.

The big companies have been doing their best to suggest that snacks are part of healthy living. Snacma – the Snack, Nut and Crisp Manufacturers' Association – sponsors symposia on nutrition. One of its consultants, Professor Donald Naismith, has even got himself into an imbroglio with the British Medical Association after claiming that crisps had a useful part to play in a balanced diet.

KP claims that the British family 'no longer lives as a single unit, but spends its time – including eating time – as a collection of individuals.'

We eat on the run, on average six and a half times a day, grazing through packet after packet of crisps, nuts and savouries.

'This', concludes KP, 'is good news for the snack food manufacturers.'

But is it good news for the national health? Some additives have been taken out of snacks – particularly out of plain crisps which often now contain only potatoes, vegetable oil and salt. But the snack makers have adopted what could be seen as the crafty posture of prominently 'flagging' the additives they have removed.

Claims that products are free from artificial colouring fail to mention the antioxidants (E320, E321) and the monosodium glutamate (E621) that remain.

Another 'line extension', as the industry describes new product ideas is the 'jacket crisp' which is cooked with its peel left on.

But, 'It is ludicrous nonsense to suggest that these are better for you just because the peel might add 1 per cent more fibre,' says Issy Cole-Hamilton, a dietician at the London Food Commission.

The biggest problem which snacks face is the number of calories they pack into every bite. Even the lower fat crisp is still too fattening.

On the cover of Private Eye Magazine this month an overweight working class woman stands talking to the Prime Minister. 'I reckon I'll lose four pounds,' she says in obvious reference to the social security changes. Intentionally misunderstanding, Mrs Thatcher replies: 'You should lose a stone*, you great tub of lard.'

It is easy enough in a snacking nation to be poor and overweight. A packet of crisps offers ten calories for every penny spent. That translates to early obesity on under £3 a day.

(James Erlichman, *The Guardian*)

* *stone*: a British measurement of weight; one stone = 14 pounds = 6.35 kilograms.

Article b

World of flavour on old steel site

When Roger McKechnie first visited the Newcastle upon Tyne office of 3i, the venture capital group, Phileas Fogg was just an idea, dreamt up over a beer in a Newcastle pub. Yet 3i stumped up £50,000 for a worldwide search for exotic snacks.

McKechnie and his colleagues collected hundreds of snacks, from the Far East to Mexico. They eventually started production of Phileas Fogg corn chips at their first Derwent Valley Foods factory, a hut next to the abandoned steelworks at Consett, County Durham.

That was in 1982. Last year the company, with a turnover approaching £7m, won the CBI's business enterprise award. Today it opens a £1.2m extension to a modern factory that will double capacity now running at about 2.5 million chips a day.

The new factory is a stone's throw from the site of the old steelworks, which closed in 1980. Many of Derwent Valley's 130 employees are former steelworkers; but instead of molten metal, they now work amid the whiff of spices, preparing snacks for the finest of cocktail parties.

Under the label 'Phileas Fogg – Fine Foods From Around the World', Derwent Valley has created a new market in healthier, adult-oriented snacks.

'Back in 1982 the snack industry was focused on nine-to-fifteen-year-old kids,' says McKechnie, the company chairman and managing director. 'At first we didn't know what our exotic products were going to be, but we knew they existed outside the UK and could be manufactured here.'

With the backing of 3i, McKechnie and three fellow directors, Ray McGhee, Keith Gill and John Pike, had put up £50,000 of their own money, and raised £400,000, some of it from British Steel. About £500,000 in additional finance was later provided by 3i, which has a 30% shareholding.

All four directors had experience in the savoury snack industry, which is reckoned to be worth almost £1 billion a year, and knew there was a niche for a quick-moving small firm. 'We knew that the industry was dominated by bureaucratic dinosaurs,' says McKechnie.

The first products were tortilla chips and Californian corn chips. Heavy advertising spending stressed Phileas Fogg, the Jules Verne character who went around the world in 80 days.

'When we started up we wondered whether we'd ever get into the big retailers,' says McKechnie. 'But they were all enthusiastic. We seemed to be offering them something they'd been wanting for quite a long time.' The company now supplies most of the leading food stores, including Marks & Spencer, Sainsbury and Tesco.

In 1984, disaster almost struck when the company over-expanded and ran into cash problems. No one knew it, but the evening after Prince Charles visited the factory in October 1984, the four directors had to rush to a crisis meeting to prevent the plug being pulled on the business by Barclays Bank, one of the backers.

A new product, Punjab Puri, is now coming to the shops, bringing the number of snacks to ten. Company profits are running at more than £500,000 a year, and sales are almost doubling every year.

But the big snack manufacturers are catching on to the fact that up-market snacks make money. Are they a threat?

'We've got a four-year start,' says McKechnie, 'We'd have worried about it far more in the early days than we do now.'

(Ian Williams, *The Sunday Times*)

Language awareness: euphemisms

Euphemisms are pleasant, innocuous words and phrases which are used instead of plainer, more direct expressions which may give offence. Sometimes euphemisms are used out of a sense of politeness, for example, *to pass away* instead of *to die*. Sometimes they are used to make things seem better than they really are, for example, *negotiator* instead of *salesman*; and sometimes they are used to deceive, for example, *air support* instead of *bombing raids*.

A Can you identify the euphemistic expressions in these sentences? What do they really mean?

1 'We'll have to let you go, John,' said the managing director.

2 At the end of the evening, the minister seemed to be tired and emotional.

3 The police seized a quantity of adult films.

4 The manager commented that certain members of staff were probably responsible for the stock shrinkage.

5 This house is ideal for the DIY enthusiast.

6 'This one was an own goal,' said the sergeant as he looked at the terrorist's burnt-out car.

7 The President admitted that the statement he had made yesterday was no longer operative.

8 General Custer explained that it had been necessary for his troops to engage in anticipatory retaliation.

9 'If anything should happen to me ...'

10 When the lawyer questioned him closely, the civil servant admitted that he may have been economical with the truth.

11 New Prices!

12 '... but I hope that we will always be friends.'

13 This is a unique opportunity for the discerning purchaser to acquire a property with truly enormous potential for improvement.

14 He is no longer in the best of health.

15 'The kindest thing to do would be to put Caesar to sleep,' said the vet.

16 General Custer expressed his satisfaction with the body-count.

17 Anthony has been resting since his widely-acclaimed performance as Prince Hal in Shakespeare's *Henry IV: Part 1.*

18 '... and in sixth place ...'

19 A man is helping police with their enquiries.

20 In his book he tells of his experiences as a gentleman of the road.

B Can you sort these euphemisms into *three* groups of *three*? Each group refers to a particular subject area. Say what these are and what the euphemisms really mean.

1. a surgical strike
2. to turn Queen's evidence
3. '... and how are we today, Mary?'
4. to be detained during Her Majesty's pleasure
5. an all-out strategic exchange
6. mopping-up operations
7. '... I think we'll have to go in and take a little look.'
8. my learned friend
9. negative patient care outcome

Theme two: Out on the Street

Door-to-door Selling

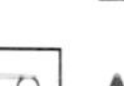

A Read the following text but do not attempt to fill the gaps until you have listened to the tape. Then complete the text with a suitable word or phrase according to the information on the tape.

Bryan thinks that door-to-door selling has .... *(1)* in recent years. He himself has a rather .... *(2)* opinion of the people who do this, believing they have a reputation for ....*(3)*. He also believes that you are unlikely to get a .... *(4)* deal from this type of sale. For major purchases, such as .... *(5)* or a new .... *(6)*, he himself would definitely not be tempted by this type of selling, but would go to a .... *(7)*. The only time he would be tempted to buy goods in this way would be in order to support a .... *(8)*.

B Discuss with a partner:

Street traders: what do they sell?

What status do they have?

What techniques do they use to attract attention?

How do they achieve a sale?

Now read the following text and see how one particular street trader operates.

Twirling the Edge

Fraz was a VIP at all the local nightclubs. He had plenty of money, and he wasn't exactly ostentatious, just not very careful about how he unrolled his notes. He always bought plenty of drinks, which, if not a good sign, is a sign nonetheless.

So one day, I was more than a little surprised to see Fraz on the pavement in Fargate in Sheffield selling furry toys. The spot was a few hundred yards from his favourite nightclub, and he wasn't even trying to conceal himself. Quite the opposite: he'd gathered a large crowd around him, and was entertaining them with his spiel. More than entertaining them, the furry dogs were going like hot cakes.

I faced the existential dilemma as to whether I should skulk off without acknowledging him, and not throw into question his alternative persona, or buy a furry dog. They were only a quid after all, and, as Fraz assured us, they were the self same furry dogs that were sold in Hamleys* and the current favourites of the Royal Princes.

But I didn't want to embarrass him, and I was just about to slink off when he caught my eye. Instead of registering embarrassment he called me over and I became the focus of his spiel. 'Here's an Irish psychologist (chuckle, chuckle) come all the way from Belfast to learn how to sell furry animals. By the way, did you hear the one about the Irish clockwork mouse ...' He was working the crowd, and using me as the straight man. I was frozen with embarrassment as he burst into song.

I learned several lessons that day. One was that guys who can spiel in a market, even fly pitchers like Fraz, are extremely proud of their abilities and their status. On a scale of social prestige of occupations – from some angles – they come out above waiters and, dare I say, psychologists, and on a par with nightclub proprietors.

Fraz had a mastery of language and techniques for selling and handling people. He described his ability as a natural gift. Researchers investigating the techniques actually employed by market pitchers have been clearly impressed by the complexity and skill involved in their communication with their customers.

Market pitchers are those market traders who explicitly rely upon their spiel to sell their products. Pitchers refer to other silent traders as 'gazers' or 'lurkers'. They may shout out the price of goods but their repetitive use of language doesn't make them pitchers. Pitchers are the cream.

They feel they have generally had a bad press, that the media and the public think they are more than a bit dodgy, and that their apparently successful selling routines rely on the presence of a large number of plants in the audience. But the use of these plants, or 'ricks' as they are called, is a lot less widespread than is popularly imagined.

The first step to success is 'pulling a pitch': that is, building a large audience. But an attentive audience is not enough. The audience has to be made to feel some obligation to buy the goods on offer. Getting them to move right into the stall is one way this is managed. Sometimes there is prolonged handling of the goods so that more people will see the one punter making the purchase. This is known as twirling the edge. A central feature is that the audience cannot buy the goods just anywhere in the pitcher's spiel, but only at certain prescribed points. These points are preceded by an announcement of the selling price. Pitchers work on the contrast between the worth of the goods on offer and the selling price; they accentuate the contrast by building up the apparent worth using a list format. The audience meanwhile may be a little puzzled by this. Is there a catch? Pitchers routinely try to forestall such thinking by explicitly assuring the audience before they have had a chance to raise their own doubts.

The spiel is very reminiscent of another type of rhetoric, that of political speeches. Oh, yes, there are enough tricks pulled at party conferences to put even the most dubious market pitchers to shame.

(Geoffrey Beattie, *The Guardian*)

* *Hamleys*: a famous children's toyshop in Regent Street, London.

C Find a word or phrase in the text which, in context, is similar in meaning to:

Paragraph 1
1 important person
2 showing off

Paragraph 2
3 place
4 sales pitch
5 selling well

Paragraph 3
6 £1

Paragraph 4
7 go away unnoticed
8 acknowledged he had seen someone
9 the joke
10 manipulating the group
11 man who assists a comedian

Paragraph 5
12 the equal of

Paragraph 6
13 sellers

Paragraph 7
14 the best

Paragraph 8
15 portrayed unfairly
16 worthy of suspicion
17 people specially placed to do a job

Paragraph 9
18 buyer
19 handling goods
20 something wrong

D Basing your answers on the text, decide whether the following statements are true or false.

1 In the nightclub, Fraz wanted everyone to see how well off he was.

2 When the writer saw Fraz at work, he expected him to be embarrassed.

3 Fraz's reaction to the writer was to involve him in his sales pitch.

4 The writer considered that Fraz's skills came naturally.

5 A pitcher is different from a gazer in that he shouts louder.

6 Pitchers consider that the public has the right idea about them.

7 The first step in getting someone to buy is to build a large attentive audience of passers-by.

8 Without a feeling of obligation, people would not buy from a pitcher.

9 The pitcher determines when goods may be bought.

10 Audiences are suspicious of the source and value of the goods sold by the pitcher.

E Using your own words, answer the following questions.

1 What was Fraz's use of notes a sign of?

2 What does the writer convey by using the phrase *'wasn't even trying to conceal himself' (line 15)?*

3 What's the meaning of *'not throw into question his alternative persona' (lines 25–26)?*

4 What made the furry dogs attractive to buyers?

5 How did the writer feel when Fraz called him over?

6 What did the writer admire about Fraz?

F In a summary of not more than 100 words, describe the sales technique of the pitcher.

The ice-cream salesman

G Choose the best answer to the following questions, according to the information on the tape.

1 People who sold ice-cream in the parks were
- *A* conspicuous for their honesty.
- *B* totally dishonest.
- *C* adept at exploiting the system.
- *D* scared of being found to be dishonest.

2 There were lots of people in the park on that particular occasion because
- *A* the weather was sunny.
- *B* a concert was going to take place.
- *C* the playing of the band attracted them.
- *D* it was a good place to relax.

3 The fact that the park was so crowded meant that
- *A* the narrator couldn't park the lorry where he wanted.
- *B* the ice-cream sellers couldn't get to the lorry.
- *C* everyone selling ice-cream felt irritated.
- *D* there was a danger of people getting crushed.

4 People queued at the back of the lorry because
- *A* they thought this was the place to buy ice-cream.
- *B* they thought the ice-cream sold there would taste better.
- *C* they couldn't reach the other ice-cream sellers.
- *D* they didn't want to be seen.

5 The dilemma was
- *A* what price to sell the ice-creams for.
- *B* whether to sell ice-cream at all.
- *C* what to do with the proceeds.
- *D* whether ice-cream should be given away.

Grammar: infinitive, -ing form, linking sentences

Infinitive

A Can you identify the *infinitive* forms in the following sentences and describe them? You will need to use these words – *full infinitive* (with *to*), *zero infinitive* (without *to*), *perfect, progressive, passive.* Do all the sentences contain infinitive forms?

1 We may be able to arrange a meeting for Tuesday.

2 Joseph must be arriving in Bombay now.

3 He says that the work will be finished by Friday.

4 All the vehicles must come in to be serviced by the end of the year.

5 He is believed to be carrying a gun.

6 I'm looking forward to seeing you.

7 She is believed to have been stealing from her employers for a number of years.

8 It is better to have loved and lost than never to have loved at all.

9 The gold bullion is thought to have been smuggled out of the country.

10 They strongly objected to cuts in their budget.

Infinitive, *-ing* form

B Complete these sentences in an appropriate way, using either the infinitive form or the *-ing* form. Only one of the two forms is correct in each case.

1 I can understand Mary ....
....

2 Sheila refused ....
....

3 I haven't asked Martin yet but I intend ....
....

4 Thomas denied ....
....

5 Unfortunately, the damage to the boat means ....
....

6 This job entails ....
....

7 We are all looking forward to ....
....

8 We all resigned ourselves to ....
....

9 I suggest ....
....

10 Martin deeply resented ....
....

11 We all thoroughly enjoyed ....
....

12 Steven is bound ....
....

13 You would be foolish ....
....

14 Professor van Helsing is generally considered ....
....

15 Peter strongly advised us to ....
....

16 The official reminded us to ....
....

17 Martin felt like ....
....

18 Margaret detested ....
....

-ing form

C Compare these four pairs of sentences. The meaning is the same within each pair.

If we take into account the end-of-year bonus, the salary is quite high.

Taking into account the end-of-year bonus, the salary is quite high.

He picked up his bags and got on the train.
Picking up his bags, he got on the train.

Because he felt hungry, he went out and bought a hamburger.
Feeling hungry, he went out and bought a hamburger.

After he had completed the interview, he began to write his report.
After completing the interview, he began to write his report.

We can see that the present participle construction can replace many other constructions.

Rewrite these sentences, using a present participle. Think carefully about what the first word will be, and note the position of the comma.

1. Before he started painting, he cleaned the walls thoroughly.
2. When I realised what was happening, I called the police. (Begin *'On ...'*)
3. While I was waiting for the bus, I completed the crossword puzzle.
4. Since he had the right tools, he started to repair the clock.
5. Despite the fact that he had very little water, he began to cross the desert.

D Why are these sentences *unacceptable* ? How can you rescue them?

1. Eating grass, I saw a cow.
2. Driving along the motorway, the sun shone in my eyes.
3. Doing the washing up, the cat sat at my feet.
4. Walking in the park, the beautiful flowers made me feel cheerful.
5. Feeling energetic, the Sports Centre seemed a good place to visit.

E Note the difference between:

Wanting to become rich, he started his own business. (Try rewriting with *'Because ...'*)

Wanting to become rich is no excuse for stealing. (What is the subject of this sentence?)

Complete these sentences in an appropriate way. Note carefully the position of the comma.

1. Finding the information he wanted, ...
2. Finding the house ....
3. Being very nosy, ...
4. Asking a lot of questions ....
5. Knowing about computers, ...
6. Doing up old cars ....
7. Signing his name on the bottom of the form, ...
8. Signing his name so many times every day ....
9. Getting up very early, ...
10. Working very late ....

Linking sentences

F Notice how these simple sentences are built up into complex ones.

a *The explorers continued their journey.*
What problems did they have?
Why did they continue?
How did they travel?

Although they were tired and hungry, the explorers continued their journey, on foot and by boat, because they wanted to reach the coast before the rains began.

b *The professor started the machine.*
When did he start it?
Was there a problem?
What was the result?

After entering the laboratory, the professor started the machine but it became so hot that it caused a fire, with the result that the laboratory was burned down.

Now try the sentences below.

1 The doctor examined the patient.
(When? Why? How?)

2 The pilot made an emergency landing. (Was it difficult? Why did he decide to do this? When?)

3 We will give a 25% discount on the normal price of a room.
(Why? Is there a condition?)

4 He played football.
(How? Why? Was there a problem?)

5 Harry threw the ball.
(With what result? When?)

6 The manager was satisfied with the new factory.
(Compared with what? Any problems?)

7 They dug a tunnel.
(How far? Why? Any problems?)

8 She mended the washing machine.
(When? How?)

Theme three: *Running a Business*

A Before reading the text consider the following questions.

What qualities do you think are necessary when people do business together?

Is a contract more important than trust?

Now read the text and answer the questions which follow.

My Biggest Mistake

William Sargent, 35, is chairman of Spitting Image productions and Managing Director of Viva Pictures. He became a financier in the television industry after taking a degree in business and legal studies at Trinity College, Dublin. In 1985, he founded The Frame Store, one of London's leading digital video post-production facilities. Recently he has put together more than £15m of funding for European programming, and acted as executive producer on Prix Italia winners and British Academy nominees.

'My biggest mistake was trying to do business on the strength of a handshake without doing my research first. In 1983, I had just sold a company which distributed video equipment around Europe, and I was looking for new opportunities. Quite idealistically, I decided I should be trying to put something back into Ireland, where I come from. I had run three businesses while I was at college to pay for my education, so I knew my way around. And over the next two years, I attempted to set up three partnerships. On each occasion I did so without a contract. It cost me around £100,000.

The first two cases involved importing various video-related goods. On both occasions they refused to pay the agreed price on delivery. Both sets of people reckoned they could renegotiate the package because the goods were already in the country. And because I had paid the freight bills to get them there, I didn't really have the option of shipping them back again. On the third attempt, the problem was that both the people selling the equipment and the potential customers were never honest with us in terms of their ability to pay. Instead of a business, we had a number of people saying they could do things which they couldn't, and at the point when I owed £40,000 to the Irish banks, I called it a day. I paid the money back, but as a result, when we started The Frame Store, my wife and I didn't have the capital to take a big enough stake. It went on to become one of the most successful companies in the industry, and in order to own the stake we deserved, we really had to pay for it.

Funnily enough, I still do business on a handshake. I never want to go into business on my own: I always look for a partner. I have neither the aptitude nor the desire to run a business on a day-to-day level. I work as a strategist, identifying opportunities and creating relationships, preferably in niche markets. If you're going to make money in the long-term, you've got to stick with someone you trust, because you don't control the chequebook and therefore you can be fiddled. After five years, it could cost you a substantial amount of money, so you might as well find out in the first twelve months if that trust is going to be betrayed. Trying to enforce contracts only creates ulcers; it's virtually impossible. If, instead, you recognise that you're never going to get what you set out to get or that you made a mistake, you save yourself a lot of angst. On that basis, I decided quite early on that I would try to do business with people on trust. Most times it works ...

The Germans and the Japanese understand long-term partnerships. They're not in it for this year's deal. That is the reason for doing business on a handshake. It is an incentive for the person to mislead you; so you find out in time that you shouldn't be in partnership. No one person has all the skills to create a successful business. It has to be a team effort. I've learnt to spend a lot more time on research before entering a partnership. You have to be partners in spirit, not in contract. And if the partnership can't be based on a handshake, then when the pressure is on, your business will fall apart.'

(William Sargent, *The Independent on Sunday*)

B Find a word or phrase in the text which, in context, is similar in meaning to:

Paragraph 2
1 based on
2 aware of what to do

Paragraph 3
3 transport costs
4 there was no choice
5 an interest or share in something

Paragraph 4
6 specialist areas
7 tricked
8 worry

Paragraph 5
9 something which makes you want to do something
10 collapse

C Now read the text again and choose the best answer to the following questions.

1 William Sargent's biggest mistake was

A overstretching himself financially.
B trusting unreliable partners.
C failing to investigate the situation thoroughly.
D running too many ventures at the same time.

2 When the goods had been delivered, what did his first two partners do?

A Pressed for an early delivery date.
B Refused to pay the shipping costs.
C Attempted to impose alternative terms.
D Expressed concern about the style of packaging.

3 What problem existed after William and his wife had set up The Frame Store?

A The bank was pressing them for payment.
B The company's development costs were higher than anticipated.
C Shortage of funds slowed down the rate of development.
D They had to pay to increase their holding.

4 What observation does William Sargent make about his way of doing business?

A He is reluctant to trust colleagues. responsibilities.
B He dislikes administration.
C He needs moral support from a partner.
D He hates worrying about finance.

5 For William Sargent, the key factor in a partnership is

A a binding legal agreement.
B the possibility of switching roles and
C a shared vision of the project's goal.
D the ability to withstand pressure.

Talking points

A Look at the advertisements below and on the next page and discuss the following with a partner:

What is advertised in each case?
Who is the advertisement aimed at? How do you know?

What do the advertisements depend on to make their impact?

How successful do you think each advertisement is?

Do seat belts restrict your thinking?

Somehow you can't quite imagine Albert Einstein mulling over a mind-bogglingly brilliant concept strapped into a plane with a pre-packed lunch on a plastic tray.

Or Wolfgang Amadeus Mozart composing his Horn Concerto in E flat in a car in a contraflow.

Can you picture a tycoon planning his next take-over whilst overtaking in the rain?

Some forms of transport, it seems, are just not conducive to constructive thought.

Consider an alternative. Consider InterCity.

First Class passengers sit relaxed watching Britain whizz past at up to 125 miles per hour.

They order food and drink from attentive waiters.

Briefcases snap open. Reports, previously rendered incomprehensible by jangling office phones, suddenly make sense.

Someone scribbles figures on a scrap of paper, devising a budget with tax at 20 pence in the pound. (We should be so lucky.)

Someone else attempts to recall Arnold Palmer's 18 best golf holes in the world.

Crosswords are cracked, often in record time.

A brilliant response to Karpov's latest opening gambit comes like a bolt from the blue.

People catch up on their reading, go for a stroll or formulate strategies. They arrive feeling fresh, relaxed, more alert.

Their minds have been stimulated, sometimes by doing nothing.

Makes you think, doesn't it?

INTERCITY

B Read the following extract.

> When men go shopping alone, they become women. Confronted by fifteen brands of washing powder or coffee, they instinctively reach for the names that the 'experts' trust – that's their wives, lovers, mothers. A similar metamorphosis hits lone women straying into a DIY store.
>
> That is the prevailing wisdom, gleaned from scores of market and advertising research studies, and it partially explains why, although advertising is a game largely played by men, its chief quarry is women.
>
> The New Man, who cares as passionately about household dust as his place in the company car-park, sounds suspiciously like one of those fictional stereotypes dreamed up by an adman after a long lunch. In fact, the industry wants no truck with him.
>
> (Virginia Matthews, *The Guardian*)

1 What is your view of the opinions expressed here?

2 Describe a brand of goods you are familiar with and discuss its image.

3 What is it that makes particular brands attractive to certain groups of people?

4 What persuades you to buy one brand rather than another?

C Working with a partner, discuss the best way to advertise:

- water purifiers
- freezers
- sweets
- jewellery

Writing

Letter of complaint

A You recently made a journey by train and were so dissatisfied that you wish to write a letter of complaint to the railway company.

These are some of the problems you encountered on the journey:

- the train arrived 20 minutes late.
- it was not the high-speed train scheduled in the timetable.
- there should have been a buffet car, but there was not so you had to spend two hours on the train without refreshments.
- the train was old and dirty.
- it had not been cleaned since the previous journey; there were drink cans and packaging all over the place.
- there was no heating, in November!
- the train was 30 minutes late at its destination.

Hints
Letters of complaint are often ineffective because they lack detail or display bad temper by sounding unreasonable or aggressive.

1 *Organisation:*
Before you begin the letter, make notes which answer the following points:

When did you travel?
Where to? Where from?
When did the train leave and arrive?
What *exactly* do you want to complain about?
Who will you address the letter to?
Where will you put your address and the railway company's address?
What do you want the railway to do?

2 *Tone:*
The tone you use will be very important here. Common faults that lead to the wrong tone are:

- being rude and insulting
- being unreasonable
- overgeneralising
- exaggerating
- not being specific enough about details.

3 *Extracts:*
Look at these three extracts from letters of complaint. Do you think they are adequate or not? Give reasons.

a 'I went to Bristol yesterday. The bus was late. When I bought my ticket it cost £2.40. I expected it to cost £1.60. Why is it so expensive?

Smoking was not allowed on the bus. This is not fair to smokers. Will you change the rules?

b 'I wish to protest about the service in your basement restaurant, 'Choices'.

The staff are badly trained and bad-mannered. Not only are they unfamiliar with the contents of the menu, but they seem to spend most of their time talking to their colleagues instead of concentrating on the customers and their needs.'

c When I visited your museum last Friday, I was disgusted to find that I had to pay £2 for what had previously been free.

Nothing else had changed, however. Many of the exhibits were out of order or had been removed, and others were in a shabby condition.

The coffee in your so-called cafeteria must have been used to wash up yesterday's dirty dishes ...'

An advertisement

B Read this extract, describing the problems one family encountered on a holiday they had booked after seeing the details in a brochure at their travel agent's. Then write the advertisement for the holiday as you think it appeared in the brochure.

WHICH HOLIDAY?

PERSONAL SERVICE reports on the Penningtons' holiday in Jersey.

Tom and Sheila Pennington booked a two-week self-catering holiday for themselves and two-year-old Sam at Prestige Apartments in St Brelade's in Jersey.

What attracted them was the nearness of a sandy beach, just three minutes away according to the brochure. This would be good for Sam, and was near enough for Sheila, who was pregnant, to get to easily.

But in fact, the nearest beach, 12 minutes away, was a pebble beach, not much fun for a two-year-old. To get to the nearest sandy beach, the Penningtons had to travel 15 minutes in the hire car provided as part of the holiday.

Another problem was that there were no shops at all within walking distance of the apartment. This wasn't what the Penningtons had been led to believe would be the case, and getting everyday supplies from the centre of the island's capital wasn't what they had expected from this holiday.

The accommodation, two bedrooms, a lounge and well-equipped kitchen were up to standard, but the holiday was not a success.

Literary approaches

What picture of an executive emerges from this poem?

What is the poet's attitude to the executive?

Executive
by John Betjeman (1906–1984)

I am a young executive. No cuffs than mine are cleaner;
I have a Slimline brief-case and I use the firm's Cortina.
In every roadside hostelry from here to Burgess Hill
The *maîtres d'hôtel* all know me well and let me sign the bill.

You ask me what it is I do. Well, actually, you know,
I'm partly a liaison man and partly PRO.
Essentially I integrate the current export drive
And basically I'm viable from ten o'clock till five.

For vital off-the-record work – that's talking transport-wise –
I've a scarlet Aston-Martin – and does she go? She flies!
Pedestrians and dogs and cats – we mark them down for slaughter.
I also own a speed-boat which has never touched the water.

She's built of fibre-glass, of course. I call her 'Mandy Jane'
After a bird I used to know – No soda, please, just plain –
And how did I acquire her? Well to tell you about that
And to put you in the picture I must wear my other hat.

I do some mild developing. The sort of place I need
Is a quiet country market town that's rather run to seed.
A luncheon and a drink or two, a little savoir-faire –
I fix the Planning Officer, the Town Clerk and the Mayor.

And if some preservationist attempts to interfere
A 'dangerous structure' notice from the Borough Engineer
Will settle any buildings that are standing in our way –
The modern style, sir, with respect, has really come to stay.

Follow-up

A Fill each of the numbered blanks in the following passage with one suitable word.

Packaging

Like it or not, packaging influences what we buy. The package does not simply contain the product. It is part of it. And supermarket chains who once thought our main worry was keeping our shopping .... *(1)* as low as possible are catching .... *(2)*. Where, ten years ago, their own label lines were simple and utilitarian, their presentation is now as sharp as .... *(3)* of their branded rivals. Own label has come of age.

Supermarkets like selling own brand goods. They offer the retailer better margins – up to 20%. And the proportion of total spending .... *(4)* own brand goods is expected to increase, particularly of non-food items. But, more importantly, ... *(5)* very approach to own label has changed. Robert Moberly, one half of the Lewis Moberly design partnership, says: 'You can see three phases .... *(6)* own label package design. There is the utilitarian approach. Don't try to compete head-on with the brand leader. .... *(7)* offer simple lettering, no frills. Look honest-to-goodness, yes. But rely largely on the product .... *(8)* and the very fact that it is so very conspicuously own label so people think they .... *(9)* be getting good value.

The .... *(10)* own label approach is to mimic the brand leader. Says Moberly: 'This is the me-too approach. Go for the packaging .... *(11)* is as near as legally possible to .... *(12)* of the brand leader. People will either pick up the own brand product by .... *(13)* or they will compare it on price against the brand leader, suspect that the contents of the two bottles are the same and think they are saving money. But it is the third approach which is most interesting: making an own label product look attractive in its own .... *(14)*. Don't feel embarrassed that your jar of coffee is not Nescafé. Give it a strong identity of its own. So .... *(15)* can be done with packaging to mould people's perception of what they are buying. You need to show authority. Packaging is part of the product. It reflects people's aspirations and .... *(16)* a significant degree it enhances the perception of the whole product. The package and the product must each reflect the other, ... *(17)* there is a risk of disappointment.'

Lewis Moberly were asked to redesign the box for Buxted Chicken Kiev. The .... *(18)* stayed the same. So did the size of the box and the quality of the cardboard. All that was altered .... *(19)* the graphics. The redesigned box showed the chicken on light, elegant plates with a few asparagus tips to suggest freshness and dispel .... *(20)* idea of stodginess. Sales rose more than 300 per cent.

B Finish each of the following sentences in such a way that it is as similar as possible in meaning to the sentence printed before it.

1 The inspector explained the situation briefly.
The inspector gave ....
....

2 He contributed generously to charity.
He made ....
....

3 It is impossible to say what problems might arise in the future.
Future problems cannot ....
....

4 Among the sales staff, there was widespread opposition to the new proposals.
Most ....
....

5 Although John can understand these calculations, he is not a mathematician.
John may ....
....

6 Even the best samples you have shown us do not meet our standards.
None ....
....

C Fill each of the blanks with a suitable word or phrase.

1 His ideas soon .... of the Prime Minister.

2 We had no idea what the taste of the new crisps .... until we tried them.

3 In terms of status, his job is considered to be .... with that of a nightclub proprietor.

4 In 1990 disaster .... when most of the factory was destroyed in a fire.

5 When talking to the Vegetarian Society, the chairman .... of mentioning that all his company's products were additive free.

6 This particular model .... three versions.

D For each of the sentences below, write a new sentence as similar as possible in meaning to the original sentence, but using the word given. The word must not be altered in any way.

1 I think everyone got a lot out of the training course.

worthwhile

....

....

2 With this machine you can do all the calculations that you need.

enable

....

....

3 This company stands a very good chance of winning an Export Award.

highly

....

....

4 When the police arrived, he didn't even try to hide himself.

effort

....

....

5 The speaker was soon surrounded by a large crowd.

gathered

....

....

6 Martin suddenly started to sing.

burst

....

....

E Choose the word or phrase (*A*, *B*, *C* or *D*) which best completes each sentence.

1 By the time he got to page 26 of the handbook, Martin was completely .... by the complex instructions.

A lost *B* alarmed
C baffled *D* shaken

2 This software can be .... to suit the needs of each customer.

A tailored *B* manipulated
C directed *D* cut

3 The new chairman was quite .... by the difficulty of the task ahead of him.

A unafraid B undaunted
C unheeded *D* unaware

4 The offer Brian had received seemed too good to be true and he wondered if there was a ....

A catch *B* weakness
C trick *D* lack

5 Do feel .... to write or telephone if you have any further questions.

A willing *B* ready
C happy *D* free

6 This particular product is .... at the teenage market.

A directed *B* aimed
C launched *D* pushed

7 The design of our new offices is .... of Gaudi's buildings in Barcelona.

A thinking *B* remembering
C reminiscent *D* memorable

8 'By the end of this course, you will have .... all the techniques of selling to people,' said the training manager.

A mastered *B* overcome
C conquered *D* handled

9 Before this act, the magician .... an assistant in the audience.

A used *B* concealed
C planted *D* located

10 This hand-held computer can perform tasks .... from translation to complex number-crunching.

A spreading B ranging
C going *D* searching

11 The market is dominated by two large corporations but there are some small but very aggressive companies .... at the edges.

A biting *B* snapping
C nibbling *D* scratching

12 The lack of proper documentation .... doubts in Tim's mind about the legality of the deal.

A raised *B* brought
C made *D* produced

13 The chairman tried to .... criticism by freely admitting that the company had not performed well in recent years.

A anticipate *B* forestall
C forewarn *D* dodge

14 'This is one of our most .... contracts,' said the sales manager.

A lucrative *B* money-making
C profiteering *D* rewarding

15 When it comes to tricking people, some politicians put market traders to ....

A guilt *B* despair
C disgust *D* shame

Unit ten

Other Worlds

Lead-in

A What are the people in these pictures doing, and why?

B Do you know why these places are famous?

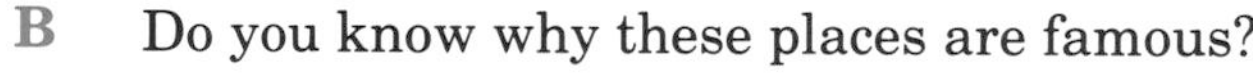

C Can you match the words on the right with the descriptions which follow?

1	vampires	*5*	poltergeists
2	flying saucers	*6*	witches
3	fortune telling	*7*	seances
4	ghosts	*8*	monsters

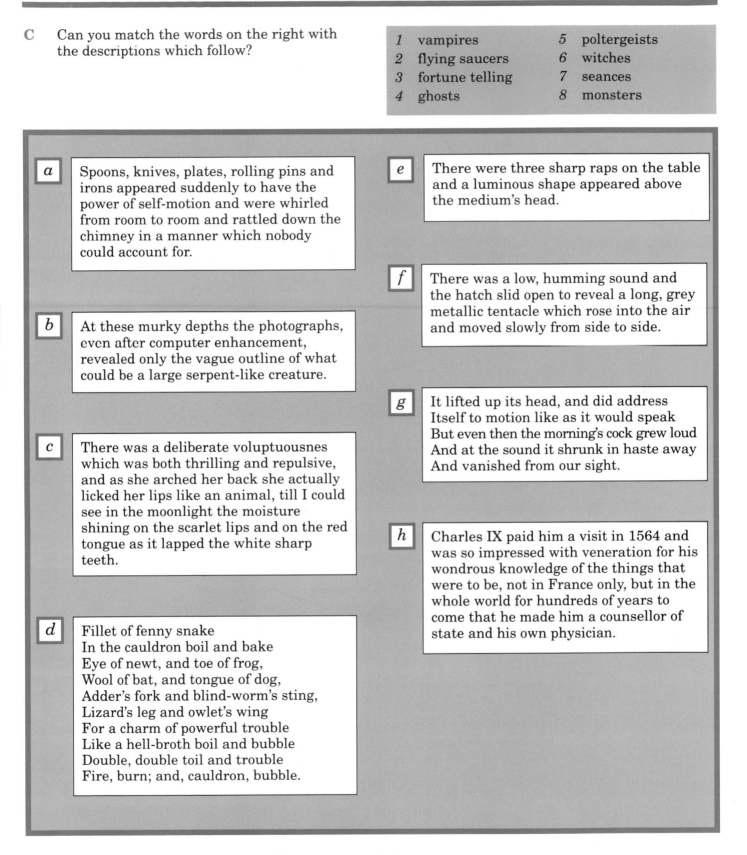

a Spoons, knives, plates, rolling pins and irons appeared suddenly to have the power of self-motion and were whirled from room to room and rattled down the chimney in a manner which nobody could account for.

b At these murky depths the photographs, even after computer enhancement, revealed only the vague outline of what could be a large serpent-like creature.

c There was a deliberate voluptuousnes which was both thrilling and repulsive, and as she arched her back she actually licked her lips like an animal, till I could see in the moonlight the moisture shining on the scarlet lips and on the red tongue as it lapped the white sharp teeth.

d
Fillet of fenny snake
In the cauldron boil and bake
Eye of newt, and toe of frog,
Wool of bat, and tongue of dog,
Adder's fork and blind-worm's sting,
Lizard's leg and owlet's wing
For a charm of powerful trouble
Like a hell-broth boil and bubble
Double, double toil and trouble
Fire, burn; and, cauldron, bubble.

e There were three sharp raps on the table and a luminous shape appeared above the medium's head.

f There was a low, humming sound and the hatch slid open to reveal a long, grey metallic tentacle which rose into the air and moved slowly from side to side.

g
It lifted up its head, and did address
Itself to motion like as it would speak
But even then the morning's cock grew loud
And at the sound it shrunk in haste away
And vanished from our sight.

h Charles IX paid him a visit in 1564 and was so impressed with veneration for his wondrous knowledge of the things that were to be, not in France only, but in the whole world for hundreds of years to come that he made him a counsellor of state and his own physician.

Do you Believe in Ghosts?

D Listen to the tape and summarise the views on ghosts expressed by the three speakers.

E Complete each sentence with one of the words or phrases given.

levitated	far-fetched	charlatans	haunted
extravagant	suppressed	dowser	glossed
sceptic	scrap	scoffed	fringe medicine
aliens	jiggery-pokery	premonition	sleight of hand
catch out	fabulous	seance	cover-up
burden of proof	dabble	solid evidence	illusion
medium	predicted	duped	

1 Many people who believe in the paranormal make .... claims that are not supported by ....

2 Griffins and unicorns are examples of .... beasts.

3 There was not a(n) .... of evidence to support his claim that he had been abducted by .... and taken to Mars.

4 The priest warned us that it was dangerous to .... in black magic and the occult.

5 As far as UFOs are concerned the .... lies with those who believe in them.

6 The psychic refused to demonstrate his powers in front of magicians on the grounds that they were try to .... him ....

7 He claimed that the sinking of the *Titanic* had been .... in a novel published fourteen years before the event actually happened.

8 The castle is believed to be .... by the ghost of a Roman soldier.

9 Professor Helsing described himself as a hard-boiled .... and dismissed the paranormal as all trickery and ....

10 We were invited to attend a(n) .... at which Mr Sludge, the .... would communicate with the dead.

11 Mr Evans said that the government had .... the facts regarding its programme of psychical research. 'It's a(n) ....,' he said.

12 Professor Helsing .... at the spurious claims of psychics, dismissing them all as .... and cheats.

13 Many reliable witnesses reported that Mr Sludge had .... two metres above the ground.

14 The Water Board called in a(n) .... to help locate the underground stream.

15 The day before the disaster, she had a(n) .... that something dreadful was going to happen.

16 To perform card-tricks convincingly, conjurers have to be very good at ....

17 Mr Brown .... over the inconsistencies in his testimony. He denied that his story was ....

18 John O'Neill claimed that his faith-healing was absolutely genuine and that his patients had not been ....

19 The speaker claimed that .... could often help where orthodox medicine had failed.

20 'The statue doesn't really move. It's just an optical ....,' said Professor Helsing.

F Complete the text using the words or phrases given.

gullible	telepathy	shoddy	evidence
body	event	non-psychic	telepathic
exempt	tricksters	occult	investigators
doings	devoted	quailed	clairvoyance
fraudulent	telekinesis	bogus	occupational hazard

The Charlatans Who Fooled Scientists

From Conan Doyle to Shirley Maclaine by way of Arthur Koestler, there's one born every minute. These are only three of the 75% of people in the western world who are or were .... *(1)* enough to believe in the paranormal. Even prestigious universities are not .... *(2)*: to their shame Cambridge recently awarded a doctoral degree for a thesis on parapsychology while Edinburgh has just established a new chair in the subject. The armed forces are just as credulous. Both in Russia and America they have .... *(3)* vast sums to psychic research in the curious belief that .... *(4)* communications, unlike radio waves, cannot be intercepted.

Physicists are pretty shrewd at distinguishing a *pi meson** from a *muon**, but are easily fooled by .... *(5)* like Uri Geller. They do not notice the invisible thread that moves objects thus demonstrating .... *(6)*, the peeking that underlies .... *(7)* and the miniature radio telephones that produce .... *(8)*. Indeed, it takes a magician to catch a magician.

The most eminent living magician, James Randi, who dislikes seeing his own tricks misused, has become a(n) .... *(9)* for psychics. Having demonstrated that Uri Geller's marvels could be replicated by completely .... *(10)* means, he sent two of his associates to a newly-established laboratory of parapsychology at a university in St Louis. He told them not to reveal how they produced their 'psychic phenomena' unless asked. If questioned, they were to say they were magicians. For two years they fooled their .... *(11)*, none of whom thought to ask them how they did it. When Randi recalled them and published an article on their .... *(12)*, the university had the good sense to close the laboratory down. But for every phenomenon shown to be .... *(13)*, two more spring up thanks to the public's zeal for the .... *(14)*. Even Hercules might have .... *(15)* before the Hydra of the psychic.

Most paranormal research is extremely .... *(16)*: there are no results that cannot be explained by fraud and none that can be replicated. There is therefore no possibility of explaining them rigorously even in the unlikely .... *(17)* that some of them are genuine: this has not prevented members of the psychic community offering .... *(18)* explanations. Moreover, the phenomena contradict the vast .... *(19)* of scientific laws that explain so many other factors. Hence, the .... *(20)* must be particularly compelling if it is to be accepted.

* *pi meson* and *muon*: scientific terms used in physics.

Theme one: Is There Anybody There?

A What do the letters UFO stand for?

What would you expect a UFO to look like and what might be mistaken for one?

Now read the text and answer the questions which follow.

Wacky World of the Ufologists

Ladies and gentlemen, boys and girls: believe it or not but the modern religion of Ufology – the quest to interpret the mystery of unidentified flying objects – today enters its 42nd year. In short, however bizarre its foundations, Ufology continues to stake its claim as a social and global curiosity of some magnitude. Like many serious religions, it is evolving fast – adapting itself to a hostile environment with speed and panache. It has priests and missionaries, miracles and messages, though nothing, to date, resembling a grand orthodoxy. It is a religion of the space age that offers us heavenly lights, god-like aliens and flying green jellies – above all the reassurance that we are not alone: that the universe pulses with intelligence. As, of course, it might.

Recently, there has been an epidemic of UFO sightings, not only in Britain, where the number of UFO stories carried by the local and national media so far this year – more than 530 – has already exceeded any annual total for the last ten years, but from here to the South Australian bush and back. In turn, there is a craze of UFO abduction stories sweeping America. The most widely-reported UK sighting this year produced multiple stories claiming that eight policemen in Kensington, London had witnessed a grey-green-blue flying saucer through the telescope of 16-year old Zena Sfeir, and had been converted into 'complete believers' on the spot. It was later realised that all nine had been looking at Jupiter through a malfunctioning telescope.

You do not have to voyage very far into Ufology to encounter your first surprise: namely that this embryonic religion possesses a positive modern starting date – June 24 1947, when businessman-pilot Kenneth Arnold ('the man who started it all') claimed to have seen nine silvery objects travelling at great speed near Mount Rainier, Washington, fluttering and swerving and behaving 'like a saucer would if you skipped it across the water'. During June and July of 1947 there were at least 850 saucer sightings. The new religion was up and running, even though Arnold had been duped: perhaps by mirages – it hardly matters, unless you are a zealot.

A seasoned Ufologist like Hilary Evans of the British UFO Research Association is swift to offer some key admissions: that UFO witnesses deliberately lie, that some lie unconsciously, or that others are acted upon by intangible cultural or psychological influences that may bias, says Evans, 'both the ability to perceived and/or the ability to interpret what is perceive'. Nor does he gloss over Ufology's obvious weakness, the tawdriness (in fact, the non-existence) of its evidence. 'For one thing,' he says, 'almost every scrap of it is eye-witness testimony only, unsupported by any confirming evidence. When we are offered tangible evidence, it inevitably falls short of being totally convincing ...' But then he switches tack: 'On the other hand, the sheer quantity of testimony is impressive. On whatever level of reality the UFO exists, it certainly exists as a new and uniquely complex challenge.'

Does it now? Without more ado, let us plunge into the wacky world of Ufology. It is a place of exceedingly low gravity, so let us check our life-support systems lest we explode into a zillion astonished pieces.

The latest Gallup polls indicate that about 20% of Britons and almost 60% of Americans believe in flying saucers. A French group even estimated that we learn about only one UFO in 38,400 that visit Earth. These figures are worthless, of course. Serious Ufologists admit this, yet they sometimes employ them in stunning sleights of hand to underpin the claim that what-ever you think of the figures, the UFO phenomenon is global, unique, complex, awe-inspiring and deserving of serious interpretive help from physicists, astronomers, engineers, meteorologists, physiologists, sociologists, anthropologists and myth-ologists – very few of whom, however, ever answer the SOS.

We are being visited, it appears, by whole genres and massive sub-groups of foreign-looking beings – often in the same week and always ignorant of each other's presence or existence. Bless them all, for we are seeing fairies and little fat men, hairy dwarfs and giant hominids, aliens 'resembling Italians' and headless women with webbed feet and bat-like wings.

One research group analysed 'thousands of cases' and determined that there were four main types of visiting alien: small humanoids, experimental animals, humanlike entities, and robots. But how eccentrically they behave! How frequently, when they are not collecting soil or flowers or abducting innocent human beings, are they seen to be repairing their spacecraft, which are forever breaking down. 'The examples of apparent absurdity are very numerous,' one researcher concedes, 'and we find one or two absurd details in every well-reported case. Some cases are veritable festivals of absurdity.' One in five of all alleged close encounters with UFOs and their occupants is claimed to leave some sort of trace: burnt ground, footprints, powdery residues, metallic fragments, etc. None of this alleged evidence is worth a brass farthing.

There is a modern folk-tale that holds that numerous governments are hoarding crashed saucers and/or alien bodies (generally mutilated) and that a global cover-up is in full swing. There is not a scrap of evidence to support these contentions. According to researcher Andy Roberts: 'Many UFO organisations and researchers thrive on rumour and secrecy, and from this base a body of folklore has been created. Similarities can be found with other discovery/secrecy/conspiracy tales. For example, the stories in which people have stumbled on blocked-up tunnels in the London Underground train system, finding whole carriages full of corpses in Victorian clothes.'

After weeks of grappling with the rubbish-mountain of non-evidence on which Ufology is perched, my own brain has now gone on the blink, becoming spiteful and provincial. There may be no evidence for UFOs, but then there is little evidence for *anything*, least of all the notion that the galaxies pulse with life. Of course there are no flying green jellies, it says. Nor are there hominids or fairies or aliens that look like Italians. There are no bat-winged women and no talking XXXX* cans. In all the reaches of time-space, it now maintains, we will never find anyone else to talk to or play tennis with. How can this be? *Because we are alone.*

(Michael Thompson-Noel, *The Financial Times*)

**XXXX*: a brand of Australian beer.

B Find a word or phrase in the text which, in context, is similar in meaning to:

Paragraph 1
1 search
2 very strange
3 declare its importance
4 developing
5 flamboyance
6 beats

Paragraph 2
7 countryside
8 kidnapping

Paragraph 3
9 deceived
10 a fanatical believer

Paragraph 4
11 experienced
12 mention only in passing
13 bit
14 changes direction

Paragraph 5
15 fuss
16 dive

C Find a phrase in the text which, in context, is similar in meaning to:

Paragraph 6
1 hand movements used for performing magic tricks
2 respond to the emergency call

Paragraph 7
3 completely ludicrous and absurd
4 absolutely worthless

Paragraph 8
5 secretly storing crashed UFOs
6 a worldwide campaign to hide the truth
7 flourish on unproven stories

Paragraph 9
8 doesn't work properly

D What attitude does the writer convey by the use of such expressions as:

1 Ladies and gentlemen, boys and girls *(lines 1–2)*
2 As, of course, it might. *(line 23)*

Can you identify two similar expressions in paragraphs 5 and 7?

E Some of the expressions the writer uses to criticise Ufology are:

1 had been duped *(line 63*
2 unless you are a zealot *(line 67)*
3 eye-witness testimony only *(line 84)*

Can you find six more phrases or sentences in which the writer expresses his criticisms in a very forceful manner?

Using the phrases or sentences that you have found, can you speak dismissively about:

– astrology
– the Yeti
– fairies
– telepathy

F Now choose the best answer to the following questions.

1 The writer thinks that Ufology

A is a religion of the space age.
B has many of the characteristics of a religion.
C is a complex and important social phenomenon.
D is entirely a matter of hoaxes and trickery.

2 The figure of 530 sightings applies to

A Britain only.
B Britain and Australia.
C Britain, Australia and America.
D the world.

3 Hilary Evans is inclined to believe in UFOs because

A there are eye-witness accounts.
B there is a lot of tangible and intangible evidence.
C there are a lot of reports of UFO sightings.
D there are many complexities to this phenomenon.

4 What is the writer's reaction to all the UFO stories that he has heard?

A amusement
B great interest
C irritation
D anxiety

A Ghost Story

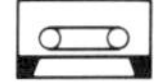

G Read the following text, but do not attempt to fill the gaps until you have listened to Stephen's story. Then complete the text with a suitable word or

Stephen tells a story in which some people were staying in a house which was not their .... *(1)* and were .... *(2)* by an .... *(3)* which rang a bell every night at .... *(4)* or .... *(5)*. They soon became .... *(6)* and put it in the .... *(7)*. But the next night, they heard it again, went .... *(8)* and found it in the place where it had been before. Stephen thinks it couldn't have been moved by the .... *(9)* because it somehow got through a .... *(10)*. He is sure this happened .... *(11)* and thinks it may have happened .... (12). He is not sure how the people in the house .... *(13)*.

Language awareness: body language

A Use these words to complete the sentences. Sometimes you will have to change the form of the words because they may be used as plural nouns, adjectives or verbs. Some words can be used twice.

nose	thumb	foot	guts
elbow	heel	toe	shoulder
neck	shin	cheek	
stomach	mouth	body	

1 I really can't .... his rudeness any more.

2 If they don't .... the line we will have to ask them to leave the club.

3 Jack .... up the tree and threw down the apples.

4 I'm not prepared to .... all the responsibility for this project.

5 Let's have another bottle of champagne. The company will .... the bill.

6 Mrs Parker is the .... woman I know. She just can't mind her own business.

7 Sebastian .... his way to the front of the queue.

8 This new injection of capital will put the company on a sound financial ....

9 They are a very good team but the goalkeeper is not so good. That's their Achilles' ....

10 That building doesn't look right at all. In fact, it sticks out like a sore ....

11 Those children are so .... They should really learn some manners.

12 Jackie looks so down in the .... Why is she so depressed?

13 Nigel asks so many silly questions. He really is a pain in the ....

14 It took a lot of .... to stand up to the boss like that.

15 This wine has plenty of .... and a very fine ....

B Can you explain what these newspaper headlines mean?

1 GOVERNMENT'S PLAN FLIES IN THE FACE OF REASON

2 JAILED FINANCIER HAD A FINGER IN EVERY PIE

3 POLICE CHIEF HAND IN GLOVE WITH GANG LEADER

4 HEADS WILL ROLL SAYS NEW CHAIRMAN

5 LIFE SENTENCES IN MURDER FOR KICKS CASE

6 HIGH INTEREST RATES: WE MUST GRIN AND BEAR IT SAYS CHANCELLOR

7 MP'S PLEA FOR HOMELESS FALLS ON DEAF EARS

8 FAMOUS AUTHOR DEMANDS POUND OF FLESH IN LIBEL CASE

9 PM AND CHANCELLOR DON'T SEE EYE TO EYE

Theme two: Strange Happenings

Dr Faustus

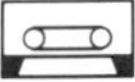

A Listen to the story and choose the best answer to the following questions.

(Note: *Dr Faustus* is a play by Christopher Marlowe (1564–1593), first performed about 1588. It tells the story of a man who sells his soul to the devil. The same story is told, in rather different ways, by Goethe and Thomas Mann. Marlowe's play is frequently performed and is quite well known. One of its most famous lines is *'Was this the face that launched a thousand ships?'* which Dr Faustus says when he sees Helen of Troy, whom the devil has conjured up at his request.)

1 At the beginning of the story, the speaker doesn't name the director because

A the director was young and inexperienced at that time.
B the director has since become famous.
C he still has to work with that director.
D he doesn't have a high opinion of the director.

2 Which is the best description of the location of the studio theatre?

A It was near the main theatre in a building of architectural significance.
B It was next to a luncheon club.
C It was between an art gallery and a restaurant.
D It was on the top floor of a three-storey building.

3 After the second dress rehearsal, what did the director persuade the actors to do?

A To go straight home.
B To think of some good ideas to improve the production.
C To try to summon up the devil.
D To spend some extra time rehearsing.

4 How did the speaker first find out that the theatre had burnt down?

A He saw what had happened.
B He saw a photograph in the local paper.
C Someone called Frank told him.
D A woman told him.

5 How did the fire start?

A Hot cinders set light to everything.
B A toasted sandwich burst into flames.
C The actors had left a burning candle in the theatre.
D A cooker had overheated.

6 What was unusual about the hole in the theatre floor?

A The firemen had made it.
B It prevented the play from taking place.
C It was in the place the actors had placed a candle.
D It was a sign of diabolic intervention.

B What sort of things do people with psychic powers claim that they can do?

What is a seance?

Now read the text and answer the questions which follow.

Daniel Dunglas Home

For twenty years, with only occasional gaps when his powers deserted him, Home gave seances to his friends and acquaintances, two or three times a week. The effects varied, and sometimes nothing happened; but usually rapping noises could be heard from around the room, and in due course the seance table could be felt by the sitters to shudder, before starting to move around, rear up on two legs, and rise in the air while the sitters' finger tips were on top, touching it lightly (or not at all). Musical instruments, brought by visitors and left in a corner of the room, would begin to play, often soulfully. Disembodied hands appeared and circled round the table; sitters could inspect them, touch them, shake them (they felt like real hands, but if anybody tried to cling to them they melted away). If pen and paper were on an adjacent table, the pen might write messages, purporting to come from deceased persons, and apparently in their handwriting. On a few occasions, Home himself levitated, floating above the sitters' heads; or he would literally play with fire, stirring up the hot coals with his hands, carrying them around, even bathing his face in them.

It was not simply these effects, many of which were the commonplace of seances, that were striking; so, also, were the circumstances in which they were produced. There could be no question of conjuring tricks; not merely were the seances often held in houses Home had never been to before, in rooms he had never entered until the seance began; they were held in daylight, or gaslight, or by the light of a fire – good enough light, almost always, for the eight or nine people present to watch Home, and satisfy themselves that he was not using hands or feet or gadgetry of any kind. And he had no assistant to play the tricks while he himself was being watched.

Neither were the sitters credulous believers. Many of them admitted they had been sceptical, even derisive; and they represented a fair cross-section of the ruling classes, including royalty – Tsar Alexander II, the Emperor Napoleon III, and Queen Sophie of the Netherlands; members of the aristocracies of several European countries; literary lions, among them Elizabeth Barrett Browning, Thomas Augustus Trollope, Thackeray, Lytton, Ruskin; eminent scientists, Alfred Russel Wallace, William Crookes and Francis Galton – along with many other men and women whose names were familiar, even household words, in their own time. Famous conjurors, too, came to his seances hoping to be able to catch him out; but they all went away disappointed. And as he refused to take any payment for his seances, those who hoped to accuse him of cupidity could only point to a venial willingness to accept the hospitality of the rich and famous. Home's private life, too, was by all accounts impeccable. It could hardly have been otherwise without detection, as he was just about the best known international figure, bar a few crowned heads and famous statesmen, of his day.

When, towards the end of his career, Home was asked to demonstrate his powers in a laboratory, he willingly consented. In tests by Alexander von Boutlerow in Russia, and William Crookes in England, Home showed that he was able to produce telekinetic effects at a distance, which could be recorded and measured on weighing machines. And when illness terminated his career as a medium in 1874, although he had often been denounced as a trickster, nobody had ever detected him in any attempt at trickery during a seance.

(*Science and Parascience* by Brian Inglis)

C Explain the meaning of these phrases from the text.

1. purporting to come from deceased persons *(line 10)*
2. literally play with fire *(line 11)*
3. the commonplace of seances *(line 13)*
4. credulous believers *(line 20)*
5. a fair cross-section *(line 21)*
6. literary lions *(line 23)*
7. to catch him out *(line 27)*
8. a venial willingness *(line 28)*
9. bar a few crowned heads *(line 31)*

D Now read the text again and answer the following questions.

1 Make a brief list of the effects that Daniel Home could produce. Which seem to be the least plausible?

2 What was impressive about the circumstances in which Home worked?

3 Who came to Home's seances?

4 What points does the writer make in support of the genuineness of Home's special powers?

5 What is the writer's opinion of Home's character?

6 Although the writer is generally sympathetic to Home, are there any words or phrases in the passage that would indicate to a sceptic that Home might have been a trickster?

A strange host

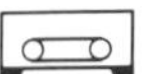

E Listen to this extract from a well-known novel. Which novel is it from? Answer the following questions with a phrase or short sentence using your own words.

1. Why was Jonathan so surprised to see the Count?
2. Why did he cut himself?
3. What did he say to the Count?
4. How was the Count affected by something Jonathan was wearing?
5. Why did the Count open the window?
6. Why was Jonathan annoyed?
7. Where is the castle situated?
8. Why can't Jonathan leave the castle?
9. What unusual characteristics does the Count have?

Grammar: use and used to, relative pronouns

Use, used to, get/be/become used to

A Can you divide these sentences into *three* groups of *three* and say on what basis you have done so? There are ten sentences, so you will have one left over. Where will you put it?

1. We used to grow our own vegetables.
2. Christopher and Rowena have given up using aerosol sprays.
3. Didn't you use to work in the office in Fenchurch Street?
4. It's taking me a long time to get used to driving a car with automatic gears.
5. We used that firm for five years, until they raised their prices and wouldn't give us a discount.
6. Life on an Australian sheep-station was definitely not what Penelope was used to.
7. USED GARDENING TOOLS FOR SALE. OFFERS INVITED. PHONE 0234 55632.
8. Lord Fotheringham is used to being waited on.
9. Trains used to run direct to Cambridge but now you have to change at Bedford.
10. We used to use typewriters, but now we have to get used to using word-processors.

B Complete the sentences with the correct form of *to use, used to, to be/get/become used to.*

1. When he was at university, Tom .... to spend every morning studying in the library.
2. .... to the humidity was the most difficult thing about living in Singapore.
3. Employees can be dismissed for not .... the safety equipment provided.
4. 'It takes a bit of .... to,' said our instructor as he stepped over the edge.
5. Not .... to such tough questioning, the Minister began to look nervous.
6. You have already .... up your petty cash allowance for this year.
7. 'I'll never .... to these controls,' said Martin.
8. Until I read that article, I hadn't thought of .... plastic bottles to protect my young plants from slugs and snails.
9. Did Mary .... to work at Tesco's?
10. Before his retirement, Bernard .... to a much higher standard of living.

That

C Can you divide these sentences into three different groups according to the way the word *that* is used? How is it pronounced in each sentence?

1. He told me that he knew the answer.
2. The man that had snatched the handbag jumped onto the back of a motorbike.
3. Sebastian claimed that he was an expert on ancient Greek vases.
4. The train that had come off the rails was lifted by a crane.
5. That man is the President's bodyguard.
6. I have never been told that story before.
7. I didn't like that film very much.
8. It's the same story that we heard last week.
9. I'm afraid that we haven't got any more seed potatoes.

That, who, which

D Can you divide these sentences into two groups? In which sentences can you use *that* instead of *who* or *which*? Note carefully the position of the commas.

1. The passengers who had missed their flight were given a meal at the airline's expense.
2. The cows which were suffering from foot-and-mouth disease had to be destroyed.
3. The tickets, which had been forged, were confiscated by the police.
4. The keys which had numbers on were returned to reception.
5. The museum, which is one of the richest in the world, is going to hold a special exhibition of the paintings of Amedeo Modigliani.
6. The man who was arrested refused to answer any questions.

Which, whom, that

E How many of these sentences can you improve by removing the word *which*, *whom* or *that*?

1. It's a picture of the hotel that we stayed at.
2. There's the lady whom we had lunch with last Wednesday.
3. Professor Williams is the scientist who discovered the new drug that we have been reading about.
4. It's the same fox that Farmer Giles shot at last month.
5. Is it the train that goes to Barcelona?
6. The girl that knew the answer put her hand up.
7. The man that we've been negotiating with has been replaced.
8. Thomas, whom we were discussing yesterday, is the ideal man for the job.
9. You can take any book that you like.
10. It was the best meal that I have ever eaten.
11. Was this the face that launched a thousand ships?
12. Her first novel, which she wrote when she was in her twenties, was her most successful work.

Mixed relative pronouns

F Complete the gaps in the following sentences, using these words.

on which	from which	to whom	whose
in which	in whose	of which	without whose
for whose	from which	for which	for the sake of which

1 That's the policeman .... I handed the parcel.

2 This is the hospital .... I was born.

3 The passenger .... leg was broken was taken away by ambulance.

4 The company .... we bought our kitchen units is no longer in business.

5 That is the boy .... mother the police are searching.

6 James has just completed a marathon, from the effects .... he is still suffering.

7 Mrs Jones, ... house the murder took place, is staying with relatives.

8 This is the recipe for Spotted Dick, ... you will need flour, suet and raisins.

9 I'd like to introduce Chris Lockwood, ... help the project would never have been completed.

10 They took us into the mine, ... over a ton of gold had been taken in only ten years.

11 That's the treasure .... many men lost their lives.

12 The idea .... the film was based came from a little-known novel.

G Join each set of sentences together to make one sentence.

1 Jack Smith helped us to raise the money for the new venture. He has a lot of experience in these matters.

2 We visited the house. Lord Byron was born there.

3 Divers found the ship in deep water. It sank in 1905. The divers risked their lives every day.

4 Mr Morgan has lived in the village all his life. He wants to build a new house. He must get planning permission for it.

5 This is the medal. I told you about it. Grandfather gave it to me.

6 Jack has purchased a new Porsche. He paid cash for it.

7 The police want to question a man. They are treating the matter very seriously. He was seen leaving the building at 7 p.m.

8 This is the cave. In my opinion, it should be closed to the public. We found the bodies here.

9 This is the tomb of Henry VIII. His reign is a turning point in British history.

10 Nicky is a good friend. I can always turn to her for help in a crisis.

Which

H Compare these three sentences.
What does *which* refer to in each case?

He walked all the way, which was not very sensible and made his feet sore.

He gave me the book which he had just read.

He gave me the book, which was very kind of him.

How many of these sentences must have a comma?

1 He ate a whole chicken which was very greedy.

2 Tom stole a car which was very dishonest.

3 He showed me the painting which used to belong to his uncle.

Complete the following sentences.

4 Jim ran for three hours, ...
....
....

5 Martin promised to be there in time to help me prepare the food, ...
....
....

6 The food was stone cold, ...
....
....

7 I didn't recognise him at all, ...
....
....

8 He succeeded in climbing Mount Kilimanjaro, ...
....
....

Theme three: Exploding the Myth

A Crystal balls, cards and tea-leaves can all be used to predict the future or analyse the present and help people to decide what course of action to take. Can you think of any other ways, ancient and modern?

Now read the text and answer the questions which follow.

A Dampener for the Dowsers

This weekend the British Society of Dowsers will hold its annual congress at a Coventry hotel. While dowsing is normally understood as divining with a pendulum or rods for subterranean water or metals, in recent years dowsers have extended their territory to include pendulum diagnosis and treatment of human ailments. Three speakers will talk on healing, one 'known for her unique blend of Reflexology, Aromatherapy, Healing and Massage'.

Practitioners of a large number of unorthodox techniques have claimed to treat human ailments, and no doubt some successes have been achieved. But underground water has no psyche and is inaccessible, so human interaction would appear to be excluded.

The use of diviners can be traced back at least 500 years, and it comes as a shock to most people when you tell them that there is no evidence for the validity of water divining. Nearly everybody 'knows somebody who can do it', has seen a dowser find water, or has formed a favourable opinion of dowsing from what they have read in the Press or seen on television.

Dowsing has two entirely separate aspects. There is the well-known movement of the twig or rod, known as the dowsing 'reflex', and there is the prediction the dowser bases on this movement. There is ample evidence that the dowsing reflex is a reality, but there is no reliable evidence that the reflex enables the dowser to detect water or minerals.

The reader can make some simple experiments. Tie a weight to a piece of string about a foot long. Look out some snapshots of men and women and enlist the aid of two friends in separate sessions. Tell the first to rest his elbow on the table and hold the pendulum steadily over the photo of a male. Explain that the pendulum can sex photos, animals and insects, and that after a few seconds the pendulum will begin to move backwards and forwards over the photograph. The friend may be surprised that this occurs. Now substitute a female photograph and explain that, for a female, the pendulum will start to move in gradually increasing circles. The pendulum moves as predicted.

Now enjoin the first friend to silence and admit the second friend. Go through the same procedure, but this time say authoritatively that a female will elicit the forward-backward movement, a male the circular movement. The pendulum will perform accordingly.

Normally subjects of the experiment are convinced they are not exerting the slightest force on the pendulum, although experiment shows that they are. Unconscious muscular movements are the cause of the pendulum's behaviour. The movement of a dowsers's hazel twig of dowsing rod is controlled by similar unconscious muscular action which occurs when the dowser thinks he or she is walking over water.

Cogent evidence of a link between the movement of the divining rod and the actual presence of water is lacking. Water is, of course, found at sites indicated by dowsers, but not more often than would be explained by chance or by the use of normal geological indications as an aid.

Whenever controlled field experiments have been conducted, dowsers have failed to substantiate their claims. The dowsers say scientific conditions inhibit the dowsing faculty. This criticism cannot be directed at the series of records kept from 1918-1945 by the Water Resources Commission in Central New South Wales, Australia, an extremely arid area. Successful bores at points selected by dowsers were fewer than at points selected by geologists. The percentage of absolute failures among divined wells was double that for the non-divined wells.

A dowser's performance is often judged by the layman to be more successful than warranted because of the popular belief that water runs in underground streams. The dowser says 'dig here' and water is found.In fact rain water percolates downward from the ground surface and is fairly evenly spread at the 'water table'. In the British Isles there are few places where you could bore a hole without finding water.

Evon Vogt, an anthropologist, and Ray Hyman, a psychologist, set out to study dowsing as a social phenomenon. In *Water Witching USA* (1979) they made a very thorough examination of the claims of the dowsers and the published results of field tests and laboratory experiments. Their conclusion was: 'We don't have to resort to prejudice to dismiss water witching (the American term for dowsing) as invalid. The evidence for it is not merely insufficient according to current scientific standards, it is appallingly negative.'

A more recent survey of the experimental research on dowsing by George Hansen, appears in the *Journal of the Society for Psychical Research*, October 1982. He concludes, 'to prove that dowsing is a function of psi (psychic ability) more strictly controlled tests will be required'.

People will tell you gas and water boards and companies have used dowsers to trace breaks in the pipes or find minerals, although they can never give chapter and verse. The man in the street believes in dowsing because he 'knows somebody who can do it' and because he has never encountered the case against it. Whenever an item on dowsing appears in a newspaper or magazine, or on the radio or TV, the write or presenter starts from the standpoint that water divining is an established fact. To be fair they have probably never had the time to research the subject adequately and no simple account of the negative aspects has been available.

(Denys Parsons, *The Independent*)

B Find a word or phrase in the text which, in context, is similar in meaning to:

Paragraph 1
1 illnesses

Paragraph 4
2 plenty of

Paragraph 6
3 ask the help of

Paragraph 7
4 applying

Paragraph 10
5 non-expert
6 dig a hole

Paragraph 11
7 fall back on irrational dislike

Paragraph 13
8 never give precise details

C Now answer the following questions.

1 How has dowsing changed in recent years?
2 Why is orthodox dowsing a better subject for scientific investigation than unorthodox techniques?
3 Why are many people inclined to accept the claims of dowsers?
4 What does the suggested experiment prove?
5 Why is Britain not a good place to carry out a scientific investigation into dowsing?
6 Why are the Australian records particularly valuable?
7 Of the two recent reports on dowsing, which is the more sceptical?
8 How is dowsing usually presented on television or radio?
9 What do you think was the writer's purpose in writing this article?

D Summarise the case the writer makes against dowsing in not more than 100 words.

Talking points

A Describe these photographs below and on the following page. Do the photographs show people? What special powers do these characters have?

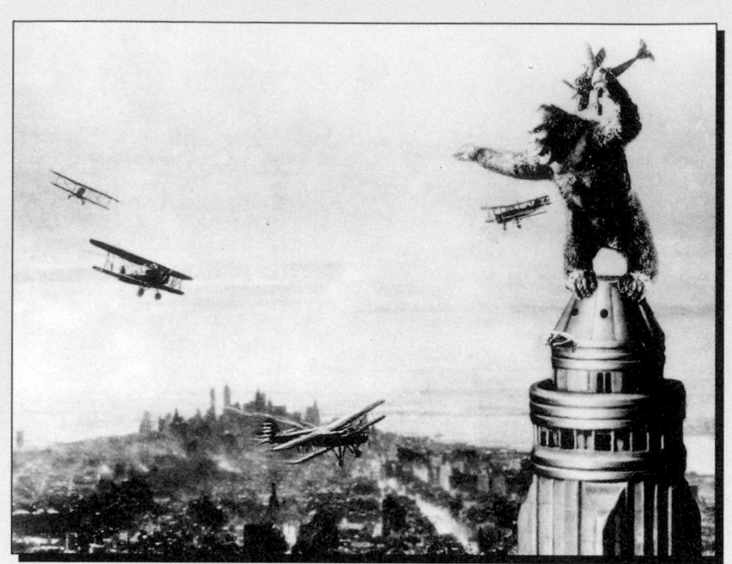

B Why are fantasy stories and films so popular? What happens in them that would not normally happen in real life?

C Working with a partner, discuss the following:

If someone claimed to have special powers such as telepathy, levitation, telekinesis or fortune telling what experiments could you set up to discover if these powers were genuine?

Writing

Letter to a friend

A A friend has recently become a convert to the idea of UFOs and extra-terrestrial phenomena and is trying to persuade other people to become believers. You feel that your friend is misguided, and because you have been close friends for a long time, feel it is up to you to help your friend 'see the light'. Write a letter to your friend pointing out what you think is wrong and trying to bring about a change of view.

Hints
The test in this letter is how able you are to treat your friend's position sensitively, yet at the same time try to bring him/her round to your point of view.

Fantasy story

B Write a short fantasy story of your own, based on the supernatural, science fiction or fantasy. Use 300 – 400 words.

Hints
English literature is full of examples of creative writers who wrote wonderful stories based on fantasy worlds. Look at the two examples (**Extract a** and **Extract b**).

Extract a
A shipwrecked sailor swims to a deserted beach and then falls asleep exhausted. This is how he described what happens when he wakes up.

... when I awaked it was just daylight. I attempted to rise, but was not able to stir: for as I happened to lie on my back, I found my arms and legs were strongly fastened on each side to the ground; and my hair, which was long and thick, was tied down in the same manner. I likewise felt several slender ligatures across my body, from my arm-pits to my thighs. I could only look upwards, the sun began to grow hot, and the light offended my eyes. I heard a confused noise about me, but, in the posture I lay, could see nothing except the sky. In a little time I felt something alive moving on my left leg, which advancing gently forward, over my breast, came almost up to my chin; when bending my eyes downward as much as I could, I perceived it to be a human creature not six inches high, with a bow and arrow in his hands, and a quiver at his back. In the meantime, I felt at least forty more of the same kind (as I conjectured) following the first. I was in the utmost astonishment, and roared so loud, that they all ran back in a fright; and some of them, as I was afterwards told, were hurt with the falls they got by leaping from my sides upon the ground. However, they soon returned, and one of them, who ventured so far as to get a full sight of my face, lifting up his hands and eyes by way of admiration, cried out in a shrill but distinct voice, 'Hekinab degul': the others repeated the same words several times, but I then knew not what they meant.

(*Gulliver's Travels* by Jonathan Swift, 1726)

Extract b
A young girl has seen a rabbit in a field and has followed him down a hole in the ground.

The rabbit-hole went straight on like a tunnel for some way, and then dipped suddenly down, so suddenly that Alice had not a moment to think about stopping herself before she found herself falling down what seemed a deep well. Either the well was very deep, or she fell very slowly, for she had plenty of time as she went down to look about her, and to wonder what would happen next. First, she tried to look down and make out what she was coming to, but it was too dark to see anything: then, she looked at the sides of the well, and noticed that they were filled with cupboards and bookshelves; here and there were maps and pictures hung on pegs. She took a jar down off one of the shelves as she passed it: it was labelled 'Orange Marmalade,' but to her great disappointment it was empty: she did not like to drop the jar for fear of killing somebody underneath, so managed to put it into one of the cupboards as she fell past it.

Down, down, down. Would the fall never come to an end? 'I wonder how many miles I've fallen by this time?' she said aloud. 'I must be getting somewhere near the centre of the earth.'

(*Alice's Adventures Under Ground* by Lewis Carroll, 1864)

Literary approaches

What did the traveller see?

What is the significance of what he saw?

Ozymandias
by Percy Bysshe Shelley (1792–1822)

I met a traveller from an antique land
Who said: Two vast and trunkless legs of stone
Stand in the desert. Near them, on the sand,
Half sunk, a shattered visage lies, whose frown,
And wrinkled lip, and sneer of cold command,
Tell that its sculptor well those passions read
Which yet survive, stamped on these lifeless things,
The hand that mocked them, and the heart that fed:
And on the pedestal these words appear:
'My name is Ozymandias, king of kings:
Look on my works, ye mighty and despair!'
Nothing beside remains. Round the decay
Of that colossal wreck, boundless and bare
The lone and level sands stretch far away.

Follow-up

A Fill each of the numbered blanks in the following passage with one suitable word.

Triumph of Mind Over Matter

Most human beings would be delighted to be written about as a remarkable example of the .... *(1)* of the human spirit over crippling physical limitations. Professor Stephen Hawking tends to be irritated at .... *(2)* a description. His cross is not so much that, ... *(3)* he is the .... *(4)* of a wasting disease that makes him unable to move, he is .... *(5)* to a computerised wheelchair with a voice synthesizer that .... *(6)* speak for him. It is that, ... *(7)* he would like people to write and read about his ideas .... *(8)* space and time, not one person in ten million could be an adequate judge of .... *(9)*.

Professor Hawking .... *(10)* an outwardly bizarre but inwardly logical press conference yesterday at Cambridge to .... *(11)* his popularised synthesis of his work in physics .... *(12)* the last twenty-five years. It is a work which immediately reveals .... *(13)* its subject and its author by admitting humorously the impossibility .... *(14)* exact proof when explaining what is happening to the universe: .... *(15)* there really was a Big Bang that started it all, and whether neutrons will implode into infinite smallness at the centre of a black hole, forcing time backwards .... *(16)* the fragments of a broken cup coming back together.

When .... *(17)* we expect him to prove that there are black holes? Professor Hawking, ... *(18)* fighting instinct and sense of humour are there behind the voice synthesizer, ... *(19)*: 'My paper on the theory of black holes was written about fifteen years ago. Observations over the last fifteen years have shown that they almost certainly do .... *(20)*'.

B Finish each of the following sentences in such a way that it is as similar as possible in meaning to the sentence printed before it.

1 These happenings may be bizarre, but the fact that they are well documented means they should be investigated.

However ....

....

2 I may forget about the meeting, so remind me about it.

Remind me about the meeting ....

....

3 Many people were conned into giving donations and very few realised even later that they had been duped.

Many people were conned into giving donations, very few ....

....

4 According to The Centre for Cosmic Consciousness, aliens from outer space are now visiting the Earth.

The Earth ....

....

5 It was possible to hear rapping noises.

Rapping noises ....

....

6 The conjurer obtained alarming effects and many of them frightened the younger members of his audience.

The conjurer obtained alarming effects, ...

....

C Fill each of the blanks with a suitable word or phrase.

1 Recently there .... an epidemic of UFO sightings.

2 One problem with Ufology is that .... on eyewitness testimony without supporting evidence.

3 There are a number of standard effects in seances, ... are frightening.

4 Practitioners of unorthodox techniques .... they are able to treat human ailments successfully.

5 The movement of the pendulum .... by the unconscious muscular movements of the person holding it.

6 Given current scepticism about the paranormal, there .... asking the government to provide finance to support research into UFOs.

D For each of the sentences below, write a new sentence as similar as possible in meaning to the original sentence, but using the word given. The word must not be altered in any way.

1 The evidence on this point is not totally convincing.

falls

....

....

2 Let's not waste any time but get down to the business in hand.

ado

....

....

3 People are now claiming that Jones is the murderer.

alleged

....

....

4 When Tom arrived, work had already started.

way

....

....

5 Francis discovered the evidence to prove his theory quite by chance.

stumbled

....

....

6 The work he has done is not up to the standard that we expect.

falls

....

....

E Choose the word or phrase (*A*, *B*, *C* or *D*) which best completes each sentence.

1 Within weeks of the first 'sighting' of a UFO, the new religion was up and ....

A running *B* racing
C hurtling *D* hurrying

2 It turned out that our telescope was ....

A shaky *B* eccentric
C inoperable *D* malfunctioning

3 Some prospectors were prepared to risk their lives in their .... for gold.

A research *B* quest
C investigation *D* pursuit

4 We couldn't record the programme about extra-sensory perception because the video was on the ....

A mend *B* fault
C blink *D* repairer's

5 Peter claimed that he had been visited by aliens but he couldn't provide a .... of evidence.

A piece *B* scrap
C trace *D* token

6 To .... such claims, considerable evidence would be required.

A rationalise *B* believe
C verify *D* stake

7 A considerable .... of folklore has built up regarding the magical properties of sites such as Stonehenge and Glastonbury Tor.

A body *B* pile
C culture *D* doctrine

8 The scientist's claim to have visited other planets was greeted with .... laughter.

A appalling *B* derisive
C amusing *D* ludicrous

9 Although many believed the faith healer to be a fraud he was never actually ....

A caught out *B* taken in
C found out *D* gone into

10 Everyone was in favour of swift and decisive action, ... for the Prime Minister.

A excluding *B* apart
C except *D* but

11 In order not to upset members, the society instigated a .... to hide the fact that funds had disappeared.

A pay-off *B* lie-in
C cover-up *D* lay-off

12 All the evidence .... to the detective's involvement in the crime.

A shows *B* refers
C attributes *D* points

13 At regular intervals, a craze such as roller-skating or skate-boarding will .... across the nation.

A speed *B* spurt
C spring *D* sweep

14 Patricia .... opposition from her parents when she said she wanted to leave home to travel around the country in a caravan.

A encountered *B* attained
C reached *D* recounted

15 In Professor Smith's opinion people who believe in fairies are fools. He says: 'There's one .... every minute.'

A created *B* born
C nurtured *D* found

Unit eleven

And Nation Shall Speak Unto Nation

Lead-in

A Can you find examples of these different types of English from the extracts (*a–f*)?

1 English written by King Alfred (849– 900)	*3* pidgin English
	4 plain English
2 English written by Geoffrey Chaucer (1345–1400)	*5* legal English
	6 jargon

a *Notwithstanding the sum for Car Tax specified in the order the sum payable by the purchaser in respect thereof shall be such sum as the seller has legally had to pay or becomes legally bound to pay for Car Tax in respect of the goods and notwithstanding also the sum for Value Added Tax specified in the order the sum payable by the purchaser in respect thereof shall be such sum as the seller becomes legally liable for at the time the taxable supply occurs.*

b *Olgeta VSO wokman ol i sitisen bilong Yunaited Kingdom o bilong Yuropian Ekonomic Komyuniti o sitisen bilong narapela hap bilong Komomwelt ol i bon dam na i stap olgeta taim long UK. Olsem na ol i gat kain kain pasin bilong sindaun na ol save mekim kain kain wok. Krismas bilong ol wan wan VSO wokman em i olsem 30 yia samting na ol i gat gutpela save long wok bilong ol. Sampela ol i marit, tasol ol i no gat pikinini. Na namba bilong ol man em i 55% (pesen), na namba bilong ol mari em i 45% (pesen).*

c *Da waes aefter manigum dagum þaet se cyning com to þaem ealande and het him ute setl gewyrcan; and het Augustinum mid his geferum þider to his spraece cuman.*

d *You must pay the Car Tax and VAT which apply when the car is delivered.*

e *Lyte Lowys my sone, I aperceyve wel by certeyne evydences thyn abilite to lerne sciences touching nombres and proporciouns; and as wel considre I thy besy praier in special to lerne the tretys of the Astrelabie.*

f *In multiple-choice item testing both the correct option and the distractors must complete the stem in a way that is grammatically correct.*

B Now can you match each of these items (*1–12*) with its example (*a– l*)?

1 runes (an early alphabet)
2 riddle (you'll have to think hard to find the answer)
3 palindrome (read it from right to left)
4 tongue-twister (how quickly can you say it?)
5 limerick (they always rhyme a, a, b, b, b, a)
6 anagram (you'll need a clue: a famous English writer)
7 pangram (these are good for practising your typing)
8 deviant spelling (common in advertisements and company names)
9 spoonerism (named after Dr Spooner (1844–1930) who, when he spoke, transposed the initial letters of words)
10 gobbledygook (whatever you do, don't write like this)
11 nursery rhyme (all English children know this one)
12 malapropism (an unintended comical confusion of words, named after Mrs Malaprop, a character in *The Rivals* by Richard Sheridan)

a *Kwik-Print*

b *'You have tasted a whole worm. You have hissed my mystery lectures. You will leave Oxford by the next Town drain.*

c *The quick brown fox jumps over the lazy dog.*

d *It is necessary to state that urban forms are a product of the modulated interaction between static determinants and the builders of urban formation subject to spatial mediation by the composite network of dynamic or functional conceptual forces. An omission of any one of these charged factors will prejudice the interrelationship in this equipotential form of causality and the result is an unbalanced formation.*

e *We all make his praise.*

f [illegible]

g *She sells sea shells on the sea shore.*

h *There was an old man from Nantucket*
Who kept all his cash in a bucket
His daughter named Nan
Ran away with a man
And as for the bucket, Nantucket.

i *Madam, I'm Adam.*

j *Why is 'smiles' the longest word in the language?*

k *A priest was called in to exercise the ghost.*

l *Humpty Dumpty sat on a wall*
Humpty Dumpty had a great fall
All the king's horses
And all the king's men
Couldn't put Humpty together again.

C Complete each sentence with one of the words or phrases given.

motto	numbers	repartee	artificial languages
genders	deciphered	aptitude test	loan words
creoles	etymological	slang	indigenous languages
coined	intelligible	official status	dead languages
purists	onomatopoeia	regional dialects	
punch line	social stigma	roots	

1 The .... of the Boy Scouts is *'Be Prepared'*.

2 Dozens of .... have been devised, the most famous being Esperanto.

3 There are a very large number of .... in England, but they are all mutually ....

4 There are three .... in the United Kingdom – English, Welsh and Scottish Gaelic.

5 Cornish and Manx must be regarded as ...., despite the efforts of enthusiasts to revive them, since the last native speakers died in the 18th century and the 1940's respectively.

6 In India, Hindi and English have .... as the languages of government and business.

7 Old English had three .... (masculine, feminine and neuter) and three .... (singular, dual and plural).

8 During the 18th century, English acquired a large number of .... from Italian, mainly to do with music.

9 In most countries, some accents have great prestige, but others have a certain amount of .... attached to them.

10 The .... of the two comedians was so fast and clever that the audience could hardly hear them for laughing.

11 *'Fab'*, and *'with it'* are .... words of the 1960's which are rarely heard nowadays.

12 Pidgin languages which develop into mother-tongue languages are known as ....

13 The sort of grammatical 'errors' that annoy .... are split infinitives and the use of *'like'* as a conjunction.

14 People who say that we should only use the word *'dilapidated'* about stone buildings (because it comes from the Latin word for stone) are guilty of the .... fallacy.

15 Until she started to study Latin, Jennifer didn't realise how many English words had Latin ....

16 Shakespeare .... many new words which entered the language and became widely used.

17 Samuel Pepys's diary was written in a code of his own invention and was not .... until 1825.

18 The trainees for the Diplomatic Service were given a language .... to see if they were likely to be successful at learning foreign languages.

19 He listened carefully to the joke but didn't laugh because he didn't understand the ....

20 Words such as *'cuckoo'* and *'cock-a-doodle-doo'* are examples of ....

D Complete the text using the words and phrases given.

linguists	grammatical	status	subordinate
common language	mother tongue	vary	vocabulary
derived	constructions	miming	developed
life span	multilingual	families	
varieties	form	lingua franca	

Pidgins and Creoles

All pidgin languages start when people who don't have a .... *(1)* try to communicate with each other. Most of the present day pidgins grew up along the trade routes of the world – especially in those parts where the British, French, Spanish, Portuguese and Dutch built up their empires. We talk of 'pidgin English', 'pidgin French', and so on, depending on which language the pidgin is .... *(2)* from.

Pidgin Englishes are mainly to be found in two big ' .... *(3)*' – one in the Atlantic, one in the Pacific. The Atlantic varieties .... *(4)* in West Africa and are still widely used. The Pacific .... *(5)* are found in a wide sweep from the coast of China to the northern part of Australia. Estimates .... *(6)*, but probably about thirty-five million people speak or understand one or other of these forms of English.

Pidgins often have a very short .... *(7)* and many which grew up for trading purposes have ceased to exist, because the countries which were in contact stopped trading with each other. On the other hand, if a trading contact is very successful, and contact builds up over the years, the people will very likely learn each other's languages, and then there will be no need for the pidgin to exist. Pidgin languages seem to be in a 'no win' situation, and it is rare to find one in existence for more than a century. But it can happen. In .... *(8)* parts of the world, the pidgin is found to be so useful that the peoples in contact find they cannot do without it. The pidgin becomes a common language or ' .... *(9)*'. This has happened in Papua New Guinea, where Tok Pisin is known or used by over a million people – more than any other language in the country.

Of course when a pidgin becomes widely used, its .... *(10)* changes dramatically. To begin with, pidgins are very limited forms of communication with few words, a few simple .... *(11)*, helped along by gestures and .... *(12)*. But when a pidgin expands, its .... *(13)* increases greatly, it develops its own rules of .... *(14)* construction, and it becomes used for all the functions of everyday life. People begin to use the pidgin at home. As children are born into these families, the pidgin language becomes their .... *(15)*. When this happens the .... *(16)* of the language fundamentally alters, and it comes to be used in a more flexible and creative way. Instead of being seen as .... *(17)* to other languages in the area, it starts to compete with them. In such cases .... *(18)* no longer talk about pidgin languages but about creoles.

Theme one: *It's The Way That You Say It*

Received Pronunciation

A Listen to the speaker talking about RP and choose the best answer to the following questions according to the information on the tape.

1 An RP accent is primarily a sign that the speaker

A comes from the south-east of England.
B has a high social position.
C is well-educated.
D is polite and respectable.

2 In the sixteenth century RP was spoken by

A most people in London.
B all noblemen and gentlemen.
C people with influence and power at court.
D everyone who moved to London from the north.

3 Why did the BBC adopt RP for radio broadcasting?

A it was acceptable to most listeners.
B It conveyed a sense of authority.
C Most of the newsreaders had been to public schools.
D Other accents could not be understood by many people.

4 One important recent development in RP is that it is spoken by people who

A could not be described as upper-class.
B are fashionable and trendy.
C are generally over sixty years old.
D live in the vicinity of Sloane Square, London.

5 Compared with fifty years ago, the pure form of RP is spoken by fewer people now because

A there is some hostility towards RP.
B RP is regarded as old-fashioned.
C the BBC no longer insists that newsreaders use RP.
D most RP speakers have accents with regional characteristics.

6 Which of these statements about RP is true?

A It is no longer the subject of extensive research by linguists.
B It is taught in British schools.
C British people use it when talking to foreigners.
D The majority of speakers do not live in the United Kingdom.

B The most recent estimate of the total number of English speakers (including those who speak it as a mother tongue, a second language or a foreign language) is at least 750 million, of which about 350 million are native speakers. Only 56 million of them live in the United Kingdom.

What are the factors which have led to the widespread use of English?

In the future, what factors are likely to encourage or discourage the use of English as an international language?

Now read this extract from a review of a book called *The English Language* by Robert Burchfield.

The Mongrel Tongue

Surprisingly little is known about the history of the English Language – a fact which the abundant scholarship on the subject tends to obscure. Speech could not be recorded at all until Edison began experimenting with wax cylinders in the 1870's; and written English, a specialised, minority activity, tells us almost nothing about how the mass of people used language in any given period.

What must be still more frustrating for linguistic historians is that, though they can deduce from written records that English has always been in a state of change, the factors that cause its mutations, and how they operate, remain largely mysterious. In this respect, English is quite as problematic as astrophysics, and much less likely to become clearer with time.

An attraction of Robert Burchfield's sturdy little book is that it has no qualms about admitting ignorance. When English first reached these shores, as part of the luggage of a few thousand illegal German immigrants in the fifth century, it had grammatical gender and case endings, rather like Latin. Why these disappeared is unclear. According to one theory, when the next wave of invaders, the Scandinavians, arrived, the Anglo-Saxons strove to converse with them in a simple 'creolised' English which put paid to niceties like gender. This picture of stumbling inter-racial dialogue has obvious charms, but Burchfield firmly squashes it. How the Anglo-Saxons lost their grammar is just another secret hidden in the pre-

Edisonian silence.

Anyway, it was a lucky break for English, since a rigid grammatical structure might have cramped its talent for digesting other languages. Stylists used to revere 'pure' English, but in reality English is about as pure as factory effluent, and has displayed a mongrel toughness over the centuries by cannibalising a picturesque array of foreign tongues from Greek to Polynesian. This absorption of loan words has slowed down, Burchfield notes, in the last 200 years, and there has been a huge increase in the outflow of English words to less successful languages which are having to adapt themselves to the master speech-system.

Though linguists can identify loan words in English, they have no idea, apparently, why some foreign ideas get borrowed, and some not. An extremely complex cultural filter seems to function, which would be worth exploring. Burchfield remarks, for instance, that British English shows a resistance to Yiddish words in *sch–* (*schmuck, schnook*), common in the US.

Also unexplained is the facility some coinages have for making themselves at home in the language, while others pine unused, Shakespeare, Spenser and their contemporaries dreamed up hundreds of words which gained instant membership, but there is a pathetic graveyard of neologisms that have found no takers at all. Admittedly, the samples of these stillborn brainwaves Burchfield cites have every appearance of being non-starters: *commotrix* (a maid that makes ready her mistress); *parentate* ('to celebrate one's parents' funerals'). But what about *neverness*, another 17th-century invention, which fills a gap in the language (as 'the opposite of eternity' – a useful 20th century concept), and is also beautiful, but has been ignored by everyone, except its originator, Bishop Wilkins, and his modern admirer, Borges.

Given all these aspects that linguists are at a loss to explain, it is no surprise that they cannot account for semantic change (why words develop new meanings) either. Words move up and down league tables of respectability in wholly unpredictable ways, and have no doubt been doing so since runic times. *Boy*, for example, originally meant 'fettered person', the 'male servant', and finally 'male child', whereas *knave* drifted in the other direction, starting out as 'male child', then 'male servant', and eventually 'rascal'. Linguists often proclaim that something Burchfield calls 'the Mitford factor' controls such developments – which means that words or usages adopted by a dominant social class tend to prevail. But this only pushes the problem one step back, since you still have to explain why a word attracts a particular class. Burchfields's conclusion on the whole issue of shifting words, meanings and pronunciations is that these things 'just happen', and cannot be explained, 'any more than it is possible to say why rooks choose one tree rather than another'. That comparison may be over-hopeful, since systematic rook-watching would probably yield a solution that systematic word-watching has not.

Although the one essential feature of English, to judge from its past record, is its rampant and chaotic changeability, there are always those who believe that it achieved its true, fragile perfection in the period of their own youth, and will be irretrievably damaged if the vulgar persist in using *like* for *as*, or misplacing the apostrophe. Burchfield cheerfully kills off various illusions of the 'correct English' addicts. Infinitives have been split, he points out, since at lease the 14th century; and purists who shudder over new words which mix up Greek, Latin and English elements (*helipad, breathalyser*) would have logically to renounce *ostrich* or *plainness*, which are similar hybrids.

The language swarms with 'incorrect' formations. *Pea, burial* (and others) are mistaken shortenings of Old English singular forms (*pise, byrgels*) which were ignorantly assumed to be plurals; yet even the most fastidious refiners seem happy with them now. Foes of 'Americanisms' can rarely, if challenged, pick them out once they have been in the language for a few years. *Law-abiding*, for example, surely the most British of vocables, is American in origin.

These sound arguments for accepting the linguistic novelties that happen to surface during one's lifetime do not, of course, stop any of us from detesting a sizeable proportion of them. How can you respect someone who says *'No way'* – a sure mark of the semi-educated, now fortunately obsolescent? How can you repress a shiver at seeing the word *silo* ('a store for gain') hideously applied to underground missile sites? Since our personalities and memories are so largely composed of language, it is as difficult to feel objective about linguistic change as it is about ageing.

(John Carey, *The Sunday Times*)

C Now choose the best answer to the following questions.

1 According to the writer we cannot discuss the history of the English language with any confidence because

A we had no record of spoken English until recently.
B the written records are too specialised.
C we know nothing about spoken English before 1870.
D the scholarship on this subject is too obscure.

2 Linguistic historians must feel frustrated about the history of the English language because

A they know that language never stops changing.
B the reasons why the language changes are not clear.
C their subject is more difficult than astrophysics.
D they are very unlikely to discover more about it.

3 Robert Burchfield's book

A replaces the myths of the past with accurate, informative answers.
B avoids speculation based on inadequate evidence.
C should be in every immigrant's suitcase.
D is well-designed and strongly-bound.

4 Why did some aspects of Anglo-Saxon grammar disappear?

A Because of the influence of Latin and Scandinavian languages.
B The Anglo-Saxons simplified their language when talking to foreigners.
C Because the Anglo-Saxons stumbled over the words.
D It is not known.

5 The writer does not believe that English is a 'pure' language because

A it doesn't have a rigid grammatical structure.
B it has absorbed a large number of foreign words.
C many English words are used in other languages.
D it is a very tough language to learn.

6 The writer compares English to

A Greek and Polynesian languages.
B a dog, industrial pollution and a cannibal.
C an attractive picture.
D foreign languages in general.

7 Linguists can explain

A why words change their meaning.
B which foreign words will be borrowed and which not.
C why Shakespeare successfully invented new words.
D how words change their meanings.

8 How many people found the word '*neverness*' attractive?

A One.
B Two.
C Three.
D None.

9 What is Burchfield's explanation for semantic change?

A It is explained by the usages of the dominant social class.
B Some words are more attractive than others.
C He has no explanation.
D It is similar to changes in the behaviour of birds and animals.

10 Which of these would a 'purist' *not* object to?

A … to boldly go where no man has gone before …
B Egg's 60 pence a dozen.
C Breathalyser.
D Ostrich.

11 Which of these words does the writer find acceptable in modern English?

A Burials.
B No way.
C Silo (for missiles).
D Pise.

D Find a word or phrase in the text which, in context, is similar in meaning to:

Paragraph 1
1 hide

Paragraph 2
2 changes

Paragraph 3
3 no sense of guilt
4 tried to talk

Paragraph 4
5 a piece of good fortune
6 worship

Paragraph 6
7 quotes

Paragraph 8
8 give up
9 mixtures

Paragraph 9
10 enemies

Paragraph 10
11 strong
12 dying out

E Explain the meaning of these phrases from the text.

1 put paid to niceties like gender *(lines 42–43)*
2 firmly squashes it *(lines 42–43)*
3 cramped its talent *(line 53)*
4 cultural filter *(lines 74–75)*
5 others pine unused *(lines 85–86)*
6 stillborn brainwaves *(line 93)*
7 tend to prevail *(lines 139–140)*
8 purists who shudder *(lines 170–171)*

F In about 100 words summarise what is said in the text about people's attitude to new words and semantic change.

Speaking English Correctly

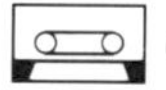

G Read the following text, but do not attempt to fill the gaps until you have listened to the tape. Then complete the text with a suitable word or phrase according to the information on the tape.

The speaker doesn't expect everybody to have a '......................................' *(1)* because, for one thing, when he was a .... *(2)* he probably didn't have one himself. He believes that .... *(3)* are to blame for the fact that some people cannot express themselves well. He thinks that speaking well is important in order to get a .... *(4)*. When he is interviewing, he doesn't like it if he frequently has to say '...................................... *(5)*' because the interviewee doesn't speak clearly enough. In court he has often found that both the prisoner and the witness were almost .... *(6)*.

He believes that you should be willing to correct the way children speak, even if they are copying what .... *(7)* say. He says that grammar should be taught in schools and he is glad that he studied .... *(8)* and in this way learned .... *(9)*. In writing by apparently well-educated people the .... *(10)* is often in the wrong place and he is particularly irritated by .... *(11)*. He refers to one occasion when, as a judge in a County Court, he noticed that a young solicitor had placed .... *(12)* words between the 'to' and the infinitive. When he complained, he discovered that she was unaware of this grammatical point. He was depressed by this because he believes that .... *(13)* should look after the English language.

Language awareness: loan words

A very high proportion of English words have Latin or Greek origins. Although many of these words are obscure scientific and technical terms, there is a huge number of everyday words which still have their original Latin or Greek form, for example, *exit*, *per annum*, *vice versa*, *et cetera*. Even such a common word as *bus* is, in fact, shortened form of the Latin word *omnibus* (meaning 'for all'). Words for technical innovation are generally coined from Greek and Latin roots, and not from Germanic roots.

Telephone, although unknown to the ancient Greeks, is a word made up from Greek elements (*tele* = 'far', *phone* = 'sound'). *Video* (as in *video-recorder*) is Latin for 'I see'.

Many more words, however, are present in the language but not in their original form. The Latin word *ferre* ('to carry'), can be seen in such words as *different*, *conference*, *infer*, *offer*, *prefer*, *proliferate*, *vociferous*. The Greek negative prefix *a-*, *an-* can be seen in such words as *abyss*, *anaesthetic*, *anonymous*, *atom*.

A Complete each sentence with one of the Latin words or phrases given.

interim	in vitro	incognito	modus vivendi
persona non grata	de facto	nem. con.	verbatim
terra firma	ad hoc	curriculum vitae	cogito ergo sum
ad lib	alias	bona fides	alibi

1 I want to know exactly what he said so write down his speech ....

2 When I was convinced of his ...., I went ahead with the deal.

3 When he applied for a new job, Christopher sent off his ....

4 Prince Rupert did not want to be recognised, so he travelled ....

5 The diplomat was declared .... and sent back to his own country.

6 Much as Walter liked sailing, he was always glad to get his feet back on ....

7 General Wallenstein may have no legal authority but he is the .... ruler of the country.

8 After he had told all the jokes he had rehearsed, the comedian began to .... so successfully that the audience roared with laughter.

9 Despite their dislike for each other, the two families eventually found a ....

10 An .... committee was set up at short notice for the purpose of organising the New Year's Eve party at the office.

11 Nobody at the meeting spoke against the resolutions, so they were all passed ....

12 There is a lot of discussion about the ethics of .... fertilisation.

13 Martin Smith, ... Maximilian von Karlstein, is wanted for questioning by Interpol.

14 '............................,' is a well-known (and much adapted) quotation from the French philosopher René Descartes (1596–1650).

15 The accused seemed to have a perfect ...., until the police investigated further.

16 All the survivors of the train crash received an .... payment of £5000, pending the result of the enquiry.

Theme two: New Words for Old

A In recent years, many of the traditional measurements used in Britain have been replaced by metric measurements. Money was decimalised as long ago as 1971 and since 1988 petrol has been sold in litres and not gallons. However, some non-metric measurements are still in common use. There are also some expressions in English which incorporate non-metric measurements. Look at the two following examples.

Give him an inch and he'll take a yard.

A miss is as good as a mile.

We cannot say 'give him a *centimetre* and he'll take a *metre*' or 'a miss is as good as a *kilometre*'. Can you think of any other common English expressions which include measurements?

Now read the text and answer the questions which follow.

Not Exactly What We Mean To Say

News came through from Brussels the other day that we are to be allowed to keep our inch, foot, yard, mile and pint. The pound, ounce, hundred-weight, stone, furlong and all the rest of the baggage, however, are to be left out for the dustman. And that, you might think, is that.

Not at all, according to Adrian Wardour-Street, British PR officer with the European Community Quantities Office. The EC thinks Britain still has a long way to go, and wants to scrap a lot more of our measurements yet.

'It's not the accurate measurements these Brussels wallahs are worried about,' says Adrian. 'If we stuck to units and measure, they'd be quite happy. What they can't stand is the way we British use very vague terms in a precise way all the time.'

How does he mean? 'Well, take the words *yonks*, for instance. When you hear an Englishman saying, "I haven't seen him for yonks," it means something very precise to us. Such as, long enough to make someone you didn't like then seem pleasant in retrospect. But if you ask an Englishman how long *yonks* is, he won't have the faintest idea how to define it.

Much worse is a word like *something*. If a wife says to a husband, "Have you left something for the waiter?", you know it means two or three quid. If a business colleague says, "Is there something in it for me?", you know it probably means five or ten thousand. If the husband says to a barmaid, "And have something for yourself?", it only means a small drink, and not any money at all.

'Well, this sort of things is impossibly imprecise, even worse than ounces and pounds and our team wants to see it all clamped down on.'

Your team? 'Ah. Yes. Perhaps I shouldn't have mentioned this, but Brussels sent a plainclothes team over to Britain last year to study the way we actually do measure and weigh things, and they discovered that we are virtually, by their standards, innumerate.

'For instance, they often heard people asking for something like, "Just over three-quarters of a pound of carrots," or "The best part of a pound of tomatoes, please".

'To begin with, they thought this was a very loose use of the word *pound*. Later, they came to realise that it was actually a very precise and private use of the expression "the best part of a pound" understood by greengrocers and customers but not by the visiting team of inquirers.

'Another test they tried was going into antique shops, picking on a bit of furniture and asking if the price on the label was final. In no case was it final – and in every case the antique seller used a different phrase to express this: "There could be some breathing space;" "I think we could find a little slack there;" "We haven't finally come into land yet;" "It's not unadjustable, I think".

'At no time did any of the dealers simply say, "Yes, I could bring the price down," or indeed mention a price.

'This sort of thing may be very charming and English but it's quite against the ideal of standardisation, so I'm afraid to say that the EC has prepared a further list of quantitative expressions it wants the British to abandon.'

Such as? 'From 1992 the EC will not permit the use of the following units of measurement peculiar to Britain:

Just a quick one, then/Not much of a day/A fair way to go yet/Not unadjacent to/A bit thin on top/A bite-sized chunk/Not a million miles from/Not by a long chalk/A drop of sherry/Just the merest hint/A little bit on the side/Selling like hot cakes/The other half/By and by/Not much upstairs/Touch it with a barge pole/A bit of a ding-dong/Straight as a die/Stiff as a ramrod/Safe as houses/As different as chalk and cheese/At the end of the day …'

'Just a moment,' I broke in. 'These ones aren't measurements. They're similes, images. You can't ban them.'

'You can if they're faulty or out-of-date, I'm afraid. Who knows what a *ramrod* or a *bargepole* looks like now?'

"*Safe as houses*" should be all right,' I said. 'Houses we still have.'

'Nothing safe about them, though, the way prices and mortgages have gone mad.'

'Well, *chalk and cheese* are still different, for God's sake.'

'When that phrase was invented, cheese was safe to eat and chalk wasn't. It's the other way round now.'

'Well, I think the British public are going to take to the streets when they hear about this.'

'They won't hear about it until we're good and ready,' Adrian told me.

'Mum's the word, eh?'

'Not an expression I am acquainted with, I'm glad to say.'

(Miles Kington, *The Independent*)

B Find a word or phrase in the text which, in context, are similar in meaning to:

Paragraph 1
1 taken away as rubbish
2 there is nothing more to say

Paragraph 2
3 abolish

Paragraph 3
4 kept to

Paragraph 6
5 firmly suppressed

Paragraph 7
6 not in uniform

Paragraph 10
7 selecting

Paragraph 12
8 give up

C Which of the italicised expressions in *Paragraph 13* of the text can be used to refer to:

1 a fierce argument
2 a husband or wife
3 bad weather
4 something which is quite near
5 someone who is not very intelligent
6 someone who is going bald
7 an extra-marital relationship
8 a very small amount

D Now answer the following questions.

1 Which paragraph do you think contains information which is absolutely true?
2 How many meanings does the writer suggest for the word *something* and what are they?
3 In what areas did the *plainclothes team* observe unusual customer-seller interaction?
4 What is the objection the writer raises to the list of expressions in *Paragraph 13*?

Grammar: linking words

A Look at these pairs of sentences (*a–i*) and decide whether the second sentence in each pair:

1 expresses a result
2 gives an example
3 gives extra information
4 explains
5 changes the subject
6 makes a concession
7 expresses a contrast
8 imposes a condition
9 contradicts

a You must wear a tie. Otherwise, you cannot eat at the restaurant.

b Yolanda received maximum marks for every part of her performance in the World Championship. In other words, she is the highest-scoring skater ever.

c He has all the qualities that we require for this job. Moreover, he is able to start work almost immediately.

d The aircraft will take off at 9 p.m. and arrive at 2 p.m. local time. By the way, the baggage allowance on this flight is 50 kilos.

e The first two witnesses could scarcely be heard. In contrast, the third one spoke out clearly.

f 'It is the most significant novel of the twentieth century,' claimed Frank.
'On the contrary,' snapped Anthony. 'I wouldn't light a fire with it!'

g He dresses in shabby clothes and, frankly, looks like a tramp. Nevertheless, he is one of our most brilliant concert pianists.

h Your marks put you on level 3. Therefore, you will have to take the test again in six months' time.

i This candidate has quite a lot of experience of working overseas. For instance, he spent two years in Peru.

B Choose the correct word (*A*, *B* or *C*) to begin the second sentence.

1 In the nineteenth century, Edwin Chadwick ensured that London had a regular supply of fresh, clean water. ...., not many people have heard of him or his achievements.

A Therefore *B* Accordingly *C* However

2 All workers were issued with identity cards. ...., they had to sign their names on arrival.

A Consequently *B* Furthermore
C On the other hand

3 His achievements in the sport of tennis are truly impressive. ...., he won Wimbledon six times in succession.

A For example *B* What is more
C By the way

4 We must re-inforce the river banks. ...., there is bound to be flooding in the winter.

A As a result *B* Otherwise *C* In fact

5 With all the optional extras, the price of the car is £120,000. ...., it costs more than the average price for most houses.

A In other words *B* After all *C* Actually

6 He is undoubtedly the best player in the team. ...., he is very unpopular with the other members.

A In contrast *B* On the other hand
C Otherwise

7 We had several reasons for not accepting his application. ...., he was unable to produce the required documents.

A Frankly *B* At any rate
C To start with

8 'He is an expert on medieval Latin,' asserted Thomas.
'....................,' retorted Bernard, 'he has no knowledge of Latin whatsoever.'

A Otherwise *B* In contrast
C On the contrary

9 'We must be ready for fierce attacks by our opponents,' said the chairman. '...................., we must be prepared for the slanderous and hurtful stories that will undoubtedly appear in the popular press.'

A Above all *B* Altogether *C* Accordingly

10 Tim completed the race in 4 minutes 32.5 seconds, the slowest time for several years. ...., it was enough to win him the gold medal.

A In any case *B* Nevertheless
C Besides

11 '... and the coach will reach the hotel at 10 p.m. ...., it's a three-star hotel, not a two-star as it says on your booking form.'

A Anyway *B* By the way
C On the other hand

12 'The helicopter will arrive to evacuate the wounded in the morning,' said the doctor. ...., we must make them as comfortable as possible.'

A Meanwhile *B* Now *C* After all

13 'I know he is old and rather difficult,' said Mary, 'but he should be treated with more respect. ...., he was once regarded as a hero and decorated by the King.'

A Moreover *B* After all *C* All the same

14 'We appreciate the fact that Mr MacGregor is very ill,' said Matron. ' ...., he must stop being so rude to my nurses.'

A For a start *B* In any case
C All the same

15 We could put the car on the train and just drive the last hundred kilometres to the cottage. ...., we could drive all the way.

A On the contrary *B* Alternatively
C Nevertheless

C Can you finish each sentence in three different ways, using the words given?

EXAMPLE: You will be allowed to join the club ...
because although but

ANSWERS: *... because you have been recommended by existing members.*
... although you are not quite old enough.
... but only for one year.

1 Michael stayed at the hotel ...
whenever although because

2 The police searched the house thoroughly ...
but in order to after

3 You are not allowed to operate this machine ...
unless as so

4 Professor Helsing was very interested in the paranormal ...
as soon even if whereas

5 We will head for the South Pole on foot ...
as soon as providing although

Theme three: *English Around the World*

A What are some of the problems you have encountered when translating from one language into another?

How do you think machines cope with translation?

Now read the text on the next page and answer the questions which follow.

Now Cheerful Inhuman Word Swap A Wonder Be

The Japanese and westerners find each other's languages hard going. This is partly because teaching is bad, but mostly because Japanese has a strikingly different structure and alphabet from any European tongue. The two sides have plenty to talk to each other about, which is the problem. So, now, have plenty of computer scientists, and this may provide the solution. Computers can be cheap translators.

They will learn this trick only gradually. The easiest task for them is to translate material written in a simple and predictable style on a limited subject matter. Boring technical manuals fit this bill, and computers are already translating them. From such beginnings, mechanical translators might move on to scientific papers and then newspaper articles. Bravice, an independent Japanese software house – which has about 80 researchers working on machine translation, more than any of the giants – has already sold 3200 of its systems. Many of them are used to translate obscure doctoral theses. Nikkei Telecom, and English-language news service run by Japan's leading business daily farms out the translation of some of its stock market reports to a software house, which translates them by computer.

There is just one problem with all these systems: they are awful. This correspondent recently watched in embarrassment as one machine took a couple of innocent Japanese sentences and came up with:

'Like this there be we to very busy situation,' and *'All employees are able to peel to this project and be holding the fight for the plan achievement.'*

The software to achieve this sort of sentence costs around Y630,000 ($4,500)

Do not chuckle too soon. The point about both these sentences is that they are nearly intelligible. They can, at a push, be turned into decent English by somebody who does not speak Japanese. So they do not need the attentions of an expensive professional translator. Unfortunately, these sentences are the good ones. When NEC claims that its English-to-Japanese programme is '70% accurate', what it means is that seven sentences in every ten come out in reconstructible form. The rest might just as well have come from the pages of the obscurest Dadaist poet.

So, for the moment, professional translators are still needed. A better name for machine translation might therefore be 'computer-aided translation'. In principle, rewriting a semi-translated text ought to be quicker than composing a translation from scratch. Mr Hiroshi Uchida, who has run Fujitsu's machine translation project since it started nine years ago, says it is already possible to do some translation jobs in half the time it takes people on their own. It is precisely where people do worst that machines excel. Computers are good at translating technical terms – of which, according to Mr Uchida, there are already 30 million in English – and have no difficulty in ensuring that expressions are translated consistently throughout a long text. What computers are bad at is producing something that looks like a well-written sentence.

Though the results tend to be comical, they are not unimpressive – given the obstacles involved. Translating a language like English into Japanese involves three steps. First, the English sentence has to be analysed. Grammarians call this 'parsing'; it involves deciding what the subject of the sentence is, which words qualify it rather than the verb, and so forth. To do this a translation system looks up each word in a lexicon listing the possibilities. Such lexicons typically contain about 100,000 terms, including about 30,000 that can be programmed to suit each user, and a handful of idioms. Luckily, a good 20 years of work have gone into the automatic parsing of English. There is, however, little such work on Japanese or, indeed, any other tongue.

This may not delay matters too long. Japanese has a much more regular sentence structure than English. Its verbs always come at the end of sentences, for instance. And it has a helpful system of 'particles' or suffices, such as '*o*', '*wa*' and '*ni*', which indicate the grammatical role of the word they are attached to, as well as marking the end of sentences and words.

But every schoolboy knows examples of ambiguous sentences, such as: *'It is advisable to avoid flying aeroplanes'*, or *'I see the sausage rolls under the table'*. The only way to sort these out is to look at the context, which is one of the toughest problems in computing. Most systems now on the market can handle only a tiny range of examples, and will sometimes get even those wrong. If the word *screen* appears in a television manual, it is much more likely to be used as a noun than as a verb meaning 'filter or conceal', but there is chaos when it means the latter.

Once an English sentence is broken down and the individual words translated, it has to be built up again into a Japanese sentence. If the parsing has been done well, this is the easiest part. It involves nothing much more complicated than running a Japanese parser backwards. In between comes the 'transfer' stage, in which the analysed English terms must be replaced by Japanese ones with the same meaning.

At the moment there are two ways of doing this. The most sophisticated method, which is used by Fujitsu and NEC, involves an intermediate language. Instead of listing a Japanese translation for each meaning of every English word, Fujitsu uses an intermediate language based on Esperanto called Interlingua; NEC uses one based on English. This allows the system to be expanded so that Japanese can be translated into a third language, such as French. All that is needed is a dictionary that converts French to and from the intermediate language. Otherwise it would be necessary to add two new dictionaries: one to handle Japanese conversions, and one for English.

The ultimate goal is the simultaneous translation of unrestricted speech. This would involve marrying advanced machine translation to voice-recognition and voice-synthesis equipment. That is the master plan of Japan's Ministry of Posts and Telecommunications. The ministry has banded together seven big Japanese electronics firms and IBM Japan to work on the problem. It hopes that these eight might find a solution by early next century. Even if they do not – and most of the scheme's participants sound pessimistic – the imperfect by-products should be worth having. The main complaint might come from teachers. How will they persuade children to write elegant sentences when the computers they love get away with howlers?

(The Economist)

B Find a word or phrase in the text which, in context, is similar in meaning to:

Paragraph 1
1 very difficult
2 language

Paragraph 2
3 are appropriate
4 important financial newspaper

Paragraph 3
5 produced

Paragraph 4
6 laugh
7 with a struggle

Paragraph 5
8 from the beginning

Paragraph 6
9 difficulties

C What do the following words and phrases refer to?

1. the problem *(line 9)*
2. this trick *(line 14)*
3. software house *(lines 25–26)*
4. the giants *(lines 28–29)*
5. this correspondent *(line 41)*
6. and so forth *(line 107)*
7. this may not delay matters too long *(lines 121–122)*
8. when it means the latter *(line 149)*
9. the master plan *(line 190)*

D Can you rewrite the title and the two translated sentences in acceptable English?

E Now choose the best answer to the following questions.

1 Which of these is the most difficult for computers to translate?

A Doctoral theses.
B Scientific reports.
C Technical manuals.
D Newspaper reports.

2 At present computer translation software

A produces sentences that only translators can make sense of.
B can write difficult poems.
C produces accurate sentences most of the time.
D produces intelligible sentences most of the time.

3 Computer-aided translation saves money because

A a human translator need not be employed.
B computers translate technical terms consistently.
C computers help a human translator to work faster.
D computers are better at some things than human translators.

4 What is the second stage in the machine translation from English into Japanese?

A A grammatical analysis of the English sentence.
B Translating the English words into Japanese.
C Looking up the English words in a lexicon.
D Re-constituting the sentence according to Japanese grammar.

5 Teachers may not like machine translation because

A there will no longer be any need for language teachers.
B simultaneous translation of unrestricted speech will make human translation and interpreting unnecessary.
C they will have to learn how to use machine translators.
D their students may get accustomed to the poor grammar of computer-generated sentences.

F Summarise the advantages and disadvantages of computer translation, in not more than 100 words.

Australian English

G The speaker talks about the differences between British and Australian English. Using the information that he gives you, explain, in a few words, the meaning of the words and phrases below.

1 uni
2 ute
3 fair dinkum
4 she'll be right
5 no worries
6 up a gum tree
7 barbie
8 chooks
9 galah
10 drongo
11 oz
12 smoko
13 sheila

Playing the Bagpipes

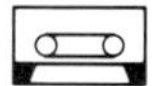

H Listen to Andrew talking about an evening class in which he teaches children to play a musical instrument. Answer the following questions with a word or short sentence.

1 How many people are there in the class?

2 What is the age range?

3 What is the earliest age children can start?

4 How does Andrew treat children the first time they come to his class?

5 How long does it take to become proficient?

6 What does Andrew say about controlling the flow of air to the instrument?

7 Why is it difficult to get people to play as a band?

Talking points

A Work with a partner. Look at what people are saying in the following cartons (a–f). Are they speaking in an appropriate way? What would you expect them to say in each situation?

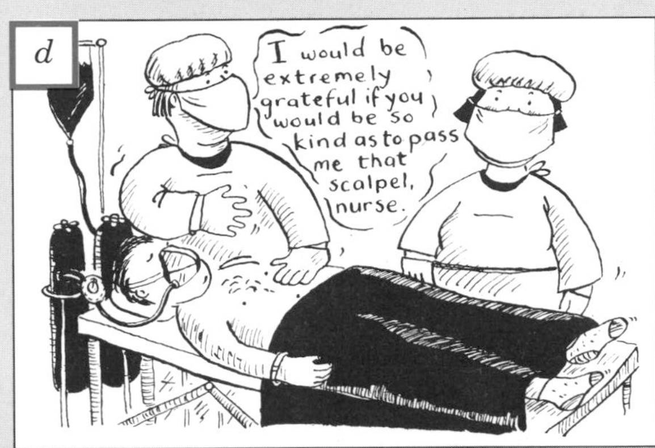

Writing

Plain English

In 1979 Martin Cutts and Chrissie Maher started the Plain English Campaign in order to persuade bureaucrats to write leaflets and forms in simple, clear, elegant and jargon-free English. They have had considerable success, and many government departments and large companies have taken up their suggestions concerning language and layout. Every year they award prizes to companies and government departments that have produced good, clear examples of forms and official letters and booby prizes to those who write in impersonal, incomprehensible, pompous and long-winded English.

Here are some of their tips for writing Plain English:

- Use everyday words. Avoid jargon and unusual words.
- Use active verbs in place of nouns, (for example, *'you must apply'* **not** *'you must make an application'*).
- Use the active, not the passive. Use the imperative when giving instructions.
- Be personal. Don't be afraid to say *'I'*, *'We'* *',You'*.
- Keep the sentences short. Use 'subject – verb – object' word order.
- Be positive. Use negative sentences only if they are essential.
- Treat the reader as your equal.

A Which of these sentences exemplify their advice?

1 Plans for the said gyratory system can be perused at the Town Hall.

2 Keep your luggage with you.

3 Applications for student grants must be submitted without delay.

4 The council has a responsibility to inform tenants of their rights according to statute.

5 Students should apply for their grants as soon as possible.

6 You can look at the plans for this roundabout at the Town Hall.

7 Passengers must be accompanied by their luggage.

8 The company is not in a position to accede to your request for reimbursement because it is not, to date, in possession of all the documents which have a bearing on this case.

9 The Council must tell tenants what their legal rights are.

10 We cannot repay you because so far we have not received all the relevant papers.

B Can you rewrite these sentences in Plain English?
An example has been done for you.

EXAMPLE: It is expected that in the foreseeable future further meetings will be arranged with the Trade Union for the purpose of conducting negotiations in relation to a reduction in working hours.

ANSWER: *We will soon be meeting the Trade Union to discuss shorter working hours.*

1 Your dwelling was visited by our inspector on 25 May but on subsequent occasions he has been unable to gain access to your premises.

2 It is regretted that your dwelling has been adversely affected by water damage consequent to the recent floods.

3 Persons who wish to receive further information should apply in writing to the Director of Housing.

4 It should be borne in mind that not all of our customers are able to speak English fluently.

5 It is now accepted that the rejection of your application should not have taken place and we would ask you to accept our apologies.

6 Failure to return your library books by the given date may lead to the imposition of a fine.

7 Unavailability of staff has necessitated the discontinuance of this service.

8 The samples will be despatched by surface mail at an early date.

9 Failure to notify the company of any outstanding bills will render the agreement null and void.

C Write a Plain English version of these three extracts.

Extract a

During the summer months, it will be necessary for me to process over 11,000 applications for awards for the academic year 1988/89. My Awards staff will, therefore, be working under very considerable pressure during the period from June to October. In an endeavour to relieve this pressure, applicants are requested to refrain from writing, telephoning or calling for information about the progress of their application, unless the enquiry is absolutely essential. In this connection, it would also be helpful if, as a general rule, telephone calls and visits to the office during the months of August, September and October could please be restricted to the afternoon period from 2 p.m. to 5 p.m. Your co-operation in this respect will considerably help my Awards staff during the busy summer months.

Extract b

In the event of any failure or malfunctioning of any component of the apparatus which renders the appliance inoperative and necessitates repair before the appliance will work normally, the company will, at the request of the customer within a reasonable period and during normal working hours, repair or replace such components free of charge.

Extract c

Virtually all those eligible to cast their votes availed themselves of the opportunity to do so, notwithstanding the exceptionally inclement weather conditions. As is customary, the result will be announced to the public by the Lord Mayor.

D Can you match these verbose and long-winded sentences with the proverbs (*a–f*) which express the same meaning much more concisely?

1 Appropriate remedial measures, even of a comparatively minor nature, if implemented at a sufficiently early stage, will obviate the necessity of very substantial repair operations which would otherwise be required in the long term.

2 Major projects involving decisions of an irrevocable nature should be undertaken only after appropriate feasibility studies have identified all possible consequences.

3 Inadequate assimiliation of the relevant data will result in a potentially hazardous situation.

4 There is a real need to ensure a sufficient diversity in resource allocation and investment decisions in order to obviate the risks inherent in over-concentration.

5 The exercise of strict economy and the optimum utilisation of all available resources will preclude the occurrence of any major shortage.

6 A tendency towards progressive sub-optimisation may become apparent before the upward trend anticipated in the longer term begins to manifest itself.

a Waste not, want not.
b Things will get worse before they get better.
c A stitch in time saves nine.
d A little learning is a dangerous thing.
e Don't put all your eggs in one basket.
f Look before you leap.

Exam hints

E

1 *Sticking to the topic:*
Focus on what the question asks for. If the title says, 'Describe a holiday that ended in disaster', then your answer must:

- *describe* – there must be a clear picture of where the holiday was and what you did before the disaster
- *be about a holiday*, not a business trip or expedition, and not about the journey to the holiday destination.
- *end with a disaster*. You must not write about a holiday that was disastrous from beginning to end.
- *be about a disaster*, something very serious, not a minor inconvenience like losing your ticket or a car breaking down.

2 *Planning:*
Think through your ideas and make a plan before you consider putting pen to paper.

3 *Timing:*
You have two hours to write two compositions. Plan your time carefully so that you have equal time for each question:
10 minutes: planning
35 minutes: writing
10 minutes: checking

4 *Length:*
The length required for each composition is usually indicated on the paper. Keep to the word limit suggested. Do not write one very long composition and one very short one.

5 *Organisation:*
Remember all the hints you have been given in this book on how to get and organise information. Don't forget the need for an introduction and conclusion.

Telexes

F You are a reporter. The newspaper where you work has received the following telexes from a news agency. Write the articles that will appear in the newspaper, using the information given in the telexes. Don't forget to provide a suitable headline for each one.

1 HURRICANE SWEEPS SOUTHERN BRITAIN. APPALLING DAMAGE. LONDON DEVASTATED. POWER LINES DOWN. ROADS BLOCKED. TREES UPROOTED. HOUSEHOLDERS TERRIFIED. STORM STRUCK AT NIGHT. NO WARNING. EMERGENCY SERVICES ALERTED. ARMY CALLED IN. PRIME MINISTER CALLS STATE OF EMERGENCY.

2 PRINCESS TO WED SOCCER STAR, PALACE ANNOUNCES. PALACE PRESS SECRETARY ANNOUNCED PRINCESS MAY, 22, TO MARRY NEXT MONTH. GROOM, BARRY GITTINGS, MANCHESTER UNITED'S GOALKEEPER. PARENTS DELIGHTED. WEDDING ST PAUL'S.

3 FAMILIES TO BE RESTRICTED TO TWO CHILDREN. PM ANNOUNCES BILL TO RESTRICT FAMILIES TO TWO CHILDREN ONLY. SEVERE TAX PENALTIES FOR THIRD AND SUBSEQUENT CHILDREN. OPPOSITION PROTESTS. RALLY EXPECTED TODAY.

4 LIVE DINOSAUR FOUND BY RESEARCH TEAM. REPORT FROM MONGOLIA. ANIMAL NOT CAPTURED, ONLY SIGHTED. HUGE SIZE. FLED FROM TEAM. TOO BIG FOR NET. HELICOPTER SEARCH IN PROGRESS. TEAM LEADER TO APPEAR ON TV TOMMORROW.

Literary approaches

On the next page are some extracts from a diary.

Which famous historical events are referred to in the following extracts?

What impression do these extracts from the diary make on you?

Some Extracts from the Diary of Samuel Pepys (1633–1703)

25 September 1660
To the office, where Sir W Batten, Colonel Slingsby and I sat a while; and Sir R Ford coming to us about some business, we talked together of the interest of this kingdom to have a peace with Spain and a war with France and Holland – where Sir R Ford spoke like a man of great reason and experience. And afterwards did send for a cupp of tee (a China drink) of which I had never drank before.

13 October 1660
I went to Charing Cross to see Major-Generall Harrison hanged, drawn and quartered – which was done there – he looking as cheerful as any man could in that condition. He was presently cut down and his heart shown to the people, at which there was great shouts of joy … Thus it was my chance to see the King beheaded at Whitehall and to see the first blood shed in revenge for the blood of the King at Charing Cross.

13 November 1660
Home to dinner. Where I find my wife making of pyes and tarts to try her oven with (which she hath never yet done); but not knowing the nature of it, did heat it too hot and so did a little overbake her things, but knows how to do better another time.

12 August 1665
The people die so, that now it seems they are fain to carry the dead to be buried by daylight, the nights not sufficing to do it in.

3 September 1665
Up, and put on my coloured silk suit, very fine, and my new periwig, bought a good while since, but darest not wear it because the plague was in Westminster when I bought it. And I wonder what the fashion will be after the plague is done to periwigs, for nobody will dare to buy any haire for fear of the infection – that it had been cut off of the heads of people dead of the plague.

16 October 1665
But Lord, how empty the streets are, and melancholy, and so many poor sick people in the streets, full of sores, and so many sad stories overheard as I walk, everybody talking of this dead, and that man sick, and so many in this place, and so many in that.

2 September 1666
Some of our maids sitting up late last night to get things ready against our feast today, Jane called us up, about three in the morning, to tell us of a great fire they saw in the city. So I rose, and slipped on my nightgown and went to her window, and thought it to be on the back side of Markelane at the furtherest; but being unused to such fires as fallowed, I thought it far enough off, and so went to bed again and to sleep.

3 September 1666
About four a-clock in the morning, my Lady Batten sent me a cart to carry away all my money and plate and best things to Sir W Riders at Bednall Green; which I did, myself riding in my nightgown in the cart.

4 September 1666
All on fire in the night, was enough to put us out of our wits; and endeed it was extremely dreadful – for it looks just as if it was at us, and the whole heaven on fire … And Paul is burned, and all Cheapside. I wrote to my father this night; but the post house being burned, the letter could not go.

24 December 1666
I this evening did buy me a pair of green spectacles, to see whether they will help my eyes or no. So to the Change, and went to the Upper Change, which is almost as good as the old one; only shops are but on one side. Then home to the office and did business till my eyes begun to be bad; and so home to supper (my people busy making mince-pies) and so to bed.

31 May 1669
And thus ends all that I doubt I shall ever be able to do with my own eyes in the keeping of my journal. I being not able to do it any longer, having done so now so long as to undo my eyes almost every time that I take a pen in my hand; and therefore, whatever comes of it I must forebear; and therefore resolve from this time forward to have it kept by my people in longhand, and must therefore be contented to set down no more then is fit for them and all the world to know; or if there is anything (which cannot be much, now my amours to Deb are past, and my eyes hindering me in almost all other pleasures), I must endeavour to keep a margin in my book open, to add here and there a note in shorthand with my own hand. And so I betake myself to that course which is almost as much to see myself go into my grave, for which, and all the discomforts that will accompany my being blind, the good God prepare me.

Follow-up

A Fill each of the numbered blanks in the following passage with one suitable word.

Learning to Read

English spelling is extremely complex, and this means that even in the early stages, reading is not a simple matter. There are two basic methods used .... *(1)* teaching children to read, the 'look and say' method and phonics. The English spelling system basically ....*(2)* speech sounds by letters and the latter teaching approach encourages .... *(3)* to match the sound to the letter. But phonics does not help with the many words in English that do not .... *(4)* phonic rules. This is where the former method .... *(5)* in. Developed in the 1930s, the 'look and say' method is designed to make use of children's visual memories and in this way give them .... *(6)* to a wider range of words. It encourages .... *(7)* of the whole word rather than its constituent parts.

However, ... *(8)* when used together, these two approaches do not teach children to read fluently. The reason is that in .... *(9)* methods, words are taught .... *(10)* of context, as individual items. Different skills are needed in order to recognise a word when it appears in a piece of continuous text. When we read .... *(11)* skilled adults, our perception of both words and letters is conditioned by what we expect the text .... *(12)* say. The more we read, the more refined this expectation becomes. When we are .... *(13)* with the subject matter of a text and with the style of writing, we can decipher even poorly printed texts with .... *(14)*. There is now a considerable amount of evidence to show that children tackle reading a continuous text in much the same way as adults do, by using the cues .... *(15)* by the context to work out the meaning of individual words and the grammatical structure of the sentence. .... *(16)*, when we are teaching children to read, we .... *(17)* not restrict the approach to the arduous need to identify individual words. .... *(18)* we should encourage them to enjoy books for their content. In that way, they will develop text processing .... *(19)* and a positive attitude to .... *(20)* books have to offer at one and the same time.

B Finish each of the following sentences in such a way that it is as similar as possible in meaning to the sentence printed before it.

1 If you want to become proficient at any skill, you'll have to put in hours of practice.
Becoming proficient in any skill involves ......
....

2 As a public speaker, John is not good at all.
What John is bad ....
....

3 It's possible that a rigid grammatical structure would have led to a different development of the language.
A rigid grammatical structure ....
....

4 It's a pity the author has not considered all the relevant facts.
I wish ....
....

5 It's easy for computers to ensure that expressions are consistently translated throughout a long text.
Computers have no difficulty ....
....

6 There is no tougher problem in computer translation than how to handle context.
How to handle context ....
....

C Fill each of the blanks with a suitable word or phrase.

1 Although purists would like to believe otherwise, the split infinitive .... in English since the 14th century.

2 .... Tony wants to come to the party is that Petra will be there.

3 This cooker .... to last at least ten years from the date of purchase.

4 There is .... with this machine: it just doesn't work properly.

5 One way of working out the meaning of an unknown word is to .... the context.

6 A major problem in machine translation is .... what class a word belongs to.

D For each of the sentences below, write a new sentence as similar as possible in meaning to the original sentence, but using the word given. The word must not be altered in any way.

1 Everyone became tired on the mountain path.
going
....
....

2 Stephen just couldn't manage to explain how he made so many spelling errors.
loss
....
....

3 He did not hesitate to report his grandmother to the police.
qualms
....
....

4 Tom comes from Yorkshire, but you couldn't tell this from his accent.
trace
....
....

5 Technical manuals are quite suitable for this purpose.
bill
....
....

6 The skier injured his back, so that was the end of his championship hopes.
paid
....
....

E Choose the word or phrase (*A*, *B*, *C* or *D*) which best completes each sentence.

1 The .... bringing about change in the meaning of words remain a mystery.
A facts *B* reasons
C causes *D* factors

2 Elaborate ministerial answers just tend to .... the basic facts of the case.
A darken *B* obscure
C cloud *D* cover

3 Simon never has any .... about pursuing his own interests at the expense of other people.
A fears *B* doubts
C qualms *D* pretensions

4 The idea that MPs should have to give up other sources of income beyond their parliamentary salaries was firmly .... by the Prime Minister.
A squashed *B* suppressed
C squeezed *D* subdued

5 Colin found it very .... living in a bed-sit.
A limited *B* cramped
C restricted *D* defeated

6 The Marketing Director could find no .... for his suggestion that free samples of the product should be distributed to schools.
A backers *B* undertakers
C catchers *D* takers

7 The Minister is such an authoritarian figure that his views tend to .... in any discussion.
A override *B* prevail
C succeed *D* triumph

8 The two sides are entrenched and any meeting between them at this stage seems unlikely to .... a solution.
A submit *B* force
C yield *D* concede

9 Purists will always .... when they encounter grammatical uses they consider inexact.
A shudder *B* shake
C tremble *D* quake

10 John's report is .... with useful information.
A thick *B* loaded
C crowded *D* packed

11 Although his knowledge of the language was minimal, the tourist .... to make himself understood.
A strove *B* fought
C laboured *D* strained

12 Searching through the shelves in a second-hand bookshop, Anna discovered the very book to fill a .... in her collection.
A space *B* hole *C* gap *D* cavity

13 The minister's resignation came in the .... of a barrage of criticism from opponents, former supporters and the Press.
A follow-up *B* wake
C train *D* background

14 This work will just about do, at a ....
A pull *B* consideration
C push *D* shove

15 All the applicants were .... to ensure that none of them represented a security risk.
A monitored *B* screened
C tested *D* selected

Unit twelve

Scruples

Lead-in

A What issues of right or wrong are suggested by the following photographs?

A Confession

B What is the worst thing you have ever done?

While you are considering this listen to the tape. What childish prank is described here?

Now discuss in groups of three any such activities you have engaged in.

C Look at this list of actions. Have you done any of them? Would you do any of them?How serious do you consider them to be?

a jumping the traffic lights
b stealing from a self-service restaurant
c travelling on public transport without paying the fare
d leaving a restaurant without paying
e leaking secret information to the Press
f betraying your country
g exceeding the speed limit when driving
h failing to stop after an accident
i drinking and driving
j burning the private diaries of a famous person
k selling a house or car which has serious defects
l buying shares on the basis of inside information

D Complete each sentence with one of the words or phrases given.

shortcomings	misdemeanour	deception	sacrificed
betrayed	ethics	principle	integrity
dishonesty	sin	loyalty	conscience
misconduct	culpable	traitor	
in disgrace	reproached	vices	
honour	corrupt	culprit	

1 .... is an indispensable quality in a lawyer.

2 John has dismissed him from his post for .... after he had been caught stealing from the cash box.

3 Wouldn't it be unusual if all politicians were not swayed by political expediency but always acted upon ....?

4 The administration always demands .... from its civil servants.

5 Although everyone agreed that Alastair was not to blame for the accident he felt he was ....

6 Any man convicted of spying for a foreign power is regarded as a(n) .... because he has .... his country.

7 It is a criminal offence to obtain money by ....

8 The British Medical Authority set up a special committee to study the .... of experimental work on human embryos.

9 Jeremy is a paragon of virtue. He seems to have no .... at all.

10 In .... societies, you can't blame individuals for working to their own advantage.

11 The doctor was accused of gross professional .... after he had demanded sexual favours from a patient.

12 A minor infringement of the law can be regarded as no more than a(n) ....

13 Who broke the window? No one is going outside to play until we find the ....

14 Charles left his job .... after being convicted of embezzlement.

15 Mary regards it as a point of .... to pay the bills on time.

16 The actress suffered pangs of .... when she was offered and accepted the part her closest friend was dying to get.

17 Andrew has many .... but misleading people as to his intentions is not one of them.

18 Telling lies is regarded as a(n) .... rather than a crime.

19 The mother .... her own life for the good of her children.

20 Tom .... himself for not having had the courage to support his friend when he was accused by the police.

E Complete the text using the words and phrases given.

undercover agent	apostasy	cloaking	groomed
defection	deceit	guise	covert
security scandal	deviously	elite	disinformation
espionage	perfidious	ambivalence	secret
realm	moles	creed	enigma

The Perfect Spy

A quarter of a century after he defected to the then Soviet Union, Kim Philby was still as much of a(n) .... *(1)* as ever. The several million words that had been written about him since 1963, when he disappeared in Beirut to surface in the USSR, seem to have compounded the mystery .... *(2)* the honourable English schoolboy who grew up to become a double agent and betray a generation. The first interview since his .... *(3)* that Philby gave to a western correspondent inevitably aroused an almost obsessive curiosity, particularly among the British establishment of which he was so intimate and so .... *(4)* a confidant. The voice that broke the silence was not just that of a 76-year-old man; in many ways, it was that of the .... *(5)* history of Europe, particularly Britain, in this century. What Philby betrayed ultimately was not his country but his class, the ruling .... *(6)*. Born in India, Harold Philby was a child of the Raj, learning to speak Hindustani before he spoke English. His father nicknamed his son 'Kim' after Kipling's hero who had also played the great game of .... *(7)*, though not as .... *(8)* as his namesake eventually would. It might not be entirely fanciful to surmise that the social and cultural .... *(9)* of those formative years may have sown the seeds of later .... *(10)*.

The interview suggested that Philby, who at one time was being .... *(11)* to be head of the British Secret Service, was deliberately allowed to defect from Beirut in a vain bid to avoid a(n) .... *(12)* at the time. Philby also hinted by implication that there were still .... *(13)* in the British crown, a ploy that could well have been an exercise in .... *(14)*. The Philby saga continued to perplex, each apparent answer reflecting a labyrinth of questions in the political .... *(15)* and beyond. In recent years popular fiction and topical fact have collaborated to project the .... *(16)* as a key symbol of the times, an elusive go-between across the unmarked border between .... *(17)* and truth, faith and betrayal, seen not as absolutes but as options of situational policy. In a world of open secrets and .... *(18)* realities, the ultimate .... *(19)* of a Judas spy is that of an apostle in search of a new .... *(20)*, a martyr on the Cross of his own treason.

Theme one: Deception

Dishonest People

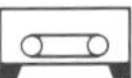

A Say whether the following statements are *true* or *false* according to the information given on the tape.

1 The speaker believes actions are either honest or dishonest.

2 He is usually able to pick out people who are likely to try and cheat him.

3 He judges harshly those who commit acts of dishonesty.

4 The speaker himself has been involved in selling stolen goods.

5 The building site where he worked featured in a TV programme about stolen goods.

6 The speaker sometimes has the chance to buy suspect goods at a reduced price.

B Have you ever been conned?

What do conmen do?

What's your opinion of conmen?

Now read the text and answer the questions which follow.

King of the Dupers

The American historian Bernard Wasserstein became curious about Trebitsch Lincoln, a dim figure of the early twentieth century who crops up in historical footnotes. Picking up clues about him in Foreign Office files, Wasserstein shrewdly scented a biographical scoop. *The Secret Lives of Trebitsch Lincoln* is the utterly improbable story of a thwarted megalomaniac who was also a champion conman. Indeed it's tempting at times to dismiss the whole thing as a hoax.

The nomadic Trebitsch was born into a Jewish merchant family in provincial Hungary in 1879. After a spell of petty crime, Trebitsch fled to Britain and became a Christian convert. At the turn of the century he was in Canada, proselytising the Jews of Montreal. By 1903, following a quarrel about his stipend, he was back in Britain, bent on self-promotion; and before long he was talking the Archbishop of Canterbury into awarding him the curacy of a village in Kent. The Archbishop was one of Trebitsch's many dupes. Promptly abandoning the clerical life, Trebitsch proceeded to bowl over Benjamin Seebohm Rowntree, the Quakermillionaire, Liberal and early social scientist. Largely through Rowntree's influence, Trebitsch became MP for Darlington in the General Election of 1910 – though at the time of his nomination he was not even a British citizen!

In less than a year, his phantom political career had ended in bankruptcy – a condition which Trebitsch rarely escaped. Accompanied by his submissive Hungarian wife and growing family, Trebitsch decamped to Rumania. There he speculated on oil wells. But this scheme – like all Trebitsch's financial schemes – failed miserably. On the eve of the First World War, he was back in Britain again – without visible means of support, yet certain he had a salient part to play in the coming conflict.

Bernard Wasserstein chronicles Trebitsch's outrageous attempts to become, first, a British, and then a German, spy. When he realised that neither side had any use for him, Trebitsch went to New York and sold a sensationally exaggerated version of his exploits to the American Press. 'Former British MP was German spy,' shrieked the credulous headlines. Originally seen as a mere nuisance, Trebitsch needled the British establishment into regarding him as a public enemy. And for British Intelligence it became a priority to stop Trebitsch's mouth.

Extradited and embittered, Trebitsch was imprisoned on the Isle of Wight* from 1916 to 1919. Behind bars he fantasised about destroying the British Empire. After the First World War, Trebitsch teamed up with European Rightists and militarists. But he was mixing with gangsters who would have distrusted even somebody who was trustworthy. With Hungarian assassins trailing him, and with his safety in Europe far from guaranteed, Trebitsch headed off for the Far East.

His most outlandish behaviour was still to come. Stricken by spiritual crisis, he converted to Buddhism, emerging in the 1930's as the abbot of

Buddhist monastery in Shanghai. With the twelve spokes of the Buddhist Wheel of Forgetting branded on his shaven skull, he proclaimed the world an illusion. All the same, he remained worldly enough to impound the belongings of the Buddhist initiates he recruited on flying visits to Europe. Moreover, when the Japanese invaded China in 1937, Trebitsch instantly espoused the Japanese cause; and as soon as the Second World War broke out in 1939 he volunteered his services as a Nazi propagandist.

The present biographer is not certain what happened to Trebitsch himself. He probably died in 1943, during the Shanghai Terror.

(Neil Berry, *The Guardian*)

* *Isle of Wight*: a small island off the south coast of England.

C Find a word or phrase in the text which, in context, is similar in meaning to:

Paragraph 1

1 appears
2 recognised
3 sensational story
4 frustrated
5 deception

Paragraph 2

6 travelling from place to place
7 trying to make converts
8 payment
9 position of minor priest in the Church of England
10 victims of deception
11 impress very favourably

Paragraph 3

12 unreal
13 absconded

Paragraph 4

14 tells the story of
15 irritated

Paragraph 5

16 surrendered for trial in another country
17 in prison

Paragraph 6

18 bizarre
19 seize
20 adopted

D Now choose the best answer to the following questions.

1 Wasserstein became interested in writing about Trebitsch Lincoln when

A he started to find footnotes about him in other books.
B the Foreign Office allowed him to consult their files.
C he realised people would be astonished by the story.
D he became aware he would be the first to tell the story.

2 Over his lifetime Trebitsch embraced many religions but he was never a

A Jew.
B Anglican.
C Quaker
D Buddhist.

3 Trebitsch's talents were best demonstrated in

A the religious life.
B politics.
C the way he took people in.
D his activities as a spy.

4 Trebitsch was extradited to the UK because he

A had given away British secrets.
B was regarded as a liability.
C had sold his story to the Press.
D wanted to spy against Britain.

5 Tebritsch went to the Far East after the First World War

A to improve his financial position.
B because he was interested in Buddhism.
C as his associates would not trust him.
D because his life was in danger.

6 The author's view of Trebitsch's years in the East is that

A he underwent a profound religious experience.
B he took a religious position to exploit others.
C he tried hard to change his way of life.
D he would have preferred to be in Europe.

Dishonesty at Work

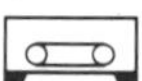

E Listen to the tape and answer the questions that follow with a phrase or short sentence.

(Note: you will hear the speaker referring to the coinage that existed in Britain pre-1971, when decimal coinage was introduced. You will not be asked questions which refer directly to this coinage.)

1. What did the shop sell?
2. What alerted the manageress to the fact that something was wrong?
3. Who first suspected Diane?
4. How did the manageress react to these suspicions?
5. How did the manageress know that goods had been paid for?
6. When the assistant realised she had been caught out, what did she do?
7. How was she cheating?
8. What did the manageress do?
9. How did the manageress feel?
10. How did the manageress justify her action?

Language awareness: clichés

A Cliches are fixed phrases which are well known to those familiar with the language. They are very common in speech, in newspapers and advertisements, but they are avoided in creative writing. What do these clichés mean?

1. You can't have your cake and eat it (too).
2. I think we should call his bluff.
3. You should know which side your bread is buttered.
4. He decided to do it on the spur of the moment.
5. Don't make a mountain out of a molehill.
6. During the war, he was involved in cloak-and-dagger work.
7. I believe in calling a spade a spade.
8. They have decided to bury the hatchet.
9. When it came to the crunch, he got cold feet.
10. Let's cross that bridge when we come to it.
11. I wouldn't touch it with a bargepole.
12. I intend to nip it in the bud.
13. It's the thin end of the wedge.
14. If you can't beat them, join them.
15. The proof of the pudding is in the eating.
16. Don't rock the boat!
17. That is certainly food for thought.
18. I'm not going to beat about the bush.
19. It was a close shave.
20. I think we are skating on thin ice.

B Match the idiomatic expressions in **List a** with the sentences in **List b** that have a similar meaning.

EXAMPLE; You must put your foot down.

ANSWER: *You must be very firm and insist that everyone obeys the rules.*

List a

a I'd like to pick your brains.

b It was a sight for sore eyes.

c I wash my hands of it.

d We watched with bated breath.

e I racked my brains.

f She worked her fingers to the bone.

g We had to pay through the nose.

h We'll have to keep our noses to the grindstone.

i He's got one foot in the grave.

j It makes my blood boil.

k It made my hair stand on end.

l Keep your eyes peeled.

List b

1 I get really angry when I see such things.

2 It was the most frightening experience I have ever had.

3 It's time to get down to some really hard work.

4 The manager is very old and very sick, so you'll soon have a chance to apply for his job.

5 The petrol cost far more than the normal price but out there in the desert we had no choice.

6 I'd like you to give me the benefit of your expert knowledge.

7 Watch carefully for any snakes that might be in the trees.

8 I thought really hard about it but I couldn't find the answer.

9 I will no longer accept responsibility for this matter.

10 There was an atmosphere of tense expectation as we waited for the astronauts to emerge from the capsule.

11 We had been filming all day without a break and were overjoyed to see the food truck coming towards us.

12 She worked extremely hard for five years to establish her own business.

Theme two: *Social Questions*

A Do you think it is justifiable to tell lies?

Does it depend on the circumstances?

In your opinion, do people in public life lie?

Germaine Greer versus the Tooth Fairy

Not long ago a highly regarded lady novelist gave an interview in which she said that among the things she was ashamed of was the fact that she was a habitual liar. This was of course a lie. She was clearly not ashamed of it at all.

Since I wrote a book describing my disgust and panic at discovering my father's whole life was based on a fabrication, I have had to read hundreds of letters written in his defence. Lying, it would appear, is good for people. Lying represents the creative approach to life. The dangerous people are the people who imagine that they themselves are not lying, the people who cling to their own distorted view of the world and call it the truth. An invented life-history may fit you better than the real one, and so on.

Well, phooey to all that. Let's be quite clear about what lying is. Lying is saying something that you know to be untrue. Lying is making statements in which you yourself do not believe in order that others should believe them. There are no good reasons for doing this. There is no good reason, for example, for telling a person who is terminally ill that he isgetting better. The assumption behind this kind of benign lying is that the person concerned is not equal to his own fate. To be sure, he may not be, but the liar who is withholding the truth from him is not entitled to assume that to be the case. When people ask questions it is because they want to know. To answer with an untruth is to exercise power over the questioner. Its real motivation is not sympathy but contempt. The doctor who lies to his patient assumes that his patient has been candid with him. His right to lie is an index of his power over this patient, who may not lie. Why do we lie to children? Why do we foist upon them nonsense about Santa Claus and Easter Bunnies and Tooth Fairies if not in some way to revenge ourselves for their candour? Our lying to small people again reflects our superior knowledge, pushes them down and away from us.

No wonder so many people are addicted to lying. Lying gives power to the powerless. Lying is instant revenge. But living a life of lies takes skill. Expert liars avoid ever having actually to utter an untruth, for they say very little that might relate to matters that they wish to conceal. At the same time, they cultivate the appearance of candour, artlessly blurting out details carefully selected to give a mistaken impression. This is regarded as enlightened self-promotion. Such liars are painfully surprised if they are rumbled. Only by keeping the people they manipulate in separate compartments can they function at all. Collusion among the candid would reveal that they are rotten to the core.

Kamikaze liars are, if anything, more corrupting than the experts. These liars are convinced that they can turn the untruth to truth by force or rhetoric, though they know that by translating their real feelings into shifting verbal constructs they falsify the feelings themselves. Lying in these cases is a sophisticated technique of self-destruction which seeks to implicate others in the process. Such liars do not seek the command over their faces and voices that the experts deploy; their blushing serves to embarrass others with more regard for the truth into pretending that they believe them.

Both kinds of liars would say that they do not expect to be believed. To them, a conversation that simply states facts instead of hinting and side-stepping is simply unintelligent and unexciting. They certainly would not understand my conviction that talking to people who do not mean what they are saying is simply a waste of time. They might also say that they lie in their different ways not out of a feeling of superiority but out of fear, fear of being judged and found wanting, as even the most honest of us lie to policemen, customs officers and landladies.

I don't believe it. A recent study has indicated that robbers steal for pleasure and become dependent upon the thrill of stealing. Just so liars lie for pleasure. The bigger the whopper, the more delicious the reminiscence. The adrenaline rush that comes with the risk of exposure, the breath-taking excitement of producing lie after lie to baffle the sceptic, these are the joys of lying. Lying cannot be reconciled with trust, or with respect or with love. Lying is hostile, malicious and fundamentally destructive.

All liars exploit and devalue the candour of others; they spread moral pollution by teaching the candid that candour is stupid. The worry is that in our public culture not even the appearance of candour is encouraged. Our leaders want to be seen to lie more adroitly than the other fellow. They hire publicity experts to instruct them in the arts of self-promotion at the expense of truth. An easy lie is a better answer, politically, than hard truth. Our children, born honest, soon learn that the prizes go to the boldest, the least blushing liars.

(adapted from Germaine Greer, *The Independent*)

B Find a word or phrase in the text which, in context, is similar in meaning to:

Paragraph 1
1 well thought of

Paragraph 2
2 something made up
3 false and inaccurate

Paragraph 3
4 not revealing
5 easily taken in

Paragraph 4
6 speak
7 hide
8 suddenly revealing
9 found out

Paragraph 5
10 involve
11 use

Paragraph 6
12 suggesting
13 lacking

Paragraph 7
14 a huge lie
15 perplex

C Now answer the following questions.

1 What is Germaine Greer's view of the lady novelist?

2 How did she feel when she discovered the truth about her father?

3 What response did she get from readers of her book?

4 What is her attitude to lying?

5 What kind of behaviour do expert liars adopt?

6 What's the difference, according to the writer, between 'expert' and 'kamikaze' liars?

7 In what way do liars devalue other people?

8 What criticism in made of public culture?

Grammar: *sentence structure*

A Can you identify the subject in the following sentences?

The train crashed into the signal box.

It had faulty brakes.

Maintaining trains is not an easy task.

The subjects of these sentences are very short, consisting of only one or two words. However, the subject of a sentence can be much longer than in these examples, and can express complex and abstract ideas. Identify the subjects in the following sentences.

1 That more people do not complain about the poor service is surprising.

2 Whatever you request will be provided for you immediately.

3 To travel all the way to India and not see the Taj Mahal is ridiculous.

4 How he manages to grow so much food in such a small garden really amazes me.

5 What must not be forgotten is that we provided all the technical support for this project.

6 Whoever asks for help will be given it without question.

7 Where he hid the money may never be known.

8 That she refused to give evidence against her husband was only to be expected.

9 What he told you about the events that took place in the village in 1960 is simply not true.

10 Whether he has experience or not will make no difference to his chances of getting the job.

B Can you write a new sentence, as similar in meaning as possible to the sentences given? The first word is provided.

1 Not many people completed the questionnaire. It is disappointing.
That ....
....
....

2 You can see many things on display. They can all be purchased.
Whatever ....
....
....

3 She was prepared to accept the job. This surprised everyone.
What ....
....
....

4 He found the treasure. We don't know where. We will never know.
Where ....
....
....

5 He lived in Spain for ten years. He didn't learn Spanish. This is surprising.
To ....
....
....

6 The car is very old. It continues to run well. This is amazing.
How such ....
....
....

7 He may be rich. He may be poor. It will make no difference to his application to build a house in the village.
Whether ....
....
....

8 People can invest £1000 now. they will receive £1700 in five years' time.
Whoever ....
....
....

9 He wrote in his diary. The diary contains nothing but false information.
Whatever ....
....
....

C Use these words and phrases to complete the advertisement below. Some of the answers have already been done for you.

on the other hand	curiously	and because	it goes without saying
for more information	each	let alone	and what's more
so whichever	mind you	both	for a start
for example	anyway	hardly	

Hungarian goulash and peach tart for eight? .... *(1)* a meal you'd consider cooking every day of the week. Certainly not with an ordinary oven *anyway*..............................*(2)*.

For a start.............................. (3), any ordinary stew worth its seasoning gently bubbles away at about 140°C. Close to 190°C is rather more comfortable for peaches. .... *(4)*, with most ovens you usually find there's a shortage of space.

On the other hand..............................*(5)* should a Belling Formula Turbo take centre stage under your kitchen's spotlight, you'll notice the peaches pop perfectly into one fan oven while the goulash slips straight into the other.

.... *(6)*, until the Formula Turbo, nobody had every put two full-sized fan ovens together, ... *(7)* with their own separate controls, ... *(8)* capable of roasting a 23lb turkey. (And that's enough to feed almost forty people, ... *(9)* eight.)

.... *(10)*, a Formula Turbo, isn't just about versatility. Every surface, inside and out, is a doddle to clean. .... *(11)* it's electric, *it goes without saying*.. *(12)* that it's remarkably efficient. The grill, ... *(13)*, has a dual-circuit element which means you don't waste energy toasting a couple of crumpets for your afternoon tea.

.... *(14)* double oven you go for (either the built-in version or the slot-in) everything from goulash and a peach tart to a midweek snack is sure to turn out perfectly.

You'll never be in a stew again.

.... *(15)*, cut the coupon or call 071-200 0200 and ask for CookElectric with Belling.

Theme three: *Whose Lifestyle is it Anyway?*

A Before reading, what responsibilities do you think parents have to their children? When do these responsibilities start, before or after birth?

A woman's rights to privacy, autonomy and freedom from assault have been enshrined in British common law and the American constitution. Now these rights are in question.

Remember Pamela Stewart? She is the Californian woman who was arrested in imprisoned earlier this year, under a 1926 child protection law, following the death of her six-week-old baby. Prosecutors said that her conduct during pregnancy had led to the death. They reasoned that the law, originally intended to force fathers to pay for their children's upkeep, should also apply to pregnant women, imposing on them a similar duty to their unborn children.

Pamela Stewart had begun to haemorrhage on the day the baby was born but, police said, waited for six hours before going to hospital. According to the police, the child, born with extensive brain damage, had amphetamine and barbiturates in his blood.

The criminal charges brought against Ms Stewart carried a penalty of one year in prison and a $2000 fine. The motive of the State Prosecutor was largely a desire to do something about the growing number of newborns exposed to drugs in the womb.

Was the prosecution justified? The judge in a San Diego court didn't think so. He accepted the argument of the American Civil Liberties Union that the law did not protect unborn foetuses; nor could the state's interest in the matter outweigh a pregnant woman's right to privacy.

But that was not the end of the story. The failed prosecution inspired Senator Ed Royce to introduce the first bill in any American state which would include foetuses in child protection legislation. If passed, his bill would threaten all pregnant women in California with a criminal conviction and penalties if they did anything which might endanger the life of the child.

Almost every woman wants to do the best she can for her unborn child. Yet the bill seems to make the opposite assumption. It would place every woman's behaviour in doubt. Coffee, cigarettes, alcohol and many other legitimate substances and activities are now thought to affect foetuses. How long would it be before threats of prosecution slipped into the normal dialogue between medical authorities and women?

(Sally Hughes, *The Guardian*)

B Now answer the following questions.

1. Why was Pamela Stewart arrested and sent to prison?
2. What was unusual about the use of the law under which she was arrested?
3. What particular aspects of Pamela Stewart's behaviour caused the police concern?
4. What was the reaction of the San Diego judge to the law?

5 Whose viewpoint did he accept?

6 What is novel about Senator Ed Royce's bill?

7 Why would the passing of Ed Royle's bill be of major concern to all pregnant women?

8 What is your opinion of the proposed legislation?

A Wicked Story

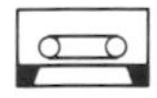

C Listen to the story and indicate whether the following statements are *true* or *false*.

1 The speaker describes an incident which happened while he was working on a cruise ship.

2 The deceased passenger had expressed a wish to be buried at sea.

3 The captain of the ship authorised the funeral.

4 The coffin itself could not be seen when it was on the ramp.

5 The bosun's mate pulled the wrong lever.

6 The bosun was in a state of panic.

7 The bosun produced three things from inside the ship in order that the funeral ceremony could go ahead.

8 The captain was present when the coffin went into the sea.

9 Five people were present at the funeral ceremony.

10 There was no indication that anything had gone wrong.

Talking points

A Look at these summaries of stories that appeared in newspapers. What is your opinion about the action described?

1 A man refused a loan by his bank manager wreaked vengeance by demolishing the bank with a bulldozer.

2 A sales representative spent money on meals, clothes and holidays after a computer assessed her salary at £70,000 p.a. instead of £7000.

3 Police stopped looking for $700,000 dollars that spilled from the back of an unlocked security van onto the roadway. Motorists who passed the van with the money flooding from it skidded to a halt and leapt out of their cars to grab the bags in which the money was contained.

4 Passengers travelling on luxury cruise liners who have tried to kill themselves and have failed are now suing the company organising the trips, on the grounds that they hurt themselves while travelling on the ship.

B What would you do in the following situations?

1 You work in a bank and have access to the bank's main computer. You know how you could set up a programme to allow a transfer of funds to your own account that would not be detected.

2 You find a £20 note on the pavement.

3 A relative of yours urgently needs an organ transplant. Someone offers to supply an appropriate organ in return for a large sum of money. What would you do?

4 You want to build a luxurious house and have heard that the only chance of obtaining permission to build is to pay a substantial amount of money in secret to the Planning Officer.

C Look at this article describing various aspects of shoplifting.

What are your views about the morality of shoplifting?

What do you think of the way suspected shoplifters are treated?

Are shops responsible for making people want to take things?

Watching the Detectives

My neighbour, discussing his 11-year-old son, said the other day: 'Daniel's got into a bit of trouble. I had to go and get him from the police station – he'd been caught shoplifting in Woolworth's. They were changing the price on the sports bags. Well, what can you say? We've all nicked stuff from Woolies when we were kids, haven't we?'

Well, have we? Some of our friends do steal from shops, parading 'social injustice' or simple greed as worthwhile motives. We have all met people who tell their children that stealing from multi-million pound stores is not really stealing because 'they can afford it'. But most of the people who get in touch with Regina Dollar, chairman of Crisis Counselling for Alleged Shoplifters, have certainly never taken as much as a tin of baked beans in their lives. For them, being accused of shoplifting is a horrifying, humiliating experience which leaves them feeling permanently branded a thief.

Regina Dollar says the stereotype of the shoplifter as a confused middle-aged housewife is far from true. A Home Office study shows that ages range evenly between 11 and 59. 'We are contacted by all kinds of people, from parents worried about their children who have been shoplifting in gangs, to professional people and the elderly.' She is highly critical of the manner in which store detectives work. Customers suspected of stealing are followed outside the store, stopped and often frogmarched in front of a crowd of shoppers back to the manager's office, where they are interrogated.

The most common fear of those accused of shoplifting is that their name will get into the newspapers. Harry Kaufer, co-founder of Crisis Counselling for Alleged Shoplifting, is often contacted by those who are on the verge of suicide. 'People get to court and they cannot speak. The stand in a chasm of misery. All they can think of is what their family will say. They feel dirty. No one realises the hell these people go through.'

People often telephone him in great distress fearing that their child will end up in a juvenile court. There is some evidence that children, aged 10 to 14, are among the fastest growing group of shoplifters. In a classroom survey conducted by Nottinghamshire Police, nearly half admitted that they had stolen from shops. Harry Kaufer takes a firm line with parents. 'I tell parents they must take responsibility for instilling manners and self-discipline in their children.'

But stores are experts in temptation. Modern marketing is nothing more than an exercise in persuading us to buy something we do not need. Eyecatching displays offer attractive goods teasingly near entrances; supermarkets load up sweet racks at check-outs where children are encouraged to reach out and grab what they want. Stealing from shops is wrong and stores must act reasonably to prevent shop-lifting. But out on the shopfloor, an attitude prevails that would not be tolerated outside in the street. As customers, we are the reason a shop makes a profit. Shops that are anxious to relieve us of our money should not be so anxious to relieve us of our innocence until proved guilty.

(Jane Ellison, *The Guardian*)

Writing

Discursive essay

A *'I hate the idea of causes, and if I had to choose between betraying my country and betraying my friend, I hope I should have the guts to betray my country.'*
(E M Forster, 1879–1970)

Discuss this statement.

Letter of advice

B Here is an extract from a letter you have received.

I just don't know what to do for the best. Since Mother came to live with us six months ago, it's been little short of hell.

As you know, Mother sold the house and could have afforded to have moved into quite a comfortable home; there are loads around here full of people just like her. But no, she had to come and live with me and Jake. She keeps interfering, and making comments about any little thing I do.

But the main problem is the kids. We've always encouraged them to be independent and to lead their own lives, you know, have their own friends and develop their own interests. And now that they're in their teens - Julian's fifteen now and Tara will be fourteen next month - they really are developing fast. Mother just doesn't understand. She treats them as if they were six years old. Nothing is right; what they do, what they wear, how they speak, who their friends are.

The worst of it is, it's really getting to me. And coming between me and Jake. He says I should be more tolerant. It's all right for him, he's out of the house all day. It's got to the stage where I really feel it's a question of either my mother or my family. What on earth do you think I should do? Should Mother be forced to go into a home?

Write to your friend offering suitable advice.

Literary approaches

What story does the poem tell?

The Castle by Edwin Muir (1887–1959)

All through that summer at ease we lay,
And daily from the turret wall
We watched the mowers in the hay
And the enemy half a mile away.
They seemed no threat to us at all.

For what, we thought, had we to fear
With our arms and provender, load on load,
Our towering battlements, tier on tier,
And friendly allies drawing near
On every leafy summer road.

Our gates were strong, our walls were thick,
So smooth and high, no man could win
A foothold there, no clever trick
Could take us, have us dead or quick.
Only a bird could have got in.

What could they offer us for bait?
Our captain was brave and we were true ...
There was a little private gate,
A little wicked wicket gate.
The wizened warder let them through.

Oh then our maze of tunnelled stone
Grew thin and treacherous as air.
The cause was lost without a groan,
The famous citadel overthrown,
And all its secret galleries bare.

How can this shameful tale be told?
I will maintain until my death
We could do nothing, being sold;
Our only enemy was gold,
And we had no arms to fight it with.

Follow-up

A Fill each of the numbered blanks in the following passage with one suitable word.

Fraud

In recent years there has been a noticeable increase in sophisticated financial fraud. This is not entirely .... *(1)* to the existence of computer technology and the opportunities it .... *(2)* for new techniques of deception. Although many fraudulent schemes involve the electronic movement of funds, ... *(3)* are simple pen-and-paper jobs which, nevertheless, are capable of .... *(4)* millions of pounds for the skilful confidence-trickster. The real reason for the increase is that many criminals, often better educated than in the past and ....*(5)* a thorough knowledge of company law and banking procedures, have discovered that robbing a bank by pretending to be a trustworthy ....*(6)* or reliable customer is a ....*(7)* more sensible than bursting in with a shotgun, grabbing the cash and jumping into the getaway car. They have no need to use violence and are often ....*(8)* with more respect by the police. Moreover, ...*(9)* it is large financial institutions that are the losers, the activities of these white-collar criminals may not arouse the same anger in the general public as the crimes ....(10) by burglars or muggers. Sometimes banks are unwilling to come ....*(11)* and admit that they have been tricked out of millions of pounds for fear that there will be a ....*(12)* of confidence in the banking system.

For this reason, many crimes go unreported and the perpetrators ....*(13)* enjoy their ill-gotten gains in ....*(14)* tropical paradise they have chosen. Not all, however, ... *(15)* justice. Those that end up behind ....(16) are likely to find that life in prison is particularly unpleasant in ....*(17)* with their former high-spending lifestyle. Until recently, sentences for fraud were quite light, ...*(18)* more than three or four years, although it has to be said that for this type of criminal the ....*(19)* of even a short time in prison is a strong deterrent. However, as judges become ....*(20)* of the prevalence of this type of crime, penalties are getting stiffer.

B Finish each of the following sentences in such a way that it is as similar as possible in meaning to the sentence printed before it.

1 The gangsters threatened Peter with violence.

The gangsters made ....

....

2 Mark does not intend to pay back the money he has borrowed.

Mark has ....

....

3 The driver behaved in such a way as to place the passengers in danger.

The passengers ....

....

4 Sheila has every chance of getting the job.

It is ....

....

5 It wasn't Jill's fault that we got lost.

Jill wasn't ....

....

6 The full story of the disaster was not told until 1990.

Not until ....

....

C Fill each of the blanks with a suitable word or phrase.

1. In the final push for the summit, the mountaineers had .... reserves of strength and determination that they didn't know they had.
2. He gave .... having recognised us.
3. He is not used .... in a house without central heating.
4. I have .... in recommending her for this post.
5. Unfortunately, grandmother treats the children .... they were still five years old.
6. The plans for the new railway line show a complete .... the interests of local residents.

D For each of the sentences below, write a new sentence as similar as possible in meaning to the original sentence, but using the word given. The word must not be altered in any way.

1. One is very much inclined to dismiss the whole thing as a joke.

   tempting

   ....

   ....

2. After a short prison sentence, he decided to go straight.

   spell

   ....

   ....

3. The right attitude to the job is as important as the right qualifications.

   less

   ....

   ....

4. He paid no regard to his own comfort.

   indifferent

   ....

   ....

5. The meals we are getting now cannot be compared to the ones we had to put up with before.

   comparison

   ....

   ....

6. We have long since ceased to keep information in printed form.

   ages

   ....

   ....

E Choose the word or phrase (*A*, *B*, *C* or *D*) which best completes each sentence.

1 References to the scandal frequently .... in private diaries of that period.

A crop up *B* come out
C look up *D* make to

2 The newspaper claimed that its story was a .... – no other newspaper had it.

A first *B* record
C win *D* scoop

3 The special alarm system .... the robbers' attempts to get into the bank's bullion vaults.

A thwarted *B* prevented
C avoided *D* sabotaged

4 In my childhood my family and I led a(n) .... existence and before the age of ten I had lived in five different countries,

A drifting *B* wandering
C nomadic *D* travelling

5 Thomas began to cut down on his consumption of animal fats for the .... of his health.

A good *B* sake
C benefit *D* future

6 The survey was .... by researchers at the university.

A carried *B* conducted
C performed *D* made

7 I am afraid that Mr Leech has no part to .... in the re-organised company.

A play *B* act
C perform *D* take

8 When he phoned it was obvious from his voice that he was in great ....

A misery *B* trouble
C distress *D* unhappiness

9 Her historical novels are highly .... by critics.

A remarked *B* reviewed
C promoted *D* regarded

10 John must be very .... if he thought such a ludicrous story was true.

A believable *B* gullible
C candid *D* accepting

11 In a thoughtless moment, Amanda .... out the truth.

A spoke *B* blurted
C uttered *D* revealed

12 Shortly after his arrest, he was .... to stand trial in his own country.

A ordered *B* exported
C extradited *D* dismissed

13 In this particular case, the freedom to report these events is .... by considerations of state security.

A outbalanced *B* outstripped
C outcast *D* outweighed

14 Although .... by a serious illness, Bernard managed to complete the musical score for his opera.

A struck *B* stricken
C upset *D* stressed

15 Cars parked here after 11 p.m. will be .... by the police.

A detained *B* held
C possessed *D* impounded

Authors' acknowledgements

The authors wish to thank the following people for their contribution to the authentic recorded material on the cassettes.

Michel Blanc; Joseph Brown; Sir Frederick Corfield; Stephen Dixon; Bryan Forbes; Philip Geddes; Brian Litchfield; Andrew Macdonald; Simon Medaney; Alice Morris; J E Morris; Helen Juliet Mosby; Robbie Ochala; Claire Skinner; Jean Smith; Betty Stankowski; Barbara Stanton; Robert Stanton; Terry Stanton.

Publishers' acknowledgements

The publishers would like to thank the following for permission to reproduce copyright material. They have tried to contact all copyright holders, but in cases where they may have failed will be pleased to make the necessary arrangements at the first opportunity.

Texts

The Guardian for the articles and extracts: 'The Odd Couple' by Polly Toynbee (page 4), 'Seven Bounden Duties' by Posy Simmonds (page 13), 'The Self Centre' by Jane Ellison (page 17), 'Death Race' by Barry Coleman (page 23), 'Hazard at Work' by Stephen Singleton (page 27), 'Debt and despair on the dark side of consumer credit' by Edward Vulliamy (page 45), 'Ten Days with the Circus' by Philippa Gregory (page 70), 'The unpopular press – the lost readers' by Roy Greenslade (page 94), 'Girl Talk – Where You Can Buy Success in the Coffee Break' by Pat Ashworth (page 90), 'Why the British Hate Fashion' by Sarah Mower (page 96), 'A Prince Who Abdicated' (Richard Burton) by Kenneth Hurren – adapted (page 134), 'Guzzling on the hoof costs Britons £1 billion a year' by James Erlichman (page 162),' 'Twirling the Edge' by Geoffrey Beattie (page 165), 'Merely Male in Admen's Markets' by Virginia Matthews (page 174), 'Paradise Aisles: how supermarkets are bottling sun, sea and sand' (Packaging) by Ben Laurance (page 177), 'The Charlatans Who Fooled Scientists' by Stuart Sutherland (page 184), 'Triumph of Mind over Matter' by Dennis Barker (page 198), 'King of the Dupers' by Neil Berry (page 228), 'Whose Lifestyle is it anyway?' by Sally Hughes (page 237), 'Watching the detectives: Shoplifting' by Jane Ellison (page 237);

The Irish Times for the article 'Little has Changed on the Streets of London' (page 7);

The Royal Army for their advertisement 'Just Another Day At the Office' (page 12);

André Deutsch Ltd. for the extract from *Sour Sweet* by Timothy Mo (page 16);

Martin Secker and Warburg for the extract from *Easy Money* by David Spanier (page 31);

The Independent for the extracts and articles: 'When The Chips are Down, Gamble' by David Spanier (page 37), 'The Steadily Shrinking Boundaries of Press Freedom' (page 99), 'Hanging: When the Debate is Just a Gloss on Gut Reactions' by Geoffrey Wheatcroft (page 115), 'Fall from Grace of a Man Who Rode his Luck Too Far' by John Karter (page 120), 'The Cockney Hero with a Difference' by Geoffrey Wheatcroft (page 123), 'A Dampener for the Dowsers' by Denys Parsons (page 193), 'Not Exactly What We Mean To Say' by Miles Kington (page 210);

Daily Mail / Solo for the articles: 'An Alternative Way to Save' compiled by Wendy Elkington (page 50), 'Hounding of the Princess' by Richard Kay (page 131);

Barclays Bank for the letter (page 45);

Daily Star for the article 'Win May Have Caused Death' (page 53);

Daily Express for the article 'Husband Walks Out On Pools Wife Who Won £369,000' (page 53);

Wayland Ltd for the extract reproduced from *Let's Discuss Animal Rights* (Animal Rights) by P J Allison (page 61) with the kind permission of Wayland (Publishers) Ltd., Hove, England;

Jonathan Cape Ltd for the extract from *Animal Liberation* by Peter Singer (page 62);

Times of India for the articles: 'Threat to Borivli Park' (page 65), 'The Perfect Spy' – adapted (page 227);

Faber and Faber Ltd. for the poems 'The Thought-Fox' from *The Hawk in the Rain* by Ted Hughes (page 76) and 'The Castle' by Edwin Muir (page 238);

The Observer for the article 'A Furry friend to stroke may keep heart attacks away' by Sarah Lonsdale (page 77);

Epson (UK Ltd.) for the extract from their advertisement (page 84);

Penguin Books Ltd for the extracts from *The Presentation of Self in Everyday Life* by Irving Goffman (page 88) and *The English Language* (Pidgins and Creoles) by David Crystal (page 205);

Olwyn Hughes for the poem 'Mirror' by Sylvia Plath (page 98);

Collins Publishers for the extracts from *Arabian Sands* by Wilfred Thesiger (page 103) and *Wild Justice* by Susan Jacoby (page 104);

The Times for the obituary for Andy Gibb (page 107);

Museum of the Moving Image for the use of part of their advertisement (page 109);

John Harvey-Jones for the quotation (page 128);